CHASING EXTREME

CHASING EXTREME

A JOURNEY OF OVERCOMING

OBSTACLES & DEPRESSION TO EMBRACE

A LIFE OF EXTREME ADVENTURE

LUKE TYBURSKI

ISBN 978-1-9993166-0-0
eISBN 978-1-9993166-1-7

Published by LUKE TYBURSKI LTD

Cover photo: Darren Wheeler
Cover design: Erica Bliss
Interior typsetting: Mark Thomas / Coverness.com

Luke.
A boy with dreams.
A man with vision, determination and courage.
A son to be mighty proud of!

Libbie Tyburski (Mum)

TABLE OF CONTENTS

FOREWORD

In order to achieve a life of purpose and fulfillment, there must be a commitment made. In order to find what one is seeking and in order to withstand the inevitable trials of the seeking itself, this commitment must be made anew, every single day, no matter where one stands in relationship to where they want to be.

One of my most beloved songs is "Soldier of Love" by the incomparable Sade Adu. Here are some of the lyrics:

It's the wild wild west
I'm doing my best
I'm at the borderline of my faith
I'm at the hinterland of my devotion
I'm in the front line of this battle of mine
But I'm still alive....

I am lost but I don't doubt
Tall I ride
I have the will to survive
In the wild wild west
Trying my hardest
Doing my best to stay alive

Luke Tyburski is an absolute "soldier of love" - Luke soldiers on daily, against all odds, against debilitating pain, mental and emotional struggles, against circumstances and challenges (tons self-created!) in order to continually touch his potential as an endurance athlete, and as a man trying to live his best life.

What I love most about Luke's story and about this inspiring read, is that it is HONEST. This is a real and raw depiction of what it takes to live a life outside of your comfort zone; It's not for the faint of heart nor is it for those who appreciate a feathered nest.

A life of continual growth and expansion is built brick by brick, through blood, sweat and tears AND its foundation must be set with a mindset keen on doing whatever it takes.

Through the telling of Luke's story, we are reminded that the adventure(s) of a lifetime is not a linear, paved path - it is anything but. What Luke also reminds us is that life is meant to be an adventure of our own creating, and each adventure in life is BEST when it's shared with those we love most and when we take the time to service both the adventure and the soul behind the wheel.

You will enjoy this book! I have no doubt that it will inspire you to set off in chase for that which makes you feel ALIVE!

Kerri Walsh Jennings - Professional Beach Volleyball Player

Five-time Olympian

Three-time Olympic gold medalist

One-time Olympic bronze medalist

PROLOGUE

The ground heat is intense, my feet are badly blistered and swimming in a pool of sweat, but I am oblivious to the bubbling, peeling skin. Right now, I have a bigger drama to deal with. Despite two cortisone injections, my iliotibial band (ITB) injury has flared up and feels like a red-hot poker has been shoved in my knee. Each step is excruciating. I try not to think about the 200 kilometres still ahead, up and over the scorching sand dunes.

When we lined up at the start of the Marathon des Sables 24 hours earlier, AC/DC's *Highway to Hell* was blaring over the tinny loudspeakers. The air buzzed with excitement around the crazy challenge ahead, bring it on!

Everything about this race – the distance, the landscape, the weather – is extreme. I was running the equivalent of six marathons back-to-back across the Sahara Desert, carrying all my supplies with me. A pack strapped to my back contained my clothes, meals, a small titanium stove and lightweight sleeping bag, plus a safety flare, compass and head torch. In a smaller pack on my front I had my salt tablets, snacks and water bottles. I had forked out thousands of pounds to be part of something akin to hell on Earth. The obvious question is why would anyone *choose* to do this.

For me it was simple. I came to race this beast. I wanted to put myself up against some of the best desert runners on the planet, and see where I ended up.

In Greek mythology, there is a King called Sisyphus who, as punishment for his sins, is tasked with a lifetime of pushing a huge boulder uphill, only to have it roll back down forcing him to start over. To outsiders, the Marathon des Sables must have a similar sense of futility – run through the desert, suffer, go to sleep, wake up and do it all again. A ludicrous quest!

Running day after day in such hostile conditions was about proving to myself I had the stamina for extreme adventure. If I am being brutally honest, it was also an escape. My life had taken an unexpected turn six months earlier, and I was still desperately searching for answers.

I joked about all my competitors in this insane race having a screw loose, but in all seriousness, I did question my state of mind choosing pain and suffering as my new day job.

At the end of Day Two, I took off my socks and barely recognised my feet. They looked like something from a horror movie. There were busted blisters all over my toes, underneath my toes – even between my toes! It was a sickening sight of torn skin, raw flesh, and toes throbbing in pain; this could potentially be a serious setback. Aside from the intense stinging (imagine walking barefoot across razor blades), with so much exposed red flesh, it would be almost impossible to avoid infection.

With still five days and 185 kilometres to cover, the Sahara had many more obstacles for me to face.

1.

SMALL TOWN, BIG DREAMS

For as long as I can remember, I have wanted to win, I mean *really* wanted to win. This competitive streak runs in my family. Both parents and my older sister are talented athletes, and every one of us played to win. Where I differed was in my response to *not* winning. If a referee made a bad call, I made it known. When I played badly, nobody wanted to be around me – I was grumpy and miserable. It took me many years to learn how to be a gracious loser.

When I was 10 years old, I had a representative coach with a strong focus on discipline. He stressed the referee's decision was always final, so there is no point arguing, and told us, 'if the referee says the sky is pink today, then guess what, the sky is pink!' The message stuck, and I knew he was right, but during a match when I would question the referee's decision, I hated hearing my dad's voice from the sidelines reminding me, 'the sky is pink today Luke!'

After every game, I would replay the entire match in my mind, remembering every mistake I made, as if my memory was on a stop/start/pause sequence. I was my own worst critic. If I lost, or felt I had not played to the best of my ability, no one could speak to me. I sulked and wished for a chance to correct my mistakes. I was constantly being told by my parents to 'snap out of it!'

When I was at my worst, Mum sat me down and explained my behaviour was unfair on everyone around me. She said, 'Luke you're allowed to be upset and disappointed for the day of the game, but once you go to bed and wake up the next morning, it's all forgotten, you must be happy and act normal.'

It was one of the best pieces of advice I've had regarding my sporting career, and I continue to use it to this day. It taught me to analyse my performance efficiently – to understand where I needed to improve and not dwell on the negatives. Life is too short to beat myself up over something that's happened, where I could no longer control the outcome. I needed to move on and enjoy all the amazing things each day had to offer.

Through the guise of sport, my parents taught me a lot about life. They insisted that if I wanted to become a better player I must work hard, be dedicated, and most importantly *never, ever give up*. Those words felt like our family mantra. There was a picture on our refrigerator of a pelican swallowing a frog; the bird has the frog firmly in its mouth but the frog has an even firmer grip on the bird's neck, squeezing as tightly as possible. The frog was not going down without a fight!

I grew up in Bathurst, a country town about 200 kilometres northwest of Sydney, and like many Australians, our family life revolved around sport, with weeknights and weekends taken up by playing or training. Sporting commitments dictated when and where we had holidays, sport chose my close friends.

My Mum excelled at basketball. At one stage, she had an opportunity to train with the national squad but when forced to choose, decided to have children instead. My Dad played rugby league until the age of 40, when, given an ultimatum from Mum to either retire or face divorce (she was serious), he wisely chose to retire. He took up field hockey and incorporated selected rugby league tackling techniques. I still enjoy watching him chase unsuspecting hockey opponents to tackle.

At times, I watched my parents struggle financially, but they worked harder and stayed dedicated to raising their young family. We rarely went without the necessities in life, but if there was a 'want' that caught my eye, I knew I'd have to earn it. They led by example, showing year after year what hard work and dedication could achieve. They are fantastic role models who gave me some amazing life tools.

My older sister, Amanda, was the star athlete in our family when we were growing up. She was always the first to be selected for representative teams across different sports, including field hockey, basketball, athletics - even tap dancing. I admired her athletic ability, but at the same time, envied her achievements. After my parents, she was my first true sporting role model. She played local, district, regional, and state level sports in a town that was truly obsessed with sporting achievements. Most people in the Bathurst sporting community knew of Amanda's accomplishments. I was simply Amanda's little brother.

Bathurst has a strong reputation for producing talented athletes, and with such high standards in local competition; it is no wonder most local athletes are extremely competitive – it's hardwired into our systems. There is a strong correlation between community status and sporting achievement; even those not interested in sport identified success by the colour of the representative tracksuit you wore.

I fell in love with football (soccer) from an early age, and set my sights on becoming a professional athlete, with dreams of being paid to play anywhere in the world. As a kid, I wasn't exactly a natural athlete, if anything I was a little awkward – chubby, knocked-kneed and highly emotional, I would cry at anything. I played basketball and Australian rules football, and excelled at cricket, but my true love was football, even though I would barely make the local district representative team. Most of the time I was the last kid to be picked, but I didn't care – I was in the team, I got the tracksuit, and was able to play, or at least sit on the bench. Other times, I'd be left standing with a few kids at the end of the tryouts, sent home with a 'thanks for coming, better luck next year' by the coach.

But I wanted to be part of the team, and was prepared to go *all in* to be picked!

Each year I would ask the coaches how I could improve myself to increase my chances of making the team next year. And each year I would go home and train in my back yard; kicking a tennis ball against the fence, passing the football literally thousands of times against any surface that would return it to me, dribbling any type of ball in circles on our back lawn. Hours would pass until Mum called time on my training session to come inside for dinner.

My determination, resilience, and ability to want to improve would set me up for a chance to be picked the following season; this fuelled my desire for success.

My parents never once pushed me to do the extra training, they didn't need to, I was self-motivated from a young age. But they always encouraged me. Mum would say, 'if you can stand in front of the mirror and say you've done your very best, then that's all you can do. But, if you feel you can go further, or do better, then go for it. Ultimately it's up to you.'

Mum always said I got my overwhelming determination, my high training threshold, and perhaps a touch of arrogance from Dad. She reckons her contribution is my ability to organise, and to properly understand a situation so I know when to push and when not to.

When I was growing up in Australia, football was not a mainstream sport. At a grass-roots level there was strong participation, with many parents urging their children to play soccer instead of the more physical rugby codes, but our top league was barely professional. Football was overshadowed by the more popular, better-funded and long-established sports of rugby league, rugby union, cricket and Australian rules.

Football only started to become a more popular sport after the Second World War when many immigrants from Europe settled in Australia and brought with them a passion for the game they loved. Local clubs were founded by Greek, Croatian, Italian, Maltese, Hungarian, and Jewish communities, who eventually helped form Australia's first full-time professional competition. Today many of these clubs are still participating in the semi-professional leagues throughout the bigger cities of the country.

At 14 years old, I joined the local gym so I could train before school. Dad would drop me off on his way to work and not once did I miss the 6.30 a.m. departure. I would swim, run on the treadmill and do hopping and jumping plyometric training two or three times a week. My grandma would pick me up from the gym, take me back to her place, make me breakfast, and then drive me to school.

It takes a certain type of person to happily get up before sunrise on a freezing winter's morning, and exercise for several hours before starting their day. My routine may not have been particularly normal for a teenager, but it was normal for me.

Being self-motivated was a valuable quality for my athletic development. There were many better players than me with vast amounts of raw talent whose career chances fizzled out in their teenage years. I had all the usual distractions of a teenager including peer pressure, girlfriends and household chores, but none of these inhibited my internal drive to work towards my potential.

I was beginning to understand that if I wanted to achieve a goal in life, I needed to give 100% effort, and be dedicated to the cause, as no one else was going to do the work for me!

* * *

1998 began like any other year in Bathurst, with pre-season training in the scorching January heat. Along with a few of my mates, who had played at higher representative levels than me, we tried out for the Bathurst 75s Under 18s team and were excited by the prospect of being coached by a man we knew simply as 'Judgey'.

Joe Judge was a slightly built Scotsman around 60 years of age, with a vast knowledge of the game, and loudspeakers for lungs. He had a phenomenal ability to get the best out of every player he coached. Judgey had several successful years coaching the club's first grade team, and helped develop many players over his time in charge. He knew as much about the physical and psychological demands of the game, as he did about the technical attributes needed for a player to make it to the top. When Judgey spoke, you listened.

After several years away from coaching, Judgey returned as coach of the Under 18s for a combination of reasons; he wanted to help develop the local talent, he missed coaching, and he needed a post-retirement hobby – and I'm forever thankful he did.

It was a talented group of footballers who tried out for the team, including my mates, Kurt, Assi, Stoney and Hardness. Stoney was the most gifted player in the region in our age group, and was already being considered by development squads and clubs from Sydney, so he was a strong chance to make the team. The other boys were definitely in the running but as we were still young, only a couple of us would be picked to train with the older boys, and travel to Sydney to play against city teams.

I was showing signs of talent during the local representative competition the previous year, but I hadn't considered stepping up three age groups and playing against some of the best 18 year olds in the state. I remember Dad suggesting I join pre-season training at the club, but I simply laughed off the idea. He thought I could use the training to develop my fitness, learn a few things, and work with a top coach. This made sense to me. I was doing all this extra work alone, so I thought why not. I will simply go there to get fitter, and enjoy training with my mates.

We trained three times a week in the intense heat of the Australian summer; it was tough but fun, I really enjoyed myself. As the weeks ticked by, a few players stopped coming, and others were asked not to come back, but I was still there. Judgey told us he would soon name the final team. I carried on training in my usual style, running every sprint like it was the 100 metre final at the Olympics, listening to and following every instruction or piece of advice he offered. When he sat us all down after the last training session and thanked everyone for their efforts over the previous weeks, he said one of two things that I will never forget. He said that this group of players had immense talent, and the team he picked would win the league that year. He started to read out the names of the players who made the cut. The next moment I heard the name 'Luke Tyburski'. I didn't move and showed no emotion, I was stunned. Not for a second did I think I would make the team.

I was ecstatic, but also felt for the players whose names weren't read out, and were left feeling rejected. I had been there many times. With the exception of Stoney, none of my mates made the team. I think they were all as shocked as I was when my name was called out.

As I helped pack up the equipment and load it into the back of Judgey's car, my new coach said the second thing I've never forgotten. He told me I had great potential, and if I continued to work hard and stay focused, I could become a quality player. I told Judgey my main goal was to make the regional team that year. He looked at me and said in his strong Scottish accent, 'Luke, don't worry about the regional team, I know you will make that, I think you also have a fantastic chance of making the state team as well!' I instantly felt taller, stronger, fitter, and more determined than I had ever felt before. Here was someone outside my family who believed in me, and encouraged me to go after big goals and play the game at a higher level. It was a moment that changed the way I viewed my life, and the way I saw myself.

From that day, my mantra went from 'I want to be a footballer when I grow up'; to 'I *will* be a footballer when I grow up.' I felt a newfound confidence that I could achieve absolutely anything if I set my mind to it.

In the 12 months that followed, Joe Judge guided the Bathurst 75s Under 18 team to the league title, as promised. And after many years of hard work and dedication to improve as an athlete, my football career started to take off.

Still only 15, I was asked to become a member of the regional developmental academy even without trying out. I had tried out for the squad every year since I was 10 years old, but was never picked. I was also selected for the regional representative team and the New South Wales state squad, and then the National coaches for the Under 17 Joeys team had me in their sights. For some it may have appeared to be an overnight success story, but I had been putting in the hard work for years, with very few people, outside of my family, believing in my talent.

Bill Casey and Chris Assigal were my first two coaches who helped teach me the game, but it was my Uncle Phil who ignited the passion I have for the sport of football. Uncle Phil was a keen footballer himself, with a strong passion for the game. I remember watching him play from a young age, watching his every move, every pass, and especially his signature slide tackles. He was a tough player and I tried to imitate his style.

Sunday family barbeques were spent kicking the ball around with him in the back yard and whilst I was a lot younger, he would never *let* me win; I had to earn every kick, every possession of the ball. Some days he would control the ball under his foot, keeping me at bay with his powerful arm – this could last for the entire time before we were called in for lunch. There were many games when I didn't touch the ball at all, but I saw this as a challenge and I never gave up. If I could tackle and steal the ball from Uncle Phil, I could steal it from anyone.

The previous two years had taught me some more pivotal life lessons. I became aware of how your future can change when someone shows faith in you and can see your true potential. My never give up attitude was reinforced, while realising it was a necessity to always work as hard as you can, as you never know who is watching, and what they can see.

The following year I represented my state once more at the National Championships and was selected to play for the Wollongong Wolves youth team – a professional club located south of Sydney who played against the best Under 20 year olds in the country. This was a big family decision, as I would have to move to Sydney without them, with still a year and a half to go at high school, and was only 16 years old. But the opportunity to play for a professional football club was too good to pass up.

* * *

Another big life lesson came a few years later, with the realisation that a single moment can change everything. I was enjoying a peaceful beach holiday with family at Bawley Point, on the New South Wales south coast, when the phone rang. It was my ex-girlfriend with the devastating news that one of my best mates was fighting for his life.

'Paul has been in an accident, he's in intensive care,' she said, struggling with the words.

When I asked to speak to Paul's mother Sondra, a sobbing woman got on the phone and said, 'Luke, he is not good, he is in a coma.' I stopped walking. I was stunned and entirely numb.

Paul had been riding his motorbike when a car failed to give way at a T-intersection. Paul reacted with what he felt was his only option, by laying his bike down and sliding along the road towards the car, only stopping when he hit the driver's side door, with his head taking the brunt of the force.

I was three hours away from the hospital and I wanted to drive there immediately, but it was late afternoon and Sondra told me to stay where I was. I felt he needed me, although I knew there was nothing I could do – he was on life support. I left for the hospital the following morning.

It was outside visiting hours when I arrived, but the medical staff gave me five minutes alone with Paul in the intensive care unit of Sydney's Royal North Shore Hospital. The sound of constant beeps and the sight of blinking jagged lines on the monitors was frightening. It was surreal, yet very real. It is extremely difficult to see your best mate lifeless, with tubes going in and out of his nose, mouth and skull to relieve some of the pressure on his brain. My chest tightened and tears rolled down my cheeks. Paul's brain was injured and the swelling was not a positive sign. How his brain, and the rest of his body recovered from such trauma was up to Paul now. He had to fight for his life.

We were a tight-knit group of friends. We grew up together and were known as 'the boys' – it was an easy way for parents to collectively refer to us, especially if we got up to mischief. We laughed, joked and had plenty of fun when we were kids, but right now all I wanted to do was slap this six-foot-five, ginger-haired kid in the face and tell him to wake up, this joke was not funny anymore.

I remember holding Paul's limp, clammy hand, and saying 'Paul, you will fight, you will not give up, and I promise to do everything I can to help you.' I placed his hand back down on the white linen sheets and walked out of the hospital ward, with no idea how I could help my mate.

Paul gave us several scares during the 10 days he spent in intensive care, with the nurses telling us, on more than one occasion, his condition had worsened and the next few hours would be critical. But then he would rally and things began to improve. It was too early to know the severity of Paul's brain injury, or the impact it might have on his life. He was moved to the neurology ward, which was considered a positive step. He was alive, but the fun-loving, self-assured Paul of old was yet to return. He had a vague look plastered across his face and was unable to put more than two words together. When I looked in his eyes, the childhood mate I knew was nowhere to be seen. Paul's recovery was slow but positive.

I would visit the hospital almost every day putting the visits ahead of my football and the university degree I'd recently started. I wanted to make him laugh, tell him what we'd get up to when he got out of hospital, when life would be back to normal. This was usually met with a wry smile, a huff, or some other incoherent noise.

Slowly he began to put a few sentences together, and then to stand up. His big frame towered above the nurses, and gradually he took his first physical steps towards a very long and difficult recovery. Watching Paul trying to re-learn the basic skills he'd once mastered was tough. When asked to point to a spoon, he would pick up a fork, or if asked to show us the microwave, he'd take us to the washing machine. It was heartbreaking. Over time he moved to a full rehabilitation facility where he spent four months preparing to function again in the real world, and rediscovering his lost memory.

As part of the Exercise Science degree I was studying, I was learning about developing motor skills and the sequence of movements that work together to perform a task. Each time I visited Paul we would work on basic daily regimes, complete a series of exercises and go for walks. I would introduce new skills like kicking a football, or catching a basketball – anything to help his body re-learn key movements. Some days he hated it and didn't want to be involved, other days he was too tired and said he wanted to stay in bed. I would tell him to get out of bed NOW, and give me 10 push-ups. Everyone laughed and cheered him on, but I don't think Paul enjoyed it too much on these days.

All the boys would visit on weekends, and we'd play football out on the grass. For a laugh, we would position Paul as the goalie and kick balls at him. He had no idea what was going on, with balls flying everywhere around him. He didn't think it was as funny as we did, and I'm not sure his mum Sondra was amused either, but we were just teenage boys dealing with a terrible situation the only way we knew how.

Paul slowly improved and graduated to an apartment with a few other patients from the centre, where he learned to complete day-to-day chores. When it was his turn to cook dinner, I would help him chop and stir while he followed a recipe.

Almost six months after the accident, Paul had recovered enough to go home. He continued his rehabilitation for a further two months. The determination Paul showed throughout this horrific period gave me a perspective I would never forget. His inner strength showed no matter how difficult things became, he never *ever* gave up. He fought so hard for his life, and he won the fight. It made me feel I could overcome any obstacle put in front of me. Although I was helping Paul on a daily basis to recover, he was consistently showing me how to be more resilient in the process, something I would need in years to come.

2003 was an unforgettable year. In the space of 12 months, Paul fought his way back to the land of the living and learned how to walk, talk and be Paul again. For those who knew him well before the accident, there would always be a small part of the old Paul missing, but we are all extremely happy to still have him in our lives.

In the years after his accident, Paul married a beautiful woman and has two wonderful children. He has completed marathons, as well as a tough 100 kilometre ultra-marathon through the scenic Blue Mountains west of Sydney. He continues to be an important reminder to never give up, especially when life gets tough. And oh, it gets tough.

2.

ONE-WAY TICKET

An athletic scholarship at an American college was not on my radar, but with Australian soccer league about to enter a hiatus for a major restructure, it seemed a timely consideration, and I was intrigued.

'You know they pay for everything?' My classmate at university explained. 'Your tuition, accommodation, boots, kit – everything!' After accepting a scholarship to Brescia University in Owensboro, Kentucky, spending an entire day at the US Embassy in Sydney sorting out paperwork, I came away with a US student visa. I had just turned 21, and my knowledge of the US college system and their competitions was limited, but I had an open mind. I promised my family and myself I'd give it nothing less than 100% effort.

I settled into the student-athlete life quite easily, with morning and afternoon training sessions book-ending a day of lectures and study. I loved it! We played two games a week during the soccer season but with long distances between grounds, we were often away for several days at a time.

Brescia was in the National Association of Intercollegiate Athletics

(NAIA), a governing body of small athletic programs, with fewer rules and regulations than its bigger brother, The National Collegiate Athletic Association. The NCAA was the premier inter-collegiate competition in the US, spanning four divisions, and Division 1 (D1) was the 'big show.'

The squad at Brescia was a mix of nationalities and skill levels and whilst I enjoyed my time there, the coach knew I was keen to play at a higher level and so helped pave the way to my second scholarship at the University of Louisville (UofL) a large NCAA D1 school. I spent a weekend on campus as part of a recruiting trip and met the players, the coaching staff, and toured the school's facilities. I was impressed; the whole set up was world class.

Before starting at UofL, I was picked to play during the summer for a club in Orlando, Florida in the Premier Developmental League (PDL). The PDL is a national intercollegiate-season competition that gives top college players and recent graduates an opportunity to demonstrate their skills to the three professional leagues that seeded above.

The squad had a few British nationals who provided plenty of entertainment and laughs, and whilst I didn't get as much playing time as I'd hoped, I returned to Louisville fit, strong and ready to impress the coaches.

'You've been red-flagged Luke,' said Kenny, in his trademark Irish accent. Kenny was the coach who recruited me, and made it known I was there to help get the program back on track after several lacklustre years.

It seemed I had inadvertently breached the NCAA eligibility rules as I had been paid to play back in Australia. This put me in the professional category, as I had previously signed professional contracts.

With the school year already underway in Louisville, and an immediate ban from attending classes until my status had been clarified, I felt like an outcast. No training with the team, no access to the school's facilities, I was on my own. I continued to train alone until the decision was finalised. I was incredibly dis-appointed to learn I was ineligible to play at any NCAA school – my time at UofL was over before the season even started. I was eligible to play for the NAIA, where I'd come from, but I had no athletic scholarship, and my football future was completely up in the air. I was forced to consider moving back to Australia.

In this life altering moment, I remembered a phrase both my parents had said to me on more than one occasion, 'if you want something in life, it's up to you to find a way to get it.'

I wasn't giving up, I had to exhaust all avenues, and find a way to overcome the obstacle that lay in front of me. I sprang into action calling and emailing anyone I could think of who might be able to help me find a new school – my only prerequisites, that the institution offered a soccer program and an Exercise Science degree. There was no time to sleep as I canvassed hundreds of options from east to west to build my shortlist. I came up with around 20 schools from my exhaustive online search and kept my fingers crossed one of them would have a budget for an international student, I wasn't ready to close the door on my US adventure – I was desperate to stay.

Within 24 hours, I had a breakthrough and took a call from Coach Persson from Southern Nazarene University (SNU) in Oklahoma. Although he was happy with his squad (three days before the start of the season) and had no budget remaining for athletic scholarships, he was impressed with my resume and the recommendations he'd heard. He had requested a special dispensation of funds from his boss, the school's Athletic Director to bring me to SNU. It took me less than 10 seconds to accept his offer and I rushed off to organise my flight – and Google where exactly Oklahoma was, I had no clue.

I spent three semesters in Bethany, Oklahoma, spanning two seasons, and they were some of the best times I've had playing football. The team was like a mini United Nations; Africans from Kenya and Burkina Faso, Canadians, an Iranian, two Scots, and several Americans whose parents came from all over the globe. And now SNU for the first time had an Aussie.

We had a great season my first year there – achieving a number one National Ranking and making the Final Four in the National Championship, followed by a number two National Ranking, only to lose during the second round of another National Championship in my second season. But it was the off-field learning that had a bigger impact on my life.

SNU is a Christian Liberal Arts University on the outskirts of Oklahoma City. The size of the school was noticeably larger than Brescia University in Kentucky, but with still just over 2000 undergraduates, tiny in comparison to other American universities. The campus was littered with monuments of religious figures, fountains in memory of significant past students, along with numerous grassy areas for students to sit and chat. The campus' buildings and facilities were all in the close vicinity of one another; there was a real sense of community within the school, although a little different to what I was used to, but one I still very much enjoyed.

I would consider myself more spiritual than religious and did not have a religious upbringing, so their student way of life was an entirely new experience for me.

We had to attend chapel five times a week (or risk being fined) and religious studies were compulsory subjects. The male dormitories were at one end of the campus, and the female dormitories at the other end, and visitors of the opposite sex were absolutely off limits.

There was no drinking or smoking, on or off campus, and if you were caught partaking in either, you'd be hit with a fine and be sent to a rehabilitation program, which included community service within the school. If you haven't grown up in this type of environment, it may sound restrictive, and for many students, it certainly took some getting used to.

Students and teachers would approach me on campus and ask if they could pray with me. At first I thought this was a little strange, but I closed my eyes, rested my hands in theirs and listened as they softly spoke to God and asked him to watch over me, and help me on my journey. I felt truly humbled that another human being wanted to share such a sacred spiritual moment with me.

Hearing the stories of my new friends' upbringing, and observing their large communities of friends, families and colleagues who were all affiliated with their church, I realised, in a way, it was similar to how I grew up – except our community was centred on sporting clubs, not the church. I met many happy, caring and supportive people, and we've stayed in contact over the years.

Between seasons, I wanted to spend my summer vacation exploring a new city and continue playing through the break. I found myself a place with the San Francisco Seals, once again in the PDL competition, and immediately fell in love with the city – it was like being on a movie set. The Golden Gate Bridge, Fisherman's Wharf and other famous locations reminded me of movies or TV shows I'd watched as a kid.

I lived across the road from Ocean Beach, on the western edge of the San Franciscan peninsula, and spent many afternoons with the sun streaming through the living room windows, or out enjoying the incredible fresh produce and international cuisines. It was one of those rare times when I felt completely happy in all areas of my life. The buzzing city, with its white sandy beaches, and endless activities or events to attend was a far cry from Oklahoma. The team played right up and down the west coast of the U.S.A, from Los Angeles to up past Seattle in Washington State. I instantly fell in love with this part of the country; its open spaces, forests, beaches, mountains, and friendly locals who were more than welcoming to this young 23 year old Aussie kid. I headed back to Oklahoma feeling like I was getting a very broad experience of the USA.

It was late in the season, a few games before the playoffs in my second season at SNU, and we were scheduled to play a mid-week match against our local rivals. Just as I was about to make the short walk across campus to board the team bus, my phone rang. It was my Mum, clearly upset, calling to tell me that my beloved Aunty Barb had died. My Aunty Barb and I spoke regularly on the phone, and we also liked to communicate the old-fashioned way by writing letters to each other. She had suffered ongoing health issues related to the Type 1 diabetes she'd had her entire life and was recently hospitalised, but her death was sudden and unexpected in my eyes. The news hit me with a shattering force and I collapsed to my knees in tears.

I shared the news with Coach Persson and only a few of my teammates, quickly adding that I still wanted to play that night. I only remember two things from that game – making a left-footed pass that split the midfield with precision and found the feet of our striker who poked the ball past the opposition's goalkeeper to put us in the lead. The second, a screeching whistle from the referee who waved a yellow card over my head. I looked down to see an opposing player holding his leg in pain. I didn't know if I'd made contact with the ball or just his leg, but I was substituted with just minutes remaining.

I took a few days off to deal with the loss of my Aunty Barb and will never forget the compassion from my fellow students, the teachers and my teammates during such a tough and emotional time. People volunteered to cook my meals, they offered a listening ear, and of course many prayed for me and for my family. Their warmth and love helped comfort me when I felt isolated and so far from home. The SNU community helped me through this difficult time.

On graduation day, as I received my Bachelor's degree in Exercise Science, I could hear the cheers of my team-mates yelling 'Aussie Aussie Aussie, Oi Oi Oi', and can honestly say I felt my family was there with me.

With my time in the US now over, the next destination was England to try and further my career in one of their demanding and highly competitive professional leagues. I was ready for the next challenge.

* * *

My introduction to UK football was far from the glamorous perception most have of the world game at a professional level. The reality was enduring day after day of cold and gloomy December weather in northern England, and despite giving everything I had at every training session, I was unsuccessful in securing a contract.

It takes sacrifice to chase a dream and when times get challenging, a certain type of survival mode needs to ignite. I was on a steep learning curve, with the style, pace and tactics of play very different to what I had become accustomed to in the States, but I saw this as an opportunity to become a better player and constantly called everyone

I knew to help me find a new football home. There was also the very practical reality of needing somewhere to live.

I had nothing but a backpack, a mobile phone, and a few hundred pounds in my pocket as I drifted through the UK chasing my dream. I became acquainted with distant relatives and friends of friends, and stayed on their couches or floors, grateful to have a roof over my head. I even spent one freezing night at a remote train station after I missed the last train.

At times it wasn't easy hopping from club to club dealing with constant rejection, and not knowing where I would be staying each night, or where my next pay cheque would come from. Occasionally though I would let the romance of it all take over, what I was trying to achieve would give me hope that things would take a positive turn. I told myself that to make my dreams a reality, I was willing to put everything on the line, never ever give up, and trust the process. The years of rejection I faced growing up at the hands of representative coaches served me well during this time. I would regroup mentally, and then continue to do all I could to secure a trial, and get one foot in the door of a potential new employer.

There were plenty of times when I had to swallow my pride and reach out for financial help. I hated doing this as it made me feel helpless, but a few pounds quite literally went a long way. I was immensely grateful to those who believed in me, and helped me on my journey. Growing up my parents continually reminded my sister and I to always be kind to others. Although not my intention, I felt that kindness coming back around to me during these tough times.

Friends and family in my close-knit circle knew I would never ask for help unless I was in desperate need, and at times, desperation was the only word for it. But it was a good lesson about the basic needs in life – most things on our 'needs' list are actually 'wants'. Food, good health and shelter are core to survival, little else.

Desperation also spawns resourcefulness. As a teenager, I learned to cook dinner for my family and that passion for cooking never left me. It's a skill that saw me through some financially tight moments. Eating out was too expensive, but knowing how to turn a few affordable ingredients into a delicious meal was something that gave me great comfort during tough times.

After several months, I had exhausted all my contacts and still had no club to play with, and no place to live. There were times I would just turn up at a club's training facility in the hope they might need a defender. I followed several league tables and looked for clubs with telling signs – they may be on a losing streak, conceding a considerable number of goals, or suffering from injuries, but all to no avail.

My confidence was starting to slip. I constantly hit dead ends, it was time for me to think outside the box, meaning outside the UK. I made contact with a few people I knew within the professional leagues in the US, as they were about to begin pre-season training camp. I was fit and, my game had evolved after four months training in the UK – plus I had nothing but fond memories of playing soccer stateside. After a few days of calling and emailing contacts, I had a trial lined up in North Carolina.

Never ever give up.

At last I felt I was back on track. The coaching staff was happy with my training and interaction within the club, I was playing well in trial games, and the manager was including me in matches with his star players. I was hopeful of securing one of the few foreign spots on the roster but just as I started to regain my confidence, I had another setback. I was chasing down a ball at training when I felt my hamstring 'ping'. The club stood by me for several weeks, but as the season was about to begin,

I was not offered a place in their squad.

Once again, I was without a club, therefore unemployed, and with nowhere to go. I called everyone I knew in the USA soccer world, hoping to land a trial anywhere.

When I faced rejection and setbacks as a child, my Mum would challenge my drive, my ambition and my work ethic. She would ask, 'is this what you really want? If so, do everything that you possibly can to give yourself a chance to make it happen.' In my current predicament, these words could not have been closer to the truth. I visualised the 'Never Give Up' picture hanging in my family's kitchen of the frog and the pelican, and focused on giving myself every possible chance to succeed.

When an offer finally came for a central defender with a club in New Orleans, I was on the next plane to Louisiana. I had been recommended by a mutual friend and with the season start a week away, the manager wanted to see if I had what he was looking for.

It was the breakthrough I so desperately needed. I had clarity in what I wanted to achieve, I was willing to adapt and persevere when times got tough, and never give up! This is the life I chose to live, and whilst it had its moments of heartbreak, I wouldn't have it any other way. I now had a new footballing home.

New Orleans was good for me on many levels; I became good mates with our captain Stu and moved in with him and couple of other players in Old Metairie, a few miles outside of downtown New Orleans. Stu is a top bloke, charismatic and funny, and a quality player with pinpoint passing accuracy from his silky left foot – a trademark of the proud English geezer. As foreigners, we immersed ourselves within the vibrant New Orleans culture.

We met many other travellers who now called NOLA (New Orleans, Louisiana) home. Most shared a similar story; they ventured to southern Louisiana for a few weeks, but fell in love with the city its people, and simply never left. The mix of traditional Creole food, French and Spanish Creole architecture, combined with old school southern hospitality and a vibrant passion for life was irresistible.

The food was on a level I'd not tasted before; a mix of international cuisines combined with famous local dishes like jambalaya, gumbo, and a range of crawfish dishes. I continually tasted diverse flavours and exciting food pairings. With its countless restaurants, cafes and street vendors, NOLA was a true foodie heaven.

Locals and visitors alike enjoyed cultural events throughout this diverse city, from The New Orleans Jazz and Heritage Festival, to the famous Mardi Gras, where revellers poured into the party corridor of Bourbon Street to wrap up the annual Carnival season.

Beyond their hard work and strong results on the field, many players on our team helped with community efforts to rebuild housing following Hurricane Katrina two years earlier. Many residents impacted by this catastrophic event were still living in what only could be described as 'shells' of their former homes, struggling in appalling conditions. Many still without electricity or running water, it was heart-breaking to see these people in need years after the disaster; I was pleased I could help a few families slowly get back on track. In addition to this, I also organised a summer soccer camp at the local Dryades YMCA, a group that has educated and supported people within the New Orleans community for more than 100 years. Many of the kids who attended the camps were from broken homes, or lived in families that struggled to make ends meet. It was quite a challenge engaging them in a game they weren't much interested in, but with the help of a few teammates, we managed to teach a few of the kids how to correctly pass and dribble a football. The happy faces when they mastered a new sporting skill made the experience worthwhile.

One afternoon a group of players sat together in our lounge room watching a Champions League football match on the television, I took a call from my Mum in Australia who broke the news my grandmother had suffered a stroke. Gran, or Joycie, as I affectionately called her, was like a second mother to me and I felt physically sick when I heard the words from Mum.

She was my maternal grandmother and a truly remarkable woman who raised seven of her own children and continued to nurture her six grandchildren. Some of my fondest memories of Gran are walking hand in hand through the local park on a sunny spring day, stopping to smell and name each of the flowering plants. By the age of five I could name all the flowers blooming in Bathurst's Machattie Park.

I also remember sitting around Gran's wooden table with a cup of tea, chatting about life and soaking up the sun, or listening to the rain against the large window in her sitting room. She encouraged me to travel the world, but to never look down on others who are less fortunate. She taught me not to want what someone else had, but be happy and content with what I had, especially my loving family. She urged me to do my very best at everything, regardless of whether I enjoyed it or not.

But most importantly, she would fill my heart with love, and assure me that I was loved and should always reciprocate this affection. Family has continued to ground me in life throughout many difficult times and Gran was instrumental in making sure I knew how much I was loved.

When I looked at Gran, I didn't see an ageing woman, I saw a wise, strong, and confident human being who experienced life to its fullest. I naively hoped this remarkable woman would be with me forever.

My sister flew home from London but at such a crucial time in the soccer season, and with the club on the verge of making the playoffs, I made the decision to stay in New Orleans. I felt confident Gran would make it through brain surgery after speaking to her over the phone briefly before the operation. She sounded tired but she told me she was fine and that I should stay where I was and keep doing what I loved. She whispered, 'go get them love'.

Two nights later, Mum called again telling me Gran had died. My decision not to fly home and see her pre-surgery remains one of my biggest regrets in life. I was devastated and furious at the world for taking my beloved Gran from me. I felt like I lost a piece of myself that day, and for some reason, I was unable to get myself on a plane and be with family as my charismatic and loving grandmother was laid to rest. Part of me didn't want to witness it, as it then would be completely real, while the other part of me felt ashamed that I didn't drop everything to be by my Gran's side, and help support my family during such a difficult time.

I wasn't the same after Gran died. My mood was flat, as was my performance on the pitch. I played a match immediately after losing Gran and despite scoring the winning goal, I knew my performance was lacklustre. I was dropped to the bench for the following game, and the rest of the season.

Our captain Stu immediately noticed the shift in my personality and outlook on life. We spent a lot of time together and spoke openly with one another. He knew I was struggling, and simply knowing I had a mate there if I needed him was a huge support to me. I suffered extended periods of low energy, on occasions unable to move, or even function normally. I dismissed these lows as part of the grieving for my Gran. At the end of the season, I moved back to the UK to be with my sister.

* * *

Within 24 hours of arriving at the cosy Kent village of Benenden where my sister lived, I received an email from a university mate who I played football with in Oklahoma. Diego was playing for a lower league club in Belgium and told me the club was interested in seeing me play. Next thing I knew I was headed for the Eurostar terminal in Ashford. I bought a one-way train ticket to Brussels and then transferred to a local train for my final destination, Liège.

An immaculately dressed conductor stood over me with his hand outstretched but dismissed the ticket I presented him with a wave of his hand. My ticket said Liège and the train was going to Liège, but he wasn't happy. I spoke little French and he apparently spoke no English, so whatever the problem was, it was lost in non-verbal translation. It was a telling sign that my next adventure had begun.

Royal Racing Montegnée FC was part of the regional leagues in Belgium's lower tier football competition, and was owned by an Englishman. His strategy was to bring in foreign players to push the club up through the rankings. Unfortunately for most of the players there, he had nothing but Euro signs in his eyes, searching for one or two footballers that may shine enough to be sold to a bigger club for a hefty transfer fee.

He was big on promise but delivered little, yet the foreign contingent from Canada, the US, England and Estonia formed a tightknit group; we lived, trained and socialised together. Disappointingly, within a month of arriving my body let me down again and I suffered a major groin injury. I discovered, despite the unprofessionalism of the club's owner, the medical team and physical therapy consultants were some of the best I have ever worked with.

Three times a week I would head into the centre of Liège for a physiotherapy treatment session with Cedric. We forged a strong professional relationship, and as I was keen to learn French during many of our sessions, he introduced me to another of his athlete clients Keyidi, a talented European handball player who was in Liège playing as well as studying to be a physiotherapist. With complementary language skills, we began to meet on a regular basis around our training schedules so we could learn each other's languages. Compared to my French, her English was perfect!

It took me a while to have any sort of conversation in my new second language with her, but she was a clever teacher. We took outings together to the supermarket or to a restaurant where she pretended she couldn't speak French, leaving me to do all the talking. She encouraged me to approach strangers and ask for directions to the old town or to various landmarks that dated back to medieval times.

She once suggested I ask for directions to the Meuse River, which ran right through the middle of the city and was unmissable. Keyidi thought it was funny and I was always up for a laugh, even at my own expense. I loved learning a new language, and felt at home settling into the city's culture of food, coffee, and nightlife, but all in a moderate European way.

Now that I was finally fit, I was playing well, but I was disappointed with the overall experience at the club. The squad had a broad range of abilities training together, including many players who lacked a professional work ethic. This was frustrating but I continued to work hard throughout the second part of the season as the club had a chance for promotion. I wanted to do everything I possibly could to make this happen.

Being in Belgium also opened up new professional connections for me outside of football. I was keen to continue my personal development as a fitness coach, and studied an advanced Personal Training course online through a prestigious Fitness Institute in Australia. I used several of my teammates as case studies and helped many others develop their own extra training sessions to complete each week, tailored to the areas they needed to enhance their performance on the pitch.

I was introduced to an Osteopath and Fitness Coach by the name of Eric Houben, and arranged to meet up for coffee on a cobblestone street overlooking Liège's St Paul's Cathedral.

We clicked right away and he soon became an important mentor for me as we worked together to create innovative exercises tailored to his broad clientele of elite and everyday athletes. Eric trusted my knowledge and skills to deal with his clients while he attended conferences, giving me more professional confidence, and a deeper understanding of the human body. His mentorship came at the right time in my own journey.

The final few months of my season in Liège were tough as most of the international players had not been paid and the club seemed to be struggling financially. With my bank account shrinking, and the end of the season approaching, I began preparing to head back to England for another go at securing a football deal in the UK. But first on the agenda, a brief rest over the British summer and some much-needed family time.

3.

ALL OVER RED ROVER

Hanging out with my sister Moo, as I call her, has always kept me grounded. I felt loved and supported and could easily tell what she thought of my latest crazy plan – often just a certain look on her face would tell me all I needed to know.

After a few weeks, I was keen to find work to give me a financial buffer ahead of the UK season. London is an expensive city, but it was also my best bet of landing a job – all I needed was a stopgap until I secured a football contract.

Thank god for mates.

Like many people who have chosen a nomadic lifestyle, it's easy to let friendships slide a little. I felt lucky to have a handful of close friends who I may not see or speak to very often but when we do reconnect, we seem to pick up where we left off. Tiny is one of those friends.

He was christened Nathanael, but as a tall skinny kid, towering over all the other kids on the basketball courts of Bathurst, he earned the nickname Tiny and it stuck. I crashed on the couch in Tiny's London apartment while I established my network in the health and fitness industry, expanding on my approach of training others I'd refined in Belgium and the US.

I built up a small client base out of a gym in west London and soon moved into a shared house of my own, just before I overstayed my welcome at Tiny's place. Keeping my main goal firmly in focus, I maintained a disciplined regime and trained hard every day to get myself fit for the upcoming season. Occasionally I needed physical therapy to keep my body in one piece.

It was important for me to be readily available for my existing clients, and the new clients I was now training. Most of the time this meant sacrificing my own rest and recuperation, but I knew I had to save some cash to cover times when I had to drop everything for a period of time to go on trial with a club, who showed interest in signing me. Being part of other people's training goals and helping them overcome their struggles was gratifying and inspiring. When I saw clients bust through personal challenges it motivated me to keep pushing myself. But the setbacks kept coming.

The pain was all too familiar; a severe dull ache deep inside my left groin. I was worried I had the same injury I'd suffered in Belgium that took months to recover from. With no health insurance, and a National Health Service waiting list of several months, I had no choice but to scrape together the funds to pay a specialist, and the resulting MRI scan. An expert diagnosis would be the only way to tell for sure what type of injury I was dealing with, so I could plan my rehabilitation and recovery.

On a friend's recommendation, I made an appointment with Dr Lorenzo Masci, a leading Australian sports physician based in London. Dr Masci was a very straight to the point kind of guy, but at the same time helped you understand what the problem was, and the options you had to attempt to fix it. After looking at the MRI scan, Dr Masci confirmed I had inflamed my pubic symphysis and diagnosed Osteitis Pubis, round two. The injury is caused by tissue damage combined with severe inflammation of the pubic symphysis. The pain is debilitating. As my physiotherapist, Cedric, explained nearly 12 months earlier in Belgium, it's a common injury in sports that use a kicking motion.

I emailed Cedric to tell him the bad news and he was more than happy to help guide my rehabilitation process from across the English Channel. After some initial rest, I set off yet again on the lonely path to recovery. One positive moment was meeting up with an Australian pilates teacher who I immediately clicked with. She only had a couple of months left in London before she was moving back to Sydney. Although it was brief, our whirlwind romance caught us both by surprise, the feelings we felt for one another were surprisingly strong when it was time for her to head back to Australia.

Another British summer rolled around as I continued my rehab. The sun was a wonderful healer and I worked through my daily training sessions on the freshly cut grass at my local park. My groin felt good but now I was experiencing pain on the outside of my right foot. I was training with discomfort during my sessions, but after my body had cooled down, I was reduced to a hobble; I could barely put weight through my foot. This was not a good sign.

I saw numerous physical therapists, medical practitioners and herbalists, and tried the many weird procedures prescribed to me (like wearing a sock soaked in apple cider vinegar and wrapped in a plastic bag while I slept), but nothing seemed to work. I went back to see Dr Masci who I'd now spent so much time with I was on a first name basis. After exhausting all possible scenarios, Lorenzo in his softly spoken Aussie accent suggested exploratory surgery, and I reluctantly agreed. I honestly felt I had exhausted all other possibilities, I felt like I had no other option.

While all this was going on, I had a call from my pilates friend who was heading back to the UK for a wedding. She asked what I thought about her buying just a one-way ticket to see if we would work as a couple. She gave me a few days to think about it before I replied with an enthusiastic 'yes'!

Post-surgery, just as I was coming down from an epic dose of painkillers and general anaesthetic, the surgeon came in to see how I was feeling. At that point, I couldn't feel much at all. His first words did not fill me with hope. He told me when he opened up the outside of my right foot and looked at all my peroneal tissues, he discovered a large 'strap' like piece of tendon hanging by a few determined fibres, so he sliced it off.

My recovery required me to stay in bed with my foot elevated for 15 days. I was only permitted out of bed to use the toilet. It was a slow and tedious rehab but eventually I could walk without pain, and before long I could run and sprint. I felt like a completely different person; I was pain-free and I haven't had a problem with that area of my foot since.

This was a glimmer of light at the end of a long injury tunnel and I began to sell myself to clubs once more. The constant rejection was disheartening, but I knew I only needed one club to say they would take a look at me, and my football career could be back on track. With this mindset firmly entrenched, I continued the daily grind of internet searches, emails, phone calls, and turning up at numerous clubs' training facilities unannounced – I was willing to try anything. I was all in!

I spread my net as far as possible and contacted every club in the relegation zone of most leagues right across the UK. Every time it was, 'no thanks'.

I was determined, but there's only so much rejection anyone can take and negative thoughts started creep into my head about my ability, my motives and at times, my self-worth. My new relationship was great, we planned weekend European getaways together, and spoke daily to one another, both eager to learn all we could about each other. As I suffered the constant knockbacks in my quest to play again, I struggled to be completely open and honest. At times, I closed myself off from my partner and that occasionally put a strain on things, although she was extremely supportive, I simply didn't feel I was strong enough to share my true thoughts and feelings I was having regarding my mental health, and football career. Whether my girlfriend actually understood what I was going through, or why I was closed off, I'm not sure. What I did know was, she cared for me deeply through this difficult time, and when she smiled, it made me smile, both on the inside and out.

My body certainly wasn't doing me any favours. Walking home after a solo training session in my local park on a brisk autumn morning, I felt a bit of a niggle in my right Achilles tendon. I didn't give it too much thought but applied some ice and did a little extra self-massage on the muscles in my lower leg. The next morning it had progressed to an extreme tightening and a hot sharp pain in my heel, so it was back to see Dr Masci again, an expert in tendons which were a constant topic of his research. The great thing about Lorenzo was he never made a big deal about any injuries. It was always a matter of fact. Understand what was wrong, or identify possibilities, then come up with a range of solutions to fix or minimise lasting damage. This suited me perfectly.

Apart from inflammation, he couldn't see or feel any reason for my Achilles tendon flare up. He told me to keep an eye on it and come back if needed. Lorenzo trusted my judgment to know when I should push on with training, or back off. If I had specific concerns or questions, he was happy to answer the occasional email.

I soldiered on through the pain and with several trials lined up I needed to stay fit. On top of my painful Achilles tendon, numerous other ailments surfaced due to my body compensating for the heel pain when I ran. I had multiple cortisone injections in my hip, psoas, groin, back and knee, as well as many other manual treatments to try and keep me in one piece. Although these injuries may have set me back physically for many months collectively, I never wavered from my end goal, to sign another professional football contract. I was prepared to do whatever it took to achieve this, playing through constant pain, being relentless in my approach, and accepting there will be adversity throughout my journey. After years battling in this way, it became normal, and what I expected to face when going after my goals.

Each time I turned up to train at a prospective club, I'd smile and swallow the pain. My body was a ticking time bomb and I had no idea when it might explode, but I couldn't let on that I was performing at less than 100%. Only I knew my performance was closer to 70% of my ability, and each step sent a shock of pain shooting through my body. Dealing with the pain was simply part of the process to success. My drive, hunger, and determination to get my career back on track were as strong as ever. I was only 26 years old; I felt I still had several more good years left in me.

The rejections continued, so did the lies to managers who asked if I was carrying any injuries. A clear 'no' assured them I was ready to play if needed. It also saved at least half an hour of me explaining what was actually wrong with me! To say I was desperate to find a club would be an understatement.

I finally found a new club to train with – a semi-professional outfit doing quite well in a professional league. They were a two-hour trip away and we trained three or four nights every week, which meant for some late nights. If I made it through the front door by midnight that only gave me a handful of hours sleep before my first personal training clients started at 6.30 a.m. I was exhausted and at an all-time low due to the throbbing pain in my Achilles.

In a blink of an eye the pain from my Achilles would suck the life out of me. At times my entire body felt numb from the inside out, which triggered negative and destructive thoughts. Being injured sometimes felt like a massive dark cloud overshadowing my life, I became miserable and believed no one else had it worse than I did. Of course, this couldn't be further from the truth, but try telling that to an injured athlete and one struggling with their mental health.

My girlfriend was understanding and looked after me however she could during this time. We weren't living together, but she would often come over and cook me dinner. Although I knew she cared deeply for me, as I did for her, I still wasn't able to bring myself to explain the full extent of my mental anguish to her, or anyone else for that matter.

Even my sister and my parents, who have always been my biggest supporters, began to question if I should continue to push my body, as it was continually breaking down. They were now not only concerned for my physical health, but also my mental health as well. My parents felt my pain from the other side of the world. Mum says they would take a breath each time I called with news of another injury because they knew how devastated I would be. She said, 'we could always tell, even if you tried to be brave, we knew from your tone of voice things weren't good.'

The journey home after one training session took a little longer than usual, as I missed a connecting train and had to wait half an hour for the next one. The pace I walked between the three trains I caught each way was slower than usual as my Achilles felt like it was on fire. I had to stop and rest after every 20-30 paces, dry retching with the pain. It was close to one in the morning when I eventually made it home, as I fumbled in the bottom of my kitbag for the keys to my front door.

Turning the key then pushing open the door, I was greeted with the usual sight of a steep staircase leading up to a landing; this wasn't going to be an easy feat to conquer in my current condition. The only way was to pull myself up, letting my arms do most of the work, as my right leg was a dead weight. I couldn't put any force through my right leg without excruciating pain. When I finally reached the landing, I crawled to my bedroom, shut the door, and wept. Was this the end of my childhood dream?

After releasing some emotion that had weighed me down for many months, I regained my composure and literally hopped on my left foot to the kitchen, fetching some ice packs for an hour's worth of cold therapy before falling asleep in the wee hours.

Later that morning I made two phone calls; one to the manager of the club telling him I'd suffered an injury at training the night before and would be out for a few weeks, and the other to Lorenzo's assistant, booking yet another appointment. Deep down I knew I was headed for the operation table again - the second time in five months! Lorenzo referred me to one of the world's leading Achilles tendon specialists, Professor Hakan Alfredson. There was a two-week waitlist, so I spontaneously booked a flight to see one of my good mates who was living in Guatemala. Dave was teaching English at a school out there, and with a quick text message to see if he would mind me coming out, my flight was booked.

Random? Yes. A Band-Aid solution to my latest problem? Probably. My girlfriend was not happy and rightly so. Rather than have talk openly and face the reality of my emotional demons, I selfishly ran away to Guatemala.

The five days away gave me a chance to escape my real life. The Achilles pain was bearable (just) and I managed to climb several volcanoes (one erupted only days after I was on top of it), and trek along Lake Atitlan, a crystal-clear body of water surrounded by smouldering peaks. I thought, as I would be having surgery, I couldn't make my Achilles any worse with all the trekking I was doing. I felt liberated in my escape; like my life's problems had dissolved into the dusty Guatemalan trails I was now walking.

Dave is a Texan I played football with during my time in Oklahoma who became one of my closest friends. We spent hours reminiscing on the rooftop of his tiny apartment in Quetzaltenango about our shared experiences in Oklahoma, and briefly in London after he played a season in Austria. Dave was the best goalkeeper I have ever shared a pitch with.

Gazing up at the surrounding mountains and volcanoes with puffy white clouds strung above was hypnotic. My mind was gloriously blank for the first time in years as I marvelled at the natural beauty around me. The trip to Guatemala ignited a fire within, and gave me a much-needed boost of confidence as I pondered a return to the UK for another operation. The adventures helped me realise, for the first time in a very long time, that life without football can be beautiful and rewarding.

D-Day had arrived, and as I walked through the automatic doors at London's Princess Grace Hospital carrying my own set of crutches, I was met with some strange looks from the front desk and concierge. When it comes to fixing problems with Achilles tendons, Professor Alfredson was the best specialist around according to Lorenzo and several other health care professionals, and 30 seconds of my own online research assured me I was in excellent hands. I was slightly sedated but awake during the operation, with Lorenzo and a handful of observers there to watch Professor Alfredson work his magic.

We casually chatted as he opened up my heel to inspect the area, and after surveying the damage and speaking softly to Lorenzo and the others in the room he said, 'I see a lot of inflammation, and there is also some bone growth within the tendon.' He asked me if I wanted him to cut out the bone that had grown in my tendon

'You're the surgeon, what do you think?' I responded somewhat confused. Professor Alfredson smiled and said, 'I think I'll leave it in, as once I cut into the Achilles, it may never be the same again.'

He continued scraping out the large amounts of inflamed tissue, before sewing me up. The procedure was declared a success, and following a short recovery, I was back walking in four weeks and looked forward to being pain-free.

No such luck.

Eight weeks passed and I was doing some light training each day but was still in pain whenever I walked, and as my pace increased, so did the pain. After another month and several trips back to see Lorenzo and Professor Alfredson, I had made peace within myself that, at the age of 26, I would walk with Achilles tendon pain for the rest of my life. It had become so dampening, I thought it would be best to deal with it and try to move on. With this latest injury, I expected that my life would be a cycle of becoming injured, then working to recover from whatever ailment my body battled; this would be part of the process for my athletic career, it was very dangerous way of thinking.

Except that this time, I wouldn't recover to be pain-free.

Then Lorenzo had a thought. He had once worked with a physiotherapist who had studied an old technique called fibrolysis. Lorenzo introduced me to Martin O'Connell who had been using this technique to help his private clients, as well as footballers at an English Premiership club where he was employed.

Martin (Mo) was younger than I expected, only a handful of years older than me. His welcoming smile and comforting tone of voice put whatever reservations I had about seeing yet another practitioner to rest. We got on immediately, laughing, joking, and sharing stories about the football world. '*I won't hold it against you that you're Australian*' he joked, before taking a look at my Achilles. Mo pulled, pushed, poked and squeezed it, much to my discomfort. He believed, with some regular treatment, that he could make inroads into my pain, and maybe even remove it all together. Three or four times a week I endured scraping down of the tendon against the skin, with Mo pulling it in all directions using his stainless steel blunt hooked tools he dubbed 'fibrolysers'. With varying sizes, they could have been mistaken for instruments of torture – actually, that's pretty much what they were!

When my skin could take no more, and it began to wear thin from the furious rubbing motion of Mo's 'magic wands', our session would stop. On several occasions my skin broke, leaving the patch of raw flesh looking like an exploded blister.

I had become so accustomed to the pain in my Achilles that when

Mo said he wanted me to start running, and there was a good chance I'd be pain free, I was at first a little shocked. It was reward enough to walk without pain, but to run without any discomfort after six long months was a huge boost. Before long, I was training intensely every day, living my life pain and injury free. I was fit and strong, and started to believe I was moving forwards once again, then, the most random incident occurred.

I was cycling the usual five kilometres from my house to the gym where I trained my clients. It was a bright summer's evening and I slowed down as I approached the red traffic lights ahead on my mountain bike. I sat down on the seat, stopped pedalling and coasted slowly towards the intersection.

The weary groan of brakes signalled a red double-decker bus was right behind me. The lights turned amber then green, and I stood up on the pedals to pick up speed. In the blink of an eye, I was seeing the world the wrong way up, with the black tarmac of the road heading straight towards me, and fast!

Crunch!

My head, shoulder, and hip slammed into the road. I scrambled to my feet and turned to see the bus's windscreen only an arm's length away. It had stopped close enough for me to register the shocked expressions on the passengers' faces. I was dazed and confused but with adrenaline surging, managed to drag myself off the road.

I dipped in and out of consciousness with a sharp pain shooting through my shoulder. I knew I had broken my collarbone; it was pure agony. I was in a bad way and thought I was becoming delirious and imagining things when I heard my girlfriend's voice. Bizarrely, she had been walking along the street and was just about to yell out to me when she saw the entire accident unfold. We figured out that when I got out of my seat and pushed down hard on my pedals, the chain had snapped, which sent me flying over the handlebars with no resistance. Weirdly, she asked me if she should call for an ambulance and I was at least semi-conscious enough to tell her I thought that would be wise!

The damage was a double fracture to my collarbone, and I needed my third surgery in just 11 months to reposition it with screws and a metal plate. I called Mo later that night to tell him the news, and ask if he knew any good shoulder surgeons, his quick response put my mind at easy. 'I'll call Carlos Cobiella now mate, and sort you out an appointment for tomorrow.' Mo was not only a fantastic physiotherapist, but also a concerned friend.

The surgery went well, and after a six-week rest period, I was able to use my arm again, but severe feelings of negativity bombarded the space between my ears. I found I couldn't catch myself before a torrent of questions rocketed through my mind.

Disturbing thoughts of 'is life really worth it?' prowled around my head, sending me into deeper bouts of depression.

I tried to stay positive and remain present in each moment, but at times this only made me feel more trapped inside my head. The punishing thoughts became entangled in my mind and life began to feel unmanageable. - I asked myself the same question daily, ' is living this life really worth it?'

On the outside though, I shrugged off my cycling accident with a smile and cheeky comment of 'my legs are just too powerful', which was met with a roll of the eyes and a collective laugh from most people. I was now quite skilled at putting on a happy face, but it felt like I was battling some sort of internal force that dictated my moods and feelings. As soon as I was alone, the voice in my head would yell negative remarks, leaving me feeling worthless and disempowered. I would feel drained of energy and unable to function, hiding my true inner thoughts and emotions from the world.

After the bike accident, I developed back problems and was barely able to twist my body to the right without triggering a stabbing pain in my spine. I had all the conventional scans but neither Mo nor Lorenzo could diagnose the cause. It would need further investigation.

The scanning machine spun around me only centimetres from my body as it closely inspected my head and torso. Each revolution lasted 10-15 seconds and I had to hold my breath to stabilise my rib cage, then have a 60 second rest before going again. The process was repeated a dozen times.

The next stage was an injection of radioactive dye to highlight any lesions or tissue trauma in the next set of scans. I was curious about the icy cold liquid and asked the nurse if it really was safe. She smiled and said, 'of course it is, we do this procedure all the time, but for the next two hours, stay away from pregnant woman and new born babies, as it can be harmful to them!'

The results of my scans came through a few days later, showing I had damaged the cartilage of several facet joints in my spine when I hit the road after being thrown from my bike. Not life threatening, but enough to warrant a general anesthetic and an injection of steroids to help the damaged cartilage repair itself. This in turn allowed the vertebrae of the spine to move smoothly against one another.

A month passed before I could resume training and I took things slowly, particularly when running and switching direction – it was a long road to recovery.

Once again, the all too familiar injury, recovery, rehabilitation cycle was reinforced. It felt oddly normal, like I was to expect this sequence of events for the rest of my life. Rehabilitation continued over the Christmas period and it snowed across much of the UK. January training sessions at the local park were peaceful as the snow was knee deep in parts and most sane people were bunkered down in their warm homes. I found the time alone in the white fields had a calming effect on me.

Typical training sessions would start with a warm up, followed by variations of short sprints in different directions through the snow. As the day warmed up and the sun came out, families arrived at the park to build snowmen or create snow angels and here I was running around like a mad man in the snow. I can only imagine what others must have thought! After missing so many months of training, I was happy to move and run freely again.

A friend of a friend helped me land a position at a club not too far from where I was living in west London. I trained with the first team, and played a few reserve team games. The feedback I received from the managers of both squads was positive and my confidence grew each time I completed a crisp pass into a teammate's feet. What I thought was a genuine smile returned to my face most days, my relationship was blooming with talks of how we would spend our future together, and life was looking like it was finally coming together.

But without warning and for no reason, my mind began to wander down a gloomy trail. At times, I was barely able to drag myself to training and struggled to ignore the negative messages flying around in my head. I tried to ignore these debilitating voices and thoughts, but it was becoming increasingly draining to keep the battle I was going through mentally to myself. Still ashamed of my thoughts, and confused about why I was feeling this way, I went on pretending like everything was 'OK.'

The reserve team manager pulled me aside one morning and told me the upcoming game would drive their decision about my future with the club. This was it – the final chance I had been waiting for – all I had to do was put in another strong showing to keep the dream alive!

The day before the match we had a light training session working through set plays and a few tactics. Turning to chase down a loose ball, not running fast, I felt a tearing sensation in the middle of my right hamstring. I didn't need to speak with the manager to know my time at the club had come to an end. The close of the season was only a few games away and I had no chance of securing a deal. The bus ride home was a sombre one.

Up until this point, I remained determined not to give up, I was driven by an intense fear of failure and a deep desire to prove my ability to all those who doubted me in my younger years. I was confident I could get fit and sign another contract, and I convinced myself I could achieve anything I could put my mind to. But with this latest injury, my mood shifted heavily and I struggled to complete even simple activities. I can only describe the feeling as an overpowering force holding me back. Thoughts of self-harm returned from somewhere deep within, but I continually brushed them off as disappointment with yet another injury getting in the way of my dream.

I told myself to 'snap out of it', but the horrible suicidal and self-harming thoughts would not budge. I had always believed the best way to handle setbacks was to roll your sleeves up and get on with it. For some reason, I just couldn't manage to do this. After years of inner torment, I finally found enough courage to ask for help, and reached out to a psychotherapist for guidance.

When I was diagnosed with clinical depression it was almost a relief. Now this negative energy had been identified, I felt some of the weight begin to lift. I didn't need a label for what I was going through, the diagnosis simply gave me context for why I was feeling the way I was, and a better understanding of myself. Did it change anything? Well, not really, but with weekly sessions working with the therapist, we began piecing together the voids in my life where I simply shut myself off from the world. We worked on clarifying what I was feeling and looked for triggers that would send me into the state of emotional paralysis and despair. She helped by giving me tools to deal with life. Nobody knew about these consultations, not even my girlfriend. I felt weak and ashamed, and even more confused about how I ended up this way.

The summer came and went in a bit of a blur and I continually put on a brave face to the outside world. When I was alone, or alone with my thoughts, the volume of internal negativity would increase, a constant battle between my ears that felt like pounding against the inside of my skull. But I continued to suppress these thoughts and emotions, just as I had done for years or whenever the skills I was learning in therapy wouldn't make an impact.

As I prepared for the start of a new football season, I suffered a calf tear that needed four weeks rest. Just as I was about to hit full fitness, I then tore my other calf muscle. Even Mo, who had worked daily with professional footballers for many years, couldn't understand why I was suffering repeated injuries.

My parents had a theory, which I only learned years later. Around this time Mum remembers saying to Dad 'do you think all these injuries are happening because he's scared that he's not going to achieve the level he needs to be satisfied?'

They both thought it was possible that I was somehow 'willing' the soft tissue injuries to occur so I had an excuse – but they said nothing to me at the time. Perhaps they could see a connection between my physical fitness and my emotional health – even if I hadn't yet seen it.

It was tough keeping a relationship on track during so many setbacks. My mood was constantly low, frustration spilled out into conversations, which resulted in regular bickering between my girlfriend and I. Although we very much loved one another, and only wanted each other to be happy, my lack of communication put a strain on our relationship at times.

Once the second calf tear recovered, I was straight back into training. I completed my usual warm up with some light running in different directions and dynamic stretching, gradually increasing the intensity of my movements. I would follow this with some multi-directional dribbling with the ball at my feet. I decided to complete part of the fitness section of my session with a drill I'd done countless times.

The routine was a 70 metre run over a 30 metre course, so two laps followed by a 10 metre burst, with 15 repetitions following a 90-second rest period between repetitions.

I had just started my eighth repetition with thoughts of 'stay low, fast feet and drive' as I approached the yellow plastic cone I'd measured to be 30 metres from my starting position. I began to shorten my stride, quicken my steps and plant my foot next to the cone, before pushing off to begin the next leg of this repetition.

As I began to decelerate and take shorter quicker steps, I felt the familiar dull stretching sensation through my calf. I had torn it – again. And that was it. I made the decision to quit football there and then. I felt a wave of emotion sweep throughout my entire body. The voice in my head said, *'I'm done!'*

* * *

My professional football career was over. After three operations, an excruciating back injury, countless injections, and many different physical therapies in the space of three years I was forced to endure, I'd had enough. It was time to call it quits and end the continuous struggle to keep my body in one piece. The moment I heard the words 'I'm done', a wave of relief washed over me. I even managed a smile as I limped home from another lonely training session.

I felt a weird sense of freedom as I released the pressure and expectations I had been loading myself up with for years. There was a sense of peace in my life in this moment. A quiet, yet transformative euphoria encompassed me as I acknowledged the journey I had been on. My constant battles to overcome injury, moving away from family and friends, early morning training sessions before school and the late nights getting home after training at faraway clubs. All the sacrifices my family had made for me to live my dream were all worth it.

For the first time in my life, I felt truly proud of what I had achieved. I had given my dream everything I had – from the age of four kicking a tennis ball against the fence at my parent's house. A sense of contentment filled my soul.

Alongside this overwhelming feeling of satisfaction, extreme happiness filled my heart. I wasn't sad that my career was now over, nor did I feel any regret for the path I chose to take in my life up to this point. It was time to move on with my life, and for the first time in years, I wanted to.

I didn't know what to expect when I decided to stop playing the game I loved so much. To my surprise I felt positive about the future. I now could finally take a brief pause in life to gather myself, recover physically, and spend some time reflecting on what I deemed was a fantastic international career. It was a perfect time to reboot and rebuild my life after some initial rest.

* * *

The healing process began on my bedroom floor with my injured leg elevated and resting on a bag of ice to reduce the swelling in the torn muscle. I reached for my phone to text my girlfriend, my parents, and Mo about my immediate retirement. Then I tossed away my phone to give myself some headspace.

Before long, anxious thoughts began to fly through my head.

What's next?

Where do I go from here?

What do I want to do with my life?

Who am I?

Raz, a mate who I grew up with, once told me about an ultra-marathon across the Sahara desert, where each runner had to carry all their supplies for the week in a backpack. I remember laughing when he told me; I thought he was making it up! Despite my total lack of interest in long-distance running, this race immediately struck a chord. It wasn't that it was a running race, but a challenge, and one that would test my mental, physical, and emotional toughness – something I've been doing my entire life.

Growing up I was constantly challenged. What I have achieved in life so far didn't come easy, and I became accustomed that nothing ever would. The constant rejection, injuries, and relentless hard work became second nature to me. This is my life, and deep down I enjoyed it! In many ways, my whole life, until this point, was preparing me for endurance sports. My never-give-up attitude, willingness to endure, and ability to adapt when faced with an obstacle were traits I had as a footballer. Little did I know it's these exact same traits a person would need when running through the Sahara desert.

I have no idea why I remembered this conversation with Raz, but at such a vulnerable time when I'd barely begun to process the end of my football career, I opened my computer and typed 'world's toughest ultra-marathon in Sahara desert' into the search engine.

* * *

The Marathon des Sables (MDS) is a 255 kilometre, seven-day, self-supported, multi-stage ultra-marathon. Talk about bonkers! Despite my torn calf muscle, the confident, carefree, passionate voice in my head, the one that ran on pure emotions, took over.

All I heard was 'do it!'

It turned out I was just in time to secure a spot for the 27th edition of this annual pilgrimage – it was six months away.

'Hi, I was wondering if you had any spaces remaining for next year's Marathon des Sables?' I asked the woman who answered the phone.

'There have been a few cancellations, so if you pay your deposit now, I can secure your place.' she replied.

It was destiny. At that point, I couldn't think of a better way to escape from myself, so I took the leap and signed up to the 2012 Marathon des Sables, and completely drained my savings account with the steep entry fee.

I now had six short months to become an ultra-runner. I had absolutely no idea how this one decision would forever change my life and change my view of the world. This sudden switch of direction, to run one of the toughest races known to mankind, was fuelled by my inability to gather together my thoughts and emotions, and come to terms with the end of my football career. Life as I knew it had been flipped upside down and I felt vulnerable – my response, *run!*

I'm somewhat of a control freak, and the quickest way I could think of to get myself back on track emotionally was to take back some of the control through a new physical focus. I needed every ounce of my self-motivation to tackle this race head on, and I needed to be entirely focussed with only 24 weeks until I departed for Morocco. First of all, I had to become a runner. Race preparations took over my life and triggered a few thoughts of concern amongst family and friends, but I was happy to have the distraction.

The uncertainty of life after football terrified me. I held on tight to the idea of completing the MDS without revealing any of the emotional turmoil. It was a potential lifeline to pull myself through to the other side. I had convinced myself of this, but my parents were not so sure it was the right move.

'You can't do that, your body won't last,' said Dad.

'Is it safe? Could you die?' asked Mum.

Both wanted to know when this 'ridiculous' race would begin and when I explained it was just six months away, the simultaneous response was, 'you're mad!'

They couldn't understand why I would do something as *stupid* as running day after day through the desert. Their main concern was my safety, and with good reason, as the race did come with risks and things had ended badly for some competitors in the past.

Mum had recently returned from a trip to Egypt where she had been on the edges of the Sahara Desert. She tried to tell me there was no way I could put my body through six marathons in seven days in that environment. She also had an underlying concern about what sort of issues might pop up once I let go of my football career. Having watched me chase my dream with everything I had since I was a young boy, she immediately wondered what I would do to fill the void. Smart woman my mother.

It took two days to convince them how well organised the race was, and to explain the strict rules and safety procedures in place. We watched hours of YouTube clips of the race, the desert terrain, and of course the painful looking blisters proudly displayed by competitors like a badge of honour. In the end, all I got was a shrug of the shoulders and what I'd consider typical parental comments, 'if that's what will make you happy', and 'it's your life, but please be careful Son!'

My girlfriend also voiced her concerns, but at the same time, she was happy to see my mood lift and hear the excitement in my voice.

With my university degree in Exercise Science, and having been involved in professional sports for many years, I had some understanding of the human body and how it works, but I had no idea where to start to prepare to take on the sands of the Sahara.

I researched online, spoke with friends who were endurance athletes, and friends of friends who had completed the race.

Finally, I consulted my physiotherapist, Mo, who I trusted to be straight up when I needed to hear the truth. He knew my body better than I did, having repaired it many times over, and he was also a friend. Mo was my body's mechanic – I would break it, and he would fix it! He knew I had not given myself enough time to fully come to terms with my decision to quit football.

When he opened the door for our first session post-retirement, I interrupted his words of condolence to tell him I had a new idea.

'You're not going to do an Ironman are you?'

I was a little shocked with his response, but also found it quite funny.

'No don't worry, nothing crazy like that,' I said, '*just* the Marathon des Sables.'

Mo understood how an athlete's brain worked and he knew how my brain worked. We agreed to collaborate on the MDS project – I would be a bit of a guinea pig, with Mo testing out how my body reacted to different amounts of running, and he would monitor my progress by treating me several times a week.

After a lengthy discussion, with Mo's gentle tone being both supportive and straight to the point, he was satisfied that my body had a chance of completing the race, bearing in mind all the surgeries and injuries I'd dealt with in recent years. I then told him my goal was to finish in the elite top 50. He said we would need to monitor all my running data and discuss my training load each week, based on the information gathered and how I was feeling physically and emotionally. From an outsider's point of view, it may have seemed very scientific and structured, but we simply figured it out as we went along.

As I was leaving after my treatment, I said to Mo, 'I'm glad you feel I can finish the race, as I've already signed up and paid my deposit.'

He simply smiled, shook his head, and replied while slightly laughing 'of course you have!'

Training for the MDS progressed as planned, my body reacted well to the slow increase of run miles each week and I continued to research the race to glean any insights that might help. I watched many hours of online footage from previous events, noting the terrain and the race atmosphere. The route changed each year and competitors only found out each day's course while travelling to the start line, when the official race book was provided.

Slowly but surely, I was racking up the kilometres, 80 one week, then 100, then pushing to 130.

My peak training weeks were more than 160 kilometres over a six-day period, while carrying a six-kilogram backpack. I had plenty of strange looks wherever I trained, as I mimicked the MDS requirements – backpack on and gaiters over my shoes. I was loving the training, on my own, no music player, and just several little men inside my head telling me all sorts of things. I took up singing while I ran – as if I wasn't getting enough strange looks already!

It was a cold, wet December in London with morning frosts and frozen paths one day and icy cold rain the next – not exactly ideal for acclimatising to cross-desert running. I was finding it harder to stay motivated but the short winter days served me well in a strange way; I got used to running with a head torch – something I would definitely need while completing the 'long day' of the race.

A happy solution to the lack of hot weather training came with my sister's wedding, scheduled for the week before Christmas in Australia – the perfect summer conditions to test myself against sandy terrain and increased temperatures, and to try out the different types of kit I'd need in the desert.

I spent six weeks running along Australia's white sandy beaches, through barren bushland and along the stunning coastal trails my homeland is famous for. I trained in temperatures consistently over 30-degrees Celsius, topped up my tan, and spent time with family and friends. It had been more than two and a half years since I stepped foot on Aussie soil, and I thought it was a good idea to see everyone before I ventured out into the desert, just in case.

Returning to the UK, I felt fit and strong as I continued to run distances of up to 150 kilometres each week, now in the bitter cold and with some snow. I'd had a couple of minor physical concerns in

Australia, but apart from that I was flying – my training plan was tracking close to perfect and I was highly motivated. To pretty much everyone's surprise, my body was holding up to this type of linear, slow and steady way of training. I started to believe even further that this is the type of athlete I was meant to be.

My Morocco departure date was now only four weeks away and I was decreasing the kilometres in my weekly schedule and I felt great – I was confident I'd done enough to achieve my goal. I had tested out different kit that I would potentially wear including shoes, socks and shirts, I'd worked out how to pack my bag, what food I'd need, and got as many tips as possible from acquaintances who'd run the race.

30 minutes into one of my regular training runs through the trails of Richmond Park in London's south west, a sharp burning pain on the outside of my knee brought me to an abrupt standstill. It felt like a red-hot fire poker had been shoved into my knee each time it bent. I knew immediately what it was – my iliotibial band (ITB) – the dreaded 'runners knee.' Mo and I were so close to getting the amount of training I was doing spot on, but this type of injury is known to arise from overuse, and a sudden increase of distance. I had done both!

I ended up back in the rooms of Dr Lorenzo Masci, for a cortisone injection. He injected my knee twice before I left for Morocco and instructed me to stop running in the final weeks before the race. And he wished me luck. We were optimistic that the injections to help decrease the inflammation and swelling would last the distance across the Sahara, but deep down we both knew that it was a long shot!

4.

BAPTISM OF FIRE

THE 27TH MARATHON DES SABLES MARCH 2012

The Marathon des Sables has a catch cry of 'the toughest footrace on Earth' and I can tell you it's bloody tough. For those who actually *race* the event, it no doubt hurts in a completely different way to those who simply want to finish. Whatever people's reasons are for taking on this iconic race, we all share two things – a strong desire to finish the gruelling 255 kilometres in seven days, and the fact we all have rocks in our head!

Covering the equivalent of six marathons in a week through the desert whilst carrying all your necessities is not normal. Most events will have aid stations packed with fresh and packaged snacks, water and electrolytes; but we needed to carry our seven days worth of food from day one! Any extra clothes, equipment, or sleeping gear had to be shoved into our backpacks before we started the event. Daily temperatures can exceed 50 degrees Celsius, drinking water is rationed and given out in the mornings, at each checkpoint, and once you cross the finishing line each day. Most runners eat dehydrated meals, so if you want to use hot water to rehydrate these forms of nutrition, a small pot, lighter, and fuel tablets would also need to be carried for the entire week.

Apart from water, the only other thing that wasn't necessary to carry was the large black fabric tent, which only had two sides that runners would be sleeping under. A dusty carpet floor was laid down to create a bed of dirt and stones. So why do competitors pay thousands of pounds to go through this level of suffering?

Well, here's my reason: I went to race this beast, I wanted to put myself up against some of the best desert runners on the planet and see where I ended up. I had no other race experience to call on, or years of training data to look back through and figure out my ideal pace. I simply went into the Sahara Desert to run! Clearly this was my ego speaking to me, perhaps over confidently. The real reason I took on the MDS was because I didn't know how to handle the predicament in which I found myself. I was no longer a footballer, so I (subconsciously) made the decision to run away from it all – and ended up in the Sahara Desert!

* * *

It was a lot cooler than I expected when I arrived in Morocco, and in typical airport fashion, it took several hours to clear customs then be shuttled to the hotel. The next morning, the entire UK contingent (who flew in together on a chartered flight the day before) was up early to board a bus for the four-hour trip into the desert. We swapped the relative comfort of the bus for the equivalent of cattle trucks to stand up in for the final 30 minute off-road drive to our base camp.

We spent the first two nights in the desert getting to know our tent buddies and experiencing what life would be like in the week ahead. I shared a tent with seven other guys, none who I knew prior to landing in Morocco. Two from the Royal Navy, two Royal Marines, Adrian, Jamie and our random South African friend, Rob. We all got on extremely well and had plenty of laughs, even though the non-military guys had no idea what the military guys were talking about with all their jargon. In typical Luke fashion, I would annoy the hell out of them by simply referring to them all as army boys and asking lots of ridiculous questions.

ON THE HIGHWAY TO HELL DAY ONE

33.8 KILOMETRES

The field set off with helicopters hovering overhead and AC/DC's *Highway to Hell* blaring over the loudspeakers. I felt an immense surge of energy, courage and spirit within me that this was my race – I was ready! I ran at my own comfortable pace, my extremely full backpack weighing less than seven kilograms (which is still quite light for MDS standards) bounced along with each stride along the dusty train I was now on. Checkpoint One came and went, and then a couple of climbs up over rocky hills, and all was going well. I was feeling fresh, reminding myself it was the first day and not to push too hard too soon, I was happy to cruise along, enjoying the view, and with a feeling of being free.

I had a technical descent along sandy paths between jagged boulders, and with only 12 kilometres until today's finishing line once I reached the bottom. I still felt comfortably strong. But, as the terrain flattened out my ITB flared up badly and forced me to stop. I couldn't move at all for a few minutes, but slowly got back in motion. For the remaining 12 kilometres the pain was fiery and intense. By the time I reached the finish line of Day One, I knew my goal of a top 50 finish was out the window – now it was a matter of simply getting through the week. At the end of each day I would change into a pair of tights, my one spare t-shirt, and eat the portion of food I had allotted myself for each afternoon. Once I ate, and like most other competitors finishing before the majority of the field, I would then lay down on the tent's sandy floor, and replay the day's events in my head, waiting for the rest of my tent-mates to return home.

It was incredibly disappointing but I had to accept this level of pain would only increase each day I ran. I managed to finish in 28th position but it felt like my race was over before I even started the second day.

DAY TWO

38.5 KILOMETRES

I woke to warm weather and a positive state of mind and naively hoped my knee had settled overnight after some rest and I'd be ready to go. Then I stood up and tried to walk.

I hobbled to the start line with one goal in mind – run as fast as I could for as long as I could and only resort to walking if the pain was excruciating. In hindsight, this was one of my more stupid decisions. I believed if my head was positive my body would mirror the strength and I would make it through.

The second stage started with six kilometres of sand dunes, which exacerbated the knee injury as I had to push harder on the soft ground. I fell over plenty of times and managed a few mouthfuls of sand to add to my misery.

At the penultimate checkpoint of the day, hobbling like an old man in need of a hip replacement, the organisers called for the doctor who had a barrage of questions. I eventually told him, 'all you can do for me mate is give me a massage to try and release some tension pulling on my ITB, a few pain-killers – that's about it!' Thankfully he had a sense of humour, he laughed and complied.

After a 20 minute massage, several painkillers, and a morale boosting high five, I was out of the tent and heading across a dried-up lake to the next checkpoint. It was 10 kilometres straight ahead in heat I later discovered was 48 degrees Celsius! The first two kilometres were horrible and at times I was in tears, but I wasn't planning on slowing down or stopping, so I kept moving on. I told myself, 'Luke, you have eight kilometres to the next checkpoint, get there as quickly as possible, just deal with the pain!'

I worked hard and made the checkpoint in a decent amount of time, and surprisingly with just bearable pain levels. I now had 11 kilometres to the end of the day, but with a range of different terrains to overcome. This was not going to be much fun. Another three kilometres of dunes had me gritting my teeth but I wasn't about to give up.

Back at the tent at the end of the day, I took my shoes and socks off to discover I had blisters all over my toes, underneath my toes, even between my toes. I'd been so focused on my knee pain I hadn't noticed what I'd done to my feet. It was a sickening sight. The medics had a look, did a bit of slicing and dicing and wrapped up my feet to try and stop any infections. They were truly mummified.

DAY THREE

35 KILOMETRES

With very little sleep on the desert floor thanks to an upset stomach, the knee pain and my feet pulsing with every heartbeat, I knew Day Three would be tough.

I stood up and my feet felt like I was standing on razor blades, I still had the hot poker inside my knee that stabbed with every step and I had a near marathon-distance day in front of me – through the desert. Morale was at rock bottom and despite starting the day in the top 50, I knew I had no chance of realising my goal of top 50 overall.

One thing that helped immensely was the encouragement and support I had from my tent buddies. Their positivity really got me through the day. I did a lot more walking than running but I just kept my head down, tried to ignore how many people were running past me and stayed focused – my mantra was 'one foot in front of the other'.

It was bloody hot. The organisers provided an extra bottle of water at one checkpoint as the mercury rose above 50 degrees Celsius. *How kind of them*, I thought. The scenery was magnificent with mountains, valleys, rock cliffs and sand dunes all around me but I barely absorbed the natural beauty. All I could do was push on, deep in my pain box. The last 10 kilometres went something like this: hobble, hobble,

ARGH! Stop for 30 seconds. Walk for a minute. Hobble, hobble, ARGH! And repeat. At this point I'd stopped caring about the finish line, I just wanted the pain to go away.

To add to my woes, my stomach upset worsened, and I needed to find cover for to do my *business* (a regular occurrence). My blisters worsened and the skin began to slide off my toes, so I went to see the doctor again that evening. He cleaned and re-bandaged my bleeding feet, gave me a box of penicillin for the suspected infection, and told me to put my feet up for the rest of the day.

A short time later, a sandstorm blew in. The calm vibe of camp escalated into minor panic as the stinging sand forced all of us inside our tents, inside our sleeping bags and with sand goggles on to protect our eyes.

DAY FOUR

81.5 KILOMETRES

What's worse than facing a marathon through the desert when you're in a world of pain? How about a *double* marathon?

I was in a positive mood despite knowing I had an epic battle to get through this stage. My game plan was to run hard when I could, and walk when my body wouldn't let me run. Just keep moving forward. With a departure time of 8:30 a.m., I estimated I'd be back in camp by around eleven that night. I was preparing myself for what was going to be one of the toughest and most emotional days of my life.

The elite runners (top 50 men and top five women) were due to set off three hours later than the rest of us, and I figured they'd be back in camp at least three hours before us. The race organisers stopped in front of our tent, and said 'congratulations, there's someone in this tent in the top 50.'

To my utter disbelief, I was that 'someone'. I was confused, and gutted. I didn't think it was possible after the day I'd had yesterday, and I'd already mentally prepared myself to set off nice and early. I made my way to the start line to cheer on the mass start, before heading to the tent with the other elites to rest and share stories about our previous ultra-marathon experience.

When I told the other competitors this was my first race, their expressions were priceless. They admired my guts, but thought I was insane for choosing the Marathon des Sables as my first ultra-marathon.

A few hours later, I lined up beside this highly accomplished group of runners with 81.5 kilometres ahead of me and set myself two goals: ignore the pain, and finish the stage. So pretty much the same as the previous three days, just double the distance. I went straight to the back of the field with the rest of the stragglers – I wasn't the only one visibly hurting.

Within five kilometres, all other runners had passed me, but I wasn't bothered. Sitting at the back of the field was an interesting experience. There was no pressure, I was running my own race and there was nobody around. It was almost like I was alone in the desert – a very surreal feeling. After a huge rocky climb followed by a 20% gradient descent down a sandy passage for a couple of hundred metres, I arrived at Checkpoint One. I was feeling OK and dealing with the pain reasonably well.

I refilled my water bottles and headed off again, but after only a few small dunes, I became nauseous, light-headed and weak. I had sharp stabbing pains in my gut and was forced into a bent-over stagger. Forget running, I could barely walk. The stagger became a shuffle, and with another six kilometres to the next checkpoint, I took a turn for the worse. I began to sway like a drunk and couldn't focus. I tried eating, drinking some electrolyte filled water, but nothing made a difference, I was a mess.

A support car drove by and asked if I needed medical attention – I stupidly mumbled 'no', even though I could barely raise my head high enough to see where I was going. By Checkpoint Two and only 20 kilometres into the day, I was forced into the medical tent for rehydration. If I could keep down a full bottle of water, some salt tablets and manage to pee, they'd let me continue. If not, it was an intravenous drip and a two-hour time penalty, or be pulled out of the race.

I tried to drink the murky mix the nurse handed to me but the entire contents of my stomach shot straight up and out my mouth and nose. The remains of the six litres of water I'd already consumed that day ended up on the sand next to my feet in less than 10 seconds!

It turned out I was severely dehydrated, I suspect from the stomach bug I picked up the day before which quite literally emptied me.

The doctor told me that if I didn't have an IV drip, he wouldn't let me continue, as I still had nearly 60 kilometres to the day's finishing line. Even with a drip he made it perfectly clear that I had to demonstrate I could pee afterwards, and provided I looked OK, he'd allow me to continue.

I lifted my right arm up for the drip and said, 'let's get started!' After three litres of fluid and two hours horizontal, I was given the green light to head on to Checkpoint Three – 14 kilometres away – within three hours, due to the allocated cut off time for this stage.

I felt this next stretch of the race would define my entire MDS experience. If I struggled badly, I would be forced out of the race. This was not about getting through the next stage – it was a race to stay in the race. I had to make it, no two ways about it!

I was up against the odds, so when another sandstorm kicked in I was really in trouble. It was like an invisible force pushing me in all directions. I let out a huge roar and screamed at the desert to 'bring it ON!' I was on a mission to survive today's stage.

The battery on my watch was dead and my solar charger was full of sand from the storm, so I had no idea how I was tracking for time or what my pace was, other than very slow. All I could do was push on and hope it was enough to get me there in time.

I made it to the third checkpoint within the three-hour limit, with little time to spare. I checked in with the medics, and they gave me the go ahead to continue just as the light left the sky.

I had something to eat, refilled my water bottles, and with my head torch blazing, set off into the night.

The next two checkpoints covered a combined distance of 24 kilometres, 22 of them in huge sand dunes. It was a strange experience being in the desert at night, out in the open air with only the stars and the occasional other competitor at the back of the pack to keep me company.

I hobbled, walked, yelled, screamed and cried my way through the night, crawling up the dunes and trying not to fall on the way down. Every checkpoint was going to be a battle and each one would be different – some more difficult than others. There'd be times I knew I'd want to give up, not believing I'd get through but I just couldn't let myself do that. Somehow, I would overcome the odds and be the victor of my MDS Stage Four war!

I passed through the fourth and fifth checkpoints in reasonable shape, one more checkpoint, then a nine kilometre stretch to the stage finish – the end of the double marathon.

Immediately after the last checkpoint, I hit soft sand and with the pain in my knee and feet, I was reduced yet again to a hobble, and I was out of food. It was hard to focus and I wandered off course time and time again, catching myself as I headed in the wrong direction. I was exhausted, slightly delirious and still had seven kilometres ahead of me.

At around two in the morning, I was down to a slow walk. I was tired, cold and hungry. I had no warm clothes to put on so had to push myself to walk faster to enable my pumping blood to keep me warm. The price I paid for warmth was increased pain, and increased fatigue.

Finally, the finish line was in sight so I increased my speed to a hopping hobble and immediately came crashing down in the sand as my painful knee gave way. Up I got and kept pushing, yelling at myself to keep going. I wanted to run into the checkpoint, not walk, so I found that last bit of energy and got myself across the line.

I walked up to the webcam at the finish line and pointed to my heart. It was how I got through an incredibly tough day. A double marathon, 81.5 kilometres completed in 15 hours.

It was now three in the morning.

It took 30 minutes to remove my socks due to the swelling and bleeding of both my feet. I lay in bed knowing I had won the Day Four war, but I was unsure what price I had paid.

Thankfully, Day Five was a rest day. I managed about four hours' sleep but the body's need to pee and eat overtook its need to sleep. I spent the following day resting and I knew my inability to bend my knee was a bad sign, plus my feet were throbbing without any pressure on them. It was time to see the medics again.

If they hadn't been attached to the end of my legs, I wouldn't have recognised my feet. They were a mess of raw flesh, swollen nail beds and blisters on top of blisters. Despite all the treatment, they were getting progressively worse. They were so bad, they became celebrities in their own right! Doctors, nurses and other runners took photos of my toes and couldn't believe I was still running. Had social media been as popular in those days, my feet would have been an internet sensation!

Not to be left out, my knee also needed treatment and several doses of painkillers were pumped into it to help relieve the pain.

One thing about the desert, you're never too sure what is just around the corner.

On Day Five, we had rain and a hailstorm – yep in the middle of the Sahara Desert. We ended our rest day soaked with water and battered by a shower of ice!

DAY SIX

42.2 KILOMETRES

I was a constant source of amusement to my tent-mates, as they'd watch me peel myself off the floor each morning and will my body to keep going. So far, I'd run most of the Marathon des Sables on my own with only brief encounters and the odd chat with other runners. On Day Six, one of the guys, Jamie (or Croc as I named him after he asked me one night if Crocodile Dundee was still alive) offered to run with me. I was surprised by how relieved I felt by this offer, having someone to share the pain with.

From the start, Croc pushed me to run faster than my usual hobble as I was slowing him down. I wanted him to run his own race but he insisted on staying with me, which helped me to stay strong. We ran together for eight kilometres then he took off and I was alone again. I arrived at checkpoint one feeling relieved after getting through the rocky terrain. The pain levels were intense and I was struggling, a lot.

Two kilometres into the second section, I tore a hole in my running shorts and my skin was now rubbing on the lycra of my other leg. I had eight kilometres to the next checkpoint and thought about getting some tape to protect my chafing skin when I got there.

I went straight to the medical tent and was amazed to discover blood streaming down my leg where the skin had been rubbed raw. The doctor applied some antiseptic which stung a little (to say the least), taped it up and I was off again, pushing through the next six kilometres any way I could – hobble, walk, just keep moving forward. My mindset was to finish as fast as possible so the pain would stop. I could see Croc ahead of me at the end of the dunes and he was hurting – the huge week had caught up with him. He helped me through the first few kilometres so now it was time for me to help him through his dark patch. We shuffled on together, each encouraging the other to keep going, helping each other up when we fell flat on our faces.

Finishing Day Six was another massive achievement but my body surprised me by having plenty of energy left. The other runners were exhausted but I wasn't tired at all. I did some stretching, a bit of cooking, self-massaged my legs and ate. The injuries I was carrying prevented me from running fast enough to be tired at the end of a marathon through the desert. I spent the afternoon relaxing and watching other runners cross the finish line.

That evening, the race organisers surprised us with a live concert – a 12 piece orchestra with accompanying soprano soloist. It was surreal, sitting under the stars in the middle of the desert listening to classical music.

DAY SEVEN

15.5 KILOMETRES

Everyone was excited about the final day of the event, but with nine kilometres of the biggest sand dunes in Morocco ahead of us, it wasn't going to be easy.

I set off with Croc again but was moving very slowly, so slowly, others who were casually walking were passing me. I heard Croc yelling at me to hurry up but I told him I was running as fast as I could so he left me to fend for myself – and I don't blame him.

I was so close to the end, all I had to do was keep my mind strong for a little while longer – and I knew I had it in me. I was determined to finish what I had started. There was only one checkpoint today and with less than 10 kilometres to the end of the final stage, I sucked down some water and headed off into the golden peaks of the Sahara. The finish of this year's race was preceded by nine kilometres of some of the largest sand dunes in Morocco.

I caught up with Croc again with about four kilometres to go and we decided to finish together as we were both in a world of pain. In the final 500 metres, I really struggled so I told him I'd meet him at the finish line. There was a crowd waiting which did wonders for the spirit – it helped me realise the amazing accomplishment in completing this beast of a race.

Finally, I crossed the finish line. I had done it. I finished the 27th Marathon des Sables with only one knee working and with bloodied, blistered, infected toes.

The desert was awash with competitors celebrating their achievements – yet I couldn't help but feel flat. I was disappointed in myself for not working as hard as I wanted and to the level of fitness I knew I had. I failed by over 150 places to achieve my top 50 goal. But in sport and in life, you don't always achieve what you set out to. The true reward is what you learn from the experience.

Race organiser Patrick Bauer handed me a medal, a bag full of food, and a ticket for a bus which left in 45 minutes to take us back to the hotel – five and a half hours away. I was completely battered but I had finished what many consider the toughest footrace on earth. I was immensely relieved that I wouldn't have to keep running through such intense pain levels.

The local kids were keen to get their hands on some souvenirs so I handed over my hat and a buff as we all agreed we wouldn't be doing that race again in a hurry.

I spent two nights in Quazarate to give my feet a chance to recover. I had my first shower in nine days and was ready to eat. I inhaled a plate full of couscous, salad, chicken and rice, trying to make up for the extremely lean diet I'd intentionally been on to keep the weight of my backpack low – just 15,400 calories for the entire seven days. This boy was hungry!

The next day we attended the awards presentation and received our yellow finisher's shirts. We wandered around the local markets doing a bit of haggling for bargains, followed by an afternoon nap and our final dinner as the cohort of Tent 70. We managed a few well-deserved beers after dinner and bunked down for our last night in Morocco.

5.

RECOVERY ROAD

Despite the success of finishing what some deem the toughest footrace on Earth, I arrived home from Morocco still frustrated at not achieving my top 50 goal. I had worked extremely hard in the lead up to the race and was the fittest I'd ever been. The fact I wasn't feeling exhausted meant I hadn't given the desert everything I was capable of, the injuries I carried through the race having held me back. The following day I was back in the gym training clients, and most people told me I was crazy not taking time off to rest and recover.

In those first few weeks after the MDS I wasn't much fun to be around. I was constantly cranky and my body was broken, again. I moped around, trying to put on a brave face but I felt like I had lost everything that mattered. I was blind to reality.

The first time my podiatrist saw my feet he simply shook his head, and said 'poor feet.' He gave me a local anaesthetic, cleaned up whatever was left, salvaged bits and pieces of my nails and infected flesh. Without a hefty dose of anaesthetic, I couldn't imagine the pain I would have felt.

Next stop was a visit to Dr Lorenzo Masci to assess the damage I had inflicted on my knee. He sent me for an MRI scan so he could see exactly what my knee and ITB looked like. He decided on another cortisone injection rather than surgery as the best way forward.

My knee joint had some wear and tear from the race, but nothing too concerning; it was my ITB Lorenzo was more worried about – it was extremely inflamed and had thickened badly. After the cortisone injection, he told me to return in six weeks so he could assess the recovery.

Six weeks later, despite resting as advised, there was no improvement. My options were surgery (low success rate), more cortisone injections, or more rest then a long period of rehabilitation. The rehab was to strengthen other areas of my body to help relieve some of the strain I was putting on my ITB when running.

I discussed everything with both Mo and Lorenzo, before deciding on another injection, followed by rehab.

Running in parallel to the dramas of my body, my relationship was on rocky ground. My girlfriend was a few years older than me and was keen to know when our life would settle down. I was in love with her, but I certainly was not ready to make decisions that would change the rest of my life – I just wasn't in the right headspace. I wanted to focus on developing my idea of being an endurance adventurer, what that meant, and how I could shape what I loved doing into a sustainable career. We talked for hours about how to make it work, and decided the only way forward was for us to move back to Sydney so she could be closer to her friends and family. I agreed and did my best to feel excited about the future, but in all honesty, it didn't feel like I had much of an option if we were to stay together.

* * *

My imagination ran with the idea of becoming an adventurer. I began implementing steps to start promoting myself as Luke Tyburski the Adventurer (LTTA), a title that started out as a joke amongst friends. A nine to five job had never appealed to me, so I set out to create my own career path.

During many brainstorming sessions, I came up with plenty of ludicrous ideas, like completing the highest/coldest/hottest/wettest toughest races around the world in a single calendar year, but there was one big problem – I had no money.

I spent many days lying on the couch staring at the ceiling, mind blank, not a thought, emotion, or sensation. All I wanted was to be happy and enjoy what I did each day of my life. I tried to be positive, but with rent due and bills piling up, I had to convince myself that LTTA was like any new business, and that it would take time to start paying dividends.

The feedback was positive from people who had read my blog posts about the Marathon des Sables adventure, and I realised writing for magazines as part of LTTA could be a potential revenue stream, so I built up a list of editors I could pitch to when I had a great story. To do that, I needed new content – it was time for my next adventure, and I soon found it. I would tackle the world's highest ultra-marathon: The Everest Ultra.

2013 was the race's third year, this 65-kilometre running adventure began in Gorakshep (the final stop before Everest Base Camp) at 5164 metres above sea level, winding its way down the famous trail down to a breathable altitude of 2860 metres in Lukla.

It was exactly what I was looking for – something different and challenging – running down Mount Everest, how cool is that? It was a relatively new race on the world's ultra-running calendar, and not many people had even heard of it, let alone attempted it. I emailed the event organiser, Ramesh Bhattachan, to ask if there were any places remaining, and if I could take video plus photos to promote the race. With my first real project as LTTA in motion, I regained some enthusiasm for life.

I gave myself a tight timeline, with just six months to get fit enough to complete the Everest Ultra. I still hadn't run since finishing the MDS, and my only cardio training was through boxing, kayaking, or swimming. My knee pain took a lot longer to subside than I hoped after the injections, and I needed to find a way to ease back into some endurance training. I bought myself a road bike as a gentle way of putting in some long training days. I had never ridden a road bike before, and had no idea what to look for, but I had plenty of triathlon mates to call on for advice.

It was five months until race day and training was going well. I cycled further each week, three or four hours at a time, with no knee pain. With the consistent training, my mood lifted, I was becoming more confident, and for the first time in a long time, I was injury free.

I gave it one more month and decided it was time to run again. I started slow, painfully slow – five minutes of running, followed by two minutes of walking, repeating four times to begin with, and progressing over the coming weeks. With all the rehabilitation I'd put myself through, the last thing I wanted was to overload my knee again. I started doing longer runs, 20 minutes became 30, then 40, until I managed to run for an hour pain free. It was nothing like my preparation running six times a week for the MDS, but I was running, and that was the main thing.

I set myself a limit to run only twice a week and never on

consecutive days. Combined with three to four bike rides and a couple of swims each week, I was basically training like a triathlete. I felt fit, confident, and strong – the old Luke re-surfaced. My mind was ready and I was excited for my Nepalese adventure, even though I wasn't sure of the exact details.

Ramesh was tough to catch as he was the race director of the Everest Ultra and the Annapurna 100, as well as coach to a few of the elite local runners, some of whom would soon be travelling to Hong Kong to run in the Vibram Hong Kong 100. One of the runners was Aite Tamang, who'd finished second in the previous year's race to Ryan Sandes, one of the world's top ultra-runners.

I had been toying with the idea of travelling to Nepal several weeks prior to the Everest Ultra to live and train with one of the local runners. It was a long shot, but if you never ask, you will never know.

I eventually heard back from Ramesh and any frustration from the lack of contact soon turned to excitement as he outlined the plan he'd come up with. He had organised for me to train and stay with not one but two runners and their families in the villages where they grew up. One was Aite, and the other Upendra Sunuwar. What an incredible opportunity. I would fly to Pokhara, on the edge of the stunning Phewa lake and train with Aite in his final weeks preparing to defend his Annapurna 100 title.

After the race, I would travel with Aite to his village and stay with his family. Just over a week later, I would meet up with Upendra (who was also running the Annapurna 100) and travel to his family home, and spend nearly two weeks in a different Nepalese village. I'd then head back to Kathmandu to meet with Ramesh, and the other runners to compete in the Everest Ultra.

I couldn't believe it, the plan was amazing, I couldn't wipe the smile off my face – I had the same running-around-the-house sense of excitement as a kid waking up on Christmas morning. The adventure I was trying to find had found me.

My training continued to improve, I was up to 90 minutes running twice a week, pain-free. The fresh winter's air brushed my cheeks as I ran along the river Thames, and the constant stream of rowers gliding along the water kept me feeling relaxed as I ran. I felt better than I had in a long time.

Before I knew it, 2013 arrived. The Sydney relocation plans with my girlfriend were well underway (which I was becoming excited about), as were plans for my next series of adventures. After Nepal, I had several ultra-marathons lined up in the UK, followed by a fun weekend adventure called 'Luke Learns to Surf'. I was also sketching a plan to travel to Brazil to find an adventure in the Amazon. Wrapping up my year of adventures would be a trip to the South Island of New Zealand, attempting to summit the country's second highest peak, Mount Aspiring. I had been training a client of mine for this specific challenge, and he wanted me with him all the way to the top of the mountain!

It was an exciting year, jam-packed full of adventures to build my endurance adventuring brand. Any money I made went straight back into travel plans for further adventures – I was living one adventure at a time. At home though, things were a little less positive. Although my plans were to relocate to Sydney at the end of 2013, nine months after my girlfriend, any mention of my adventures traipsing all over the planet during this time sparked tension, so I tried to keep my plans to myself.

From my experience, relationships are all about finding a balance between the needs and wants of both people – compromising if necessary, but essentially heading in the same direction. In hindsight, we weren't heading in the same direction. As so many of us have discovered, love can be disturbingly blind.

I had reinvigorated my zest for life, and wanted to use this vitality every single day, but my positive energy was dampened as soon as talk turned with my girlfriend towards my upcoming adventures. We discussed at length moving back to Australia, but any talks about my newfound passion for life quickly fizzled out, or subject changed so to not put any unwelcomed strain on the relationship. Our long-distance relationship would begin shortly, so I made an extra effort, at the expense of my training, to make the most of our time together. We spent many weekends at our home cooking, laughing, and not leaving each other's side for the entire day. It was like time stood still as we enjoyed each other's company, and reinforced the love we had for one another.

I had my itinerary planned and my training continued well with no niggles. There was a ton of last minute running around, organising other trainers for my clients, sorting out visas, speaking with magazine editors for stories to write, and the small event of turning 30.

I was under a bit of pressure from family and friends to celebrate with a party or a dinner out, but I wasn't too fussed. I'd have been happy with a home-cooked meal with just my girlfriend. Some people freak out about turning thirty, but for me it was just another birthday.

In the end, I caved in to peer pressure and shared the celebration with my close friend Kim, who I'd known since I was about five years old. I found it hard to stay focused during the dinner, my mind kept wandering to the long list of things to do before flying to Nepal.

We jointly blew out the candles on the large red velvet flavoured birthday cake, as our friends and family belted out an energetic rendition of '*Happy Birthday*.' As we paused for the mandatory photo with the knife midway through slicing the cake, I remember thinking, 'three pairs of socks, two running shorts, three shirts …' before 'hip, hip, hooray' rang out.

Soon after my birthday dinner, my girlfriend and I said our teary goodbyes with a long loving hug at the departure gates of London's Heathrow Airport. It would be months before we would see each other again. I had my passport and a ticket to Kathmandu in my back pocket, and could feel the positive energy building.

* * *

Flying to Nepal is an adventure in itself. After an hour in Kathmandu airport, I transferred to a light plane with about a dozen other passengers for the short trip to Pokhara. Coming in to land we had a panoramic view of the snow-capped Annapurna mountain range, before we touched down and came to a shuddering, whiplash-inducing halt.

Out the front of the rudimentary terminal, a small, rusty, banged up car pulled to a stop at my feet, and the driver, wearing a *dhaka topi* (traditional Nepalese hat) peered out and gave me a toothy grin. The passenger door swung open, and a solid man wearing an orange high visibility vest with 'OFFICIAL TRAFFIC CONTROLLER' across the back got out of the car.

'Luke, Luke, hello my friend, how are you?' said Ramesh picking up my back pack. We exchanged pleasantries and set off for his house.

The dusty streets of Pokhara are best described as organised mayhem. Scooters whizzed past on either side of our car as we waited in traffic behind an ancient truck, possibly a relic from the Second World War – if not earlier. Occasionally we'd drive past a lone buffalo that stood dreamily by the roadside, watching the cars and bikes fly by.

In the more built up areas of town, locals sat on plastic chairs outside shopfronts, sipping tea and smoking cigarettes – interested observers of Pokhara as it moved throughout its daily business. Overhead, thick black cables, no higher than a few metres from the ground, were slung along the roads between crooked power poles. The lines shot out in every direction like a giant spider's web, powering the surrounding buildings for just a few hours each night. I soon discovered blackouts were a constant occurrence in Nepal – a way of life most people seem to accept.

A large brick wall fenced off Ramesh's compound, with banners identifying it as the official headquarters of the Annapurna 100, and Everest Ultra races – the heart of Pokhara's ultra-running scene. I was shown to a cosy room in Ramesh's cousin's hotel a few doors up, with the instruction to meet up in half an hour.

The room had two child-sized single beds, an armchair, a TV, and a tiny bathroom where I washed and changed before I headed downstairs where Ramesh waited in the sunny courtyard. A little while later, a slim man wearing an old tracksuit wandered in and I was introduced to Aite Tamang. I'm big on first impressions, and Aite struck me as polite and reserved and I immediately wondered if he was comfortable having a foreigner arrive from the other side of the world to train with him. Aite's weathered face made him look many years older than his 25 years, and his eyes suggested he had been through a great deal in life. They hinted at a story, and I was eager to discover more about this elite high altitude runner.

I had carried a minor chest infection with me to Pokhara, but it was a week before the Annapurna 100, so I thought it would be an easy introduction to Nepalese trail-running with Aite. I quickly learnt there is no such thing as an 'easy' run for a foreigner in Nepal.

We set off from the compound into the hills at six in the morning, with Ramesh barking orders. A few people were out and about, buses took kids to school, and a few stray animals meandered along the dusty roads. At only 900 metres above sea level, I hadn't yet felt the effects of being at altitude, but over the next 10 kilometres we climbed to 1600 metres. Either the air was thinner, or I hadn't run this far in the last few weeks, or climbed this much – whatever the cause, I struggled to keep up with Aite, who was barely jogging.

My legs felt like they weighed a ton, and on a few of the steeper climbs, I slowed to a walk. Aite would simply say 'OK, OK', along with his favourite running advice, 'slowly, slowly'.

My chest burned and felt like it was being squeezed in a vice. After a few moments doubled over with my hands on my knees, I stood upright and found myself gazing out over the most spectacular view imaginable.

A vast undulating valley, covered with dense green vegetation, stretched as far as I could see, until it met the enclosing hills. I could just make out several small villages dotted across what looked like unforgiving terrain. Ridge lines linked several slightly higher peaks, which seemed to reach forever, like pathways in the sky.

Aite and I stopped for several minutes to marvel at what lay before us. I asked if he ran here often, and in his soft voice, he told me he would run to this point most days in his training before setting off further, depending on how he felt that day. He explained he would run between four and nine hours each day, climbing and descending his way throughout the surrounds of Pokhara. I felt exhausted just hearing this, but could totally understand why anyone would want to keep running along these trails that seemed to surf the clouds.

Aite had come through the ranks of the Nepalese Army and was trained to respect rank. I had come here to learn and looked up to Aite to guide me, yet he decided that I was the higher rank, and punctuated all our conversation with 'Sir'. I tried to explain that I'd come to Nepal to run and enjoy his company and that we were equals, but it was tough to break his discipline, and he continued to address me formally. It was bizarre and felt a little uncomfortable.

During our first run, I continually asked him to call me Luke, but things got lost in translation and he addressed me the only way he knew. After about 10 or 15 attempts, he finally grasped the concept, but right away, slipped up and replied to one of my questions with 'no, Sir.'

'No, no, no,' I said, 'no call me Sir, call me Luke.' Aite threw his head back and laughed, 'OK, OK, Sir.'

We both laughed as we made our way down the tight switchbacks of the trail. The next few times Aite still would answer, 'yes Sir, no Sir', but then quickly respond with 'sorry, sorry, Luke', and give me his biggest smile.

After three hours of running, wheezing, and gasping for air, mixed with bursts of laughter, Aite finally addressed me as Luke. He seemed comfortable calling me by my first name, and although we had known each other for less than 24 hours, we connected over a minor episode of equal status. We bonded *because* of cultural differences.

A couple of days before the Annapurna 100, I met Upendra Sunuwar. Upendra was a similar height to Aite but stockier. His face was slightly sunburnt in patches across his cheeks and forehead. Upendra is a mountain guide, and takes tourists to the various peaks and base camps throughout Nepal. One week he could be knee deep in snow 6000 metres above sea level, and the next, running a 100-kilometre mountain race.

Like Aite, Upendra was courteous and said very little. We walked along the banks of the beautiful Phewa lake, one of Pokhara's main attractions, to get to know each other. My questions were initially met with single word responses and no questions in return. Upendra started running late in life, and never had any formal training, he'd simply go out and run up and down mountains all day, every day, for a couple of months. If he'd saved enough money from his guide work, he'd take time off to train, otherwise, he'd keep working right up to a couple of days prior to competition.

He loosened up a few hours into our walk and began to tell some stories. We headed down a narrow back street that felt miles away from civilization. Kids chased each other along the street as we entered a tiny shopfront that was basically sheets of iron tied to wooden poles rammed into the ground, and a corrugated iron roof.

We ordered coffee and I watched Upendra (like many Nepalese men) fill his coffee with sugar, an insane amount. Maybe that's the secret to their high altitude running – they float up the mountains on a sugar high. I counted 11, 12, then 13 spoonfuls of sugar in his coffee, wincing at the thought of the taste. He took a sip, smiled and said, 'not so bad.' We laughed, and once again, I felt closely connected to a new friend.

Upendra talked about his expectations for the upcoming Annapurna 100, and his training, but when he said he had just come down from 6000 metres guiding trekkers, only three days earlier, I nearly fell off my chair. With his deep distinct voice, and looking straight at me, he simply said, 'it's OK, I make some money, I do some running, same same.' This was one of Upendra's favourite phrases when comparing things in life – '*same same*.'

By the time we arrived back at Ramesh's house, Upendra and I were laughing, joking, and carrying on like long lost school friends. It's funny how a few hours walking and talking, and half a kilo of sugar in your coffee can change things.

Behind Ramesh's complex was an old hotel built with concrete blocks and faded rendering, where runners from across Nepal would base themselves when training or racing in the Pokhara region. Inside, the small rooms with bare concrete floors were filled with bodies lying on rickety old bed frames with thin foam mattresses, jammed next to each other. Many of the runners had travelled for hours to get to Pokhara to try and prise Aite's Annapurna 100 title away from him. Some were in the Nepalese army, some were mountain guides, a couple were at university. All of them did whatever they could to make ends meet while they trained for the race.

One thing was certain, I was in the company of *fast* runners. Some of these guys were teenagers, others in their early thirties, and a few had no idea how old they were. Most of them would be considered, in Nepalese terms, average runners, but most had marathon times around 2:30 hours. Not bad for 'average' runners.

After only a short time in Nepal, I realised most of the population thought it was crazy to run. Even crossing a busy road, with oncoming traffic, the Nepalese walk leisurely, with no thought of breaking into a jog as vehicles honk and swerve at the last second.

It was an attitude that made it difficult for any of these immensely talented runners to advance their careers, with zero government funding, and no sponsorship money. There was little opportunity to showcase their talents without the help of foreigners to promote and sponsor them. Not that it bothered them. Much as they might dream of being sponsored by Salomon or The North Face, they don't lose much sleep over it. The Nepalese runners are some of the most relaxed and cheerful people I've ever met and their attitude was highly contagious.

I was excited to share a *dal baht* (traditional local meal of rice, cooked lentil soup, and seasonal vegetables) in the dining room of the compound. Rice was piled onto the plates, smothered in *dal*, and a small serving of turmeric-coloured cauliflower, cooked in ginger and garlic, placed on the side of each plate.

We sat tightly packed on blue plastic chairs at three long tables in the dimly lit dining room. Everyone laughed while I attempted to copy how to eat this traditional meal. First, I formed a tight ball of rice, *dal*, and luminous cauliflower on my chipped porcelain plate, then scooped it towards my mouth and flicked it in using my thumb. This was the technique most Nepalese used and I wanted to adopt the same practice.

'No more knives or forks for me,' I said, 'I eat every meal *Nepali style*.' This bought rapturous laughter, before everyone resumed shovelling their mounds of *dal baht* into their mouths.

I might have mastered how to eat like a Nepalese ultra-runner, but running like them, was quite a different matter.

My alarm beeped at 5:30 am and it was barely light outside. A few roosters crowed somewhere nearby. It was the day before the Annapurna 100, but as I wasn't racing I headed out on a solo run, experimenting, trying to adopt the Nepali approach of not eating much before and during a run. My target was four hours and the distance was irrelevant – I simply wanted to coast along the ridge lines and 'float' back down the steep, rocky switch-backed trails leading into Pokhara. I knew my body could survive with minimal food after

running the Marathon des Sables on a little over 2000 calories per day, so I felt comfortable with a couple of finger-sized bananas and a small bottle of water.

I ran through the outskirts of the town and felt strong and positive, ready to enjoy whatever lay ahead. I dodged buffalos grazing on the grass that sprouted on the unsealed dirt roads. At the first part of the climb, I battled the ever-increasing elevation on the uneven path. I had been along these trails once before with Aite so I had an idea of what was ahead and it felt easier than last time. Birds chirped and tiny lizards sunned themselves on the rocks. Occasionally, I'd pass a Rhododendron tree with a few dazzling red flowers – the national flower of Nepal.

I sort of knew where I was, and felt alive with excitement, running alone in the mountains of Nepal, with minimal supplies. 'This is living,' I thought.

I maintained a steady pace, then descended into one of many small villages I would pass on my route, with no more than five or six huts and a small convenience store, stocked with bananas, water, cough drops, biscuits and a few other sweets.

Building materials were mostly bamboo, iron, mud, brick and plastic tarpaulins. One dwelling I ran past appeared to be held together by rope. Life for the happy people who lived in these hills was about being resourceful, and no two homes were the same.

Pokhara is quite a touristy place, with the beautiful Phewa lake and trails, sitting at the foot of the Annapurna mountain range. I gathered the miniature shops sold their wares to foreign trekkers who travelled the same path I was on. The villagers were so friendly, and would stop washing their clothes, chopping wood for their fires, or chatting amongst themselves to look at me. A smile, a wave, and softly spoken

'*Namaste*' were met with an excited smile, or a more reserved, and inquisitive '*Namaste*', as I jogged past.

Although I was only at 1600 meres above sea level, I felt quite a lot higher and the views were breathtaking – emerald green valleys below and the ever-changing flora of spiky shrubs, towering trees, and flowering bushes along the trail.

My watch told me I'd been running a little over two hours and I had a straight, grassy, and relatively flat trail stretching a kilometre or so before the final climb, which approached Nuwakot Bhairabsthan, the Hindu temple. I ran along one of the ridges and felt like I was balancing on a tight rope between the two valleys on either side.

I began the final ascent to the temple, the morning dew had evaporated, leaving the grassy trail slightly sticky underfoot. Stone monuments bordered the path, and even though I wasn't sure what they signified, they seemed spiritual, so I bowed my head, and muttered '*Namaste*' as I passed by.

The grassy slope turned to steps, which looked like they went up and up, into the fluffy clouds in the blue sky. The steps were unevenly placed and differing in height, so it was faster to walk up rather than run. I began to daydream about living in these mountains, a much-needed distraction, as my legs were tired and sore.

I walked around Nuwakot Bhairabsthan admiring the 360-degree views. Rows of small, delicately engraved bells surrounded the temple for people to gently ring, then pray for their loved ones, and those they had lost. I took a slow lap and caressed the bells to hear their mesmerising chime as I thought of the people I loved.

As I looked out over the trail I had come from, entranced by the beauty, I ate one of the small bananas and the sweetness was intense – it gave me an immediate boost of energy and awareness. I had run for 2:30 hours, and it was time to head back. I was careful to follow the exact trails back to Pokhara, but with the distraction of the views around me, I had several near-misses, almost taking the wrong turn where there was a fork in the trail.

I was surprised at how much energy I had. As crazy as this may sound, I felt I was being topped up with energy from the mountains as I ran through this incredible landscape. I rocketed down some of the sharp twists and turns, before I slowed myself by bending my knees even more and leaning back ever so slightly, just as I observed Aite when we ran along the same path together. Before long the mountain path delivered me onto the flat plain on the outskirts of Pokhara. It was all a bit of a blur from the time I left the top, until I naturally slowed on level ground.

As I eased back into the buzz of Pokhara, the streets were filled with rusty old cars, buses, and spluttering motorbikes bellowing smoke from their exhaust pipes. I passed an open canal 10 feet below the path where women squatted next to woven baskets and scrubbed clothes on the exposed rock above the water line. I turned at the next corner, which lead onto the road where I was staying. I glanced at my watch and it read 4:20 hours. I felt quite good, possibly even fresh. 42.5 kilometres, with an elevation gain of 1822 metres, and I wasn't even out of breath. The human body can do some amazing things – I had fuelled a 'mountain marathon' with a couple of small bananas, and half a litre of water in 30-degree weather. It shifted my ideas about fuelling for endurance training.

Back at the hotel dining room, I ate a breakfast of boiled eggs, freshly made *chapatis* (flat bread) and curried chickpeas. What a day, and it was only 11 a.m.!

Breakfast for the runners on Annapurna 100 race day was an

enormous plate of dal baht at 4.30 a.m. washed down with local water, before boarding a rickety bus for the cramped and bumpy hour-long trip to the start line. As the runners lined up, I hugged Aite and Upendra, wished them both good luck, and at 6:05 a.m. Ramesh counted down the start with a comical '3, 2, 1,' and blew his whistle. The runners had a gruelling 100 kilometres ahead of them, with 4600 metres worth of ascending and descending, but few started slowly – most of the Nepalese sprinted off into the darkness.

There were several reports via the aid station walkie-talkies of different leaders, none of whom I knew. Along with the runners staying at Ramesh's compound, several other Nepalese athletes turned up on race day ready to run, considered standard practice for these races.

The Nepalese runners did not carry running packs, water bottles, or any food. The foreign contingent of the race had to carry mandatory supplies the entire 100 kilometres. The Nepalese simply ran to a checkpoint, ate and drank what they could, and continued running. No gels, no electrolytes or carbohydrate-rich drinks lined the tables of each checkpoint, just jugs of water, a few bananas, biscuits, and occasionally, pots of ramen noodles – at least it was some sort of fuel, right?

As the hours ticked by, it became clear how the race would pan out. Aite and Tirtha Tamang (no relation), were neck and neck with 20 kilometres remaining, and no one could see that changing. By the time Ramesh and I saw the leaders, it was turning out to be a fight to the finish. Upendra was in third place, but reports said he was at least 60 minutes behind the leaders.

Aite wasn't running as freely as I had seen him up in the mountains surrounding Pokhara. I gave him some encouragement at the 10 kilometres-to-go checkpoint, and told him to be strong. He smiled and said, 'thanks Sir', with a massive grin on his face, followed by a burst of laughter. The guy is in a battle, he has just run 90 kilometres, is physically struggling and in pain, but still thinks of our past runs together and makes a joke while slurping down a bowl of noodle soup. As he signalled for another tub of ramen, I asked if he usually ate this much at one stop.

'I'm hungry and I haven't eaten in many hours', he replied, which shocked me, and made me realise why these guys fill up when they can on *dal baht*, and how much raw talent and mental tenacity they have. At the same time, they are way behind the rest of the world in terms of race nutrition knowledge, but it works for them, so who's to argue? There were no support teams, no coaches, and no guidelines – it was simply eat when you can, and keep running, fast!

If I hadn't seen what happened next, I wouldn't have believed it. Aite pulled some cash from his back pocket and went to the small shop near the checkpoint and bought two Snickers bars. He walked over to Tirtha, sat down next to him and handed him one. They sat calmly chatting to each other, while munching on their chocolate bars like the best of mates out on a casual jog together, not two competitors at the end of a race with pride, glory, and prize money at stake. When they both swallowed their final mouthful, they smiled at each other and set off for the finish line, side by side.

Over the next 10 kilometres nothing much changed as the two runners, covered in sweat with white dried salt lines caked on their faces, slowly jogged together, chatted, and even laughed at times.

The pair emerged from the final climb still looking like they were joined at the shoulder. They had 50 metres of flat dirt path, then six steps up onto a raised grassy area, 10 metres from the finishing chute.

Aite and Tirtha approached the steps looking calm and composed, and in a blink of an eye, Aite shot up the steps and across the finishing line to win by mere seconds. It wasn't just an increase of pace, but an all-out sprint for the win, in a time of 10:51:55 hours.

Aite was showered with applause and victory sashes after defending his crown, but he looked shattered, and slightly distraught. He struggled in the latter parts of the race, but he continued to dig deep, and push his body to the limits before unleashing his killer sprint finish. I was extremely proud of the determination and grit he showed, and happy for his victory.

Two days later, Aite and I began the long journey to his village where I would spend a week immersed in the high-altitude training regime of local Nepali runners. The first leg of our trip was a six-hour minivan ride into Kathmandu, followed by a two-hour cab ride to the tiny, rundown village of Khopasi. The final stretch from Khopasi was a crowded bus ride up an uneven mountain track. When we arrived at the bus terminal the only remaining seats were on the roof of the bus, so we climbed the rickety ladder and found a place to sit with around 20 other passengers. It was about as local an experience as you could get, somewhere between a game of limbo as we dodged the overhanging cables, and riding a mechanical bull, as the bus rocked and rumbled over the narrow road leading up the mountain. We travelled through several small villages, mostly only a handful of buildings, and just on dusk, about an hour and a half after we left Khopasi, Aite declared it was time to get off. We had dinner in a tiny restaurant lit by candles where Aite was warmly welcomed. It was his first trip home in more than three months so there was plenty of local chatter over noodle soup and spicy masala tea.

The sun had long set by the time we loaded up our backpacks for the long walk to Aite's home. I asked him how far it was and he said one to two hours! I thought he was joking, but no, we had a long, dark trek up the mountain ahead of us. I found my head torch, and Aite directed me along a maze of single file tracks and up steep stone stairs, at times crawling on all fours. The trail ascended for over an hour then levelled off where Aite pointed out a single light in the distance and said, 'that's my home.' A right turn and a short walk past his cousins' houses, and we were there.

Aite pushed open the wooden door and we entered the main living area of the two-storey dwelling. I could barely make out four pairs of eyes around an open fire in the corner of the room, belonging to Aite's parents, his wife Man Maya and his daughter Anjali. After *Namaste* greetings and big smiles, I was directed to sit on a rug on the smooth mud floor and was handed a tin cup of freshly brewed masala tea. As my eyes adjusted to the low light from the flames, I looked around the beautifully simple home. A few pots hung from nails on an exposed beam over the cooking area, and a ladder shot up through a hole in the ceiling to the sleeping quarters above. And that was pretty much it.

Dinner was an incredible *dal baht* with spicy homegrown vegetables and a towering heap of rice served on flat metal plates. A canister of water was passed around and we washed our hands in a small bowl before eating. Aite's family was amused with my attempts to eat with my hands like a local, but the laughter soon died down and a mellow mood descended as we enjoyed the exquisite meal.

After dinner, Aite directed me up the ladder to one of three small rooms off the landing with a tiny porthole window. I was exhausted from the long day of travel and was soon drifting into sleep on the traditional woven cane mattress.

I settled into the daily rhythm (rooster crowing at 4 a.m., sunrise at six) and enjoyed the warm hospitality of Aite's family. Breakfast was usually a dry fried rice mixture (Nepalese rice bubbles), masala tea and warm buffalo milk. All eyes were on me as I sipped my first taste of the creamy milk and when I licked my lips and said '*mitho cha*' (very nice), everyone laughed.

In Nepal, household chores are traditionally the domain of women, so Aite and I would head off after breakfast for a walk.

On occasions, Aite took a nap or helped his father with odd jobs and I'd go off on a few hours' run, doing my best not to get lost on the tracks that crossed the hills and valleys. One afternoon, I ran (slowly, slowly, as instructed by Aite) up to one of the ridges overlooking the valley. I was soon walking the steep incline, huffing and puffing with my watch telling me I was at 2600 metres above sea level. The air was thin and it was hard to get enough oxygen into my lungs. The trail along the top of the ridge had incredible views of the valleys either side with villages scattered over the lush green hills and the white-peaked Himalayas beyond. I cruised higher and higher, pushing my weary legs up to 3000 metres and on to a plateau with 360-degree views.

Whilst the outlook was stunning, I realised the light was rapidly disappearing and I had to get myself back down the mountain while I could still make out which tracks to follow. I passed several women hunched over with a *doko* (traditional cane basket) on their backs fully loaded with leaves and shrubs. When I reached where I had to turn off the main trail for Aite's house, I was faced with a choice of several tracks and in the fading light I couldn't figure out which one I'd taken on the way up. Twice I took the wrong track and had to retrace my steps, growing increasingly concerned, as daylight was fading. It was third time lucky and I soon began to pass large rocks and houses that seemed familiar. Aite was waiting for me on the now pitch black trail, not far from his house.

'I was worried you got lost,' he said.

'I did,' I replied, 'twice!'

We both laughed and I followed him home for dinner and not long after, bed. I was exhausted after my afternoon of getting lost in the magnificent Chalal Ganesthan region of Nepal.

On the day of my departure, Aite's father, Del Bahadur, gave me a *tikka*, an earthy red powder smeared on the forehead. The Hindu mark is used for special religious or spiritual occasions, or to honour an event, or person. A silk scarf was placed around my neck to bless my journey and my soul. I said '*Namaste*' with a bowed head before setting off with Aite, back down the winding trail to board the first of many bus trips to meet Upendra.

As with the trip to Aite's village, I had another long bus trip followed by a trek up the mountain to meet Upendra's family. It was an emotional goodbye as Aite handed me over to Upendra and boarded the bus to return home. We had developed our own mish-mash communication system, a mixture of English and Nepali, as well as hand gestures and facial expressions, and we understood each other, no matter what the topic or situation. We'd only known each other a few weeks but we'd grown close and I already loved him like a brother.

Upendra and I had an hour or so to kill before the bus started its four-hour journey, and after that, 'a bit of a walk, not far maybe four or five hours,' he told me. I flopped back in my seat, sending a cloud of dust puffing from the red fabric cover.

Another long day ahead.

The bus emptied of passengers and refilled twice along the way, and finally after four hours of painfully slow, stop-start travel up narrow winding roads, Upendra nudged me gently with his elbow and said, 'we get off here'. We had arrived at Dhungetar. We were both hungry, but at two o'clock most of the restaurants had closed for the afternoon. Eventually, we wandered into a dimly lit building and an older woman offered us a dented bowl of water to wash with, then after 15 minutes pottering in the almost dark cooking space, returned with some reheated rice, a few vegetables and some *dal*. It wasn't quite on par with the home cooking I'd grown accustomed to with Aite's family, but it was sustenance that would get us up the mountain to

Upendra's home.

The woman chopped a chunk of dried buffalo flesh and placed a few slices on a metal dish and slid it between us. Upendra dived straight in but I was a little cautious, wondering if my predominantly westernised stomach would handle it. With a bit of gentle coaxing from Upendra, I thought 'what the hell,' and started chewing what I'd describe as buffalo jerky, and was surprised to discover it was pretty tasty.

With a 15 kilogram backpack, the journey up the mountain to Upendra's place was tough. We slowly trekked up, up, up, mostly in silence, stopping every 45 minutes for a drink and to catch our breath. Upendra's pack was a least double the weight of mine, but he refused any help, quite used to carrying loads this size and heavier. At one point, he pointed to mountains in the distance and said, 'the third peak … one, two, three, my village is the other side of that.' I had that feeling I remembered as a child in the back of a car heading on a family holiday, when every minute seemed like an hour. This trip was going to take an eternity.

After three hours, we stopped for noodles at a teahouse in a tiny village and looking back from the crest of the mountain I noticed the panoramic valley views were no longer visible, just the multiple peaks we had climbed up and over. We both inhaled our bowl of noodles and set off again. It was getting late and as the sun dropped behind a distant mountain the air quickly cooled. We stopped to put on our jackets and continued up the increasingly difficult path, clambering over boulders and the huge trunks of fallen trees. At times, Upendra needed a light shove to get him, and his pack, over an obstacle.

At another peak, we stopped for tea and more noodles in an open-sided teahouse/supermarket. When I asked Upendra if this was his village, he said 'not yet, a little down to my village.' So long as there was no more '*up*', I was fine to keep going!

The moon was large and luminous, flooding the dark path with enough light to get us to our destination, in all, 10 kilometres and 1700 metres in elevation from the spot the bus dropped us off five hours earlier.

Upendra's home was one of only a handful of grass-roofed stone huts, with a separate small barn where the animals slept. An open fire burned through the floor of the main living area and Upendra's parents rose to greet us as we came through the door. With his work commitments and racing schedule, he hadn't been home in more than a year, but as with Aite and his family, there were no warm embraces, just a few words, and life carried on.

A couple of chickens clucked beneath upside down *dokos* (baskets) under the ladder to the upper level. The wall at the other end of the room was stacked with food, spices and pots, plus a battery-powered light. There was no electricity, no running water and no toilet (out the back, cover it with dirt), but the main living area was clean and tidy.

Our warming cup of masala tea tasted delicious but with slightly different spices to Aite's family brew. We were now in the eastern hills of Nepal and Upendra's family are indigenous Sunuwar people, so I expected a few differences in culture and cuisine.

Upendra's father, Ganbarhadur, already had a few cups of *jard* (homemade rice beer) under his belt and wanted one more, rather than the mouth watering *dal baht* his wife had cooked. Dambbar Kumari refused his request and a slightly heated discussion ensued, reminding me of my own parents when Mum, on occasions, decided Dad had drunk his last beer for the night. I asked Upendra if I had rightly guessed the conversation and he laughed and said, 'yes!'

Dambbar Kumari's *dal baht* was made with black and brown lentils and had strong aromas of turmeric, cumin, garlic, and a chilli tomato relish that warmed the body from the inside out. She served it with a side of delicious curried cauliflower, potatoes and some type of root vegetable Upendra didn't know how to translate. I even managed two small cups of the potent, sour *jard*, which prepared me nicely for a deep sleep.

After a full day of rest the following day, I was keen for a run in the hills and valleys around Upendra's village. We set off with no food or water and no real course in mind. It was already around 30 degrees Celsius and I was curious to see how my body would react with no sustenance or hydration. The trail stuck to the sweeping ridge down steep, sharp switchbacks before levelling out for a while then shooting back uphill. It felt like a rollercoaster until we got to the final long, steep climb that ended at a small cluster of huts. My watch told me we'd covered 12 kilometres in just over two hours, but it felt at least double. We immediately turned around and headed back along the same trail.

For a while we floated easily down a series of short descents but they soon became long, steep, leg-burners that seemed never-ending. There was a fair amount of traffic on the single lane trails back up the mountain as we navigated around herds of buffalo, women carrying packed *dokos*, even dogs sunning themselves. Shortly after, we were back at the ridge near home, and greeted by quite a crowd who'd come out to see the strange 'American' running. I was parched and more than ready for water and a feed, but we kept running another 15 minutes to Upendra's house, where his parents had sealed plastic bottles of water for me – where they came from I have no idea. We had run more than four hours with close to 2000 metres in climbing without food or water. It was another important lesson in fueling for long training sessions, and how resilient the body can be.

Upendra had no textbooks or nutritionists telling him what he should eat, he simply used the information passed down through generations. He cooked up beans, ginger, garlic, onions and turmeric to create a tasty snack with carbohydrates and proteins in the beans, plus anti-inflammatory and enhanced circulation benefits from the garlic and spices. He told me his father would eat this snack after a long day walking down the mountain and back, and the next day he felt strong. I was fascinated to think how long the Nepalese people had known about natural remedies for all aspects of recovery, and it made me wonder why I'd need anything but real food for endurance.

The week flew by with more challenging and memorable expeditions trekking slowly up and running full pelt back down the surrounding trails – the experience was priceless. On my day of departure, Upendra's parents sent me on my way with a hug and a traditional silk scarf for a blessed journey. Two hours later, Upendra and I arrived at the makeshift bus stop and shoe-horned ourselves into a seat on the fully loaded bus for the long journey back to Kathmandu, and after that, Lukla, for the trek up to start the 2013 Everest Ultra.

6.

MOUNTAIN HIGH

EVEREST ULTRA-MARATHON MARCH 2013

This year, only a small field of foreign runners would trek up the mountain to the start line of the Everest Ultra. Nearly 20 competitors had cancelled in the final few weeks before the race, with just four foreign runners confirmed, including me. I was disappointed, and would have preferred to be part of a bigger group trekking together, before frantically racing each other back down.

The other international runners were Scott and Lindsey, a married couple in their early thirties from Canada, and Jan in his early fifties, born in the Caribbean but raised in England. At six foot plus with broad shoulders, he didn't exactly have a runner's frame but he knew how to get from A to B. Jan had been to Nepal countless times and was the brains behind the Everest Ultra, helping to increase the profile of running and other sports in the region over many years. He was also an artist, photographer and teacher, and was on a mission to photograph stray dogs while in Nepal, which were pretty much everywhere.

Scott loved to trek and planned to walk the entire way, 65 kilometres in one day. His wife Lindsey was new to ultra-running, but had enough enthusiasm to get all four of us up and back down the mountain – she loved to run. The couple lived in Calgary on the edge of the Canadian Rockies, and told tales of heading into the woods for days at a time, leaving both sets of parents frantic, wondering if they'd been eaten by a grizzly bear.

Jan had competed in marathons, ultra-marathons, cycling races and triathlons for several decades and was extremely tough mentally, and I'm sure physically as well. He was a fountain of knowledge about the trek up to the start line and race conditions, and acted as a liaison with Ramesh who was near impossible to speak with, running around like a chicken with its head cut off, sorting out logistics. The next two days were filled with event briefings, safety reminders about altitude and the actual trek up Everest, sorting trekking permits and discussing kit.

Flights between Kathmandu and Lukla are rarely on time, primarily because of the weather. It may be sunny with no breeze in Kathmandu, but up in the mountains where we were headed, the conditions could be completely different. Fog, rain or high winds meant planes were often grounded until it was deemed safe to take off.

We checked in our rucksacks with the hundreds of other trekkers, mountaineers, and locals, moved swiftly through a basic security check to the departures area, then eventually on to our twelve-seater plane. A friend had recommended I sit front and left for the best view of the Himalayas, and as we squeezed into our seats I'm sure I wasn't the only one wondering what our chances were of making it in one piece. The propellers spun into action with a boisterous blast, and after a couple of light splutters and a gradual lift, we were airborne.

Within a few minutes, we seemed to be at our cruising altitude, which was slightly concerning as we still hadn't reached the peaks of the surrounding mountains – we flew *through* the mountain range rather than above it. The experience was surreal, almost as if I could reach out and touch the surrounding hills ... not to mention the other light aircraft whizzing across the skies – so close I could see the pilots' faces. Some planes would skim over our heads, others would dip beneath us. One plane flew at a similar altitude to us, and I could see the passengers waving at me – it was freaking crazy!

Before long, one of our group pointed through the cockpit and declared, 'Lukla!', and sure enough in the distance, literally perched on the side of a mountain, was a tiny strip of tarmac. If I squinted, I could just make out the surrounding buildings of the Tenzing-Hillary Airport, named after Sir Edmund Hillary and Sherpa Tenzing Norgay, the first people to reach the summit of Mount Everest and tell the tale.

The Lukla airstrip sits on the edge of a rugged peak at more than 2800 metres above sea level. At 460 metres long and 20 metres wide and often buffeted by gusty winds, pilots have one chance to take off or land. There is no chance of a flyby, or to go-around due to the steep terrain at one end of the runway, and an abrupt drop, plummeting down into a valley at the other.

All I can say is, flying in and out of what's considered the world's most dangerous airport, with close to zero margin for error, certainly ticks the extreme adventure box! With no door to the cockpit, we had a pilot's view of the approach and could see the steep runway (almost 12% gradient) cut into the side of the mountain. Without warning, our view disappeared and we were in a white-out of cloud cover, sparking shocked gasps from the passengers. Those few seconds with no visibility felt like minutes before we emerged and shortly after touched down with a bit of a bounce and travelled up the runway before coming to an abrupt halt with a wall of mountains only metres in front. We veered sharply to the right as another plane came hurtling down the runway in preparation for take-off, and everyone clapped and cheered. We had arrived in Lukla, in one piece - let the Everest Ultra adventure begin.

Outside the airport, hordes of mountain guides clamoured for business, each one offering cheap rates and promising the 'best' Everest experience. Beyond the hustle, the narrow streets of Lukla were lined with trekking gear shops, teahouses and convenience store for those last-minute items like soap, razors, mints, and of course bottled water.

We dodged herds of yaks heading down the mountain as we made our way over the uneven cobblestoned streets, taking care not to roll an ankle.

Horizontal strips of prayer flags, called *Lung ta*, were strung between buildings and across shop fronts. The five standard colours of blue, white, red, green and yellow, in that order, represented the five elements (space, air, fire, water, earth) or the Five Pure Lights. *Lung ta* blessed the surroundings and I hoped to see plenty more further up the mountain.

After a quick stop at the official Everest Ultra hotel, we spotted the nearby stone archway that would mark the finish line of the event in a week's time, and was also the meeting spot for our guides who would carry our main backpacks up the mountain. By hiring guides, tourists put money into the economy – it's the main source of income for families in Lukla. So even though I would have happily carried my pack the whole way, I soon understood it was a better outcome all round to provide a job to the local workforce.

Our party of seven, consisting of Ramesh, four foreign runners and two local runners, set off under the arch that marked the start of our adventure, and worked our way *down* a set of large rocky stairs. I was surprised to discover the first part of our trek up to Everest was a descent. I then realised that after running 65 kilometres downhill in the race, I would need to somehow find the energy to climb *up* these steps to the finish line.

The course for the Everest Ultra would be the same path we trekked up, and the teahouses we stayed in overnight on the way up were our checkpoints on the way down, which was both good and bad. Good that we get to see the course, learn what to expect, discover the tough parts, and bad, well for all the same reasons. Sometimes it's better not to know how steep a hill is before you tackle it.

Our constant companion both up and down the mountain was the breathtaking surroundings. We trekked towards Mount Everest, the highest mountain on Earth and all around us were rolling green hills and valleys and snow-capped peaks. The air was crisp and fresh and I buzzed with a child-like excitement. Our first stopover would be in Monjo, a pleasant few hours' walk and the whole group was relaxed and chatty along the way, covering all manner of topics from work and family to previous adventures.

A herd of yaks appeared on the trail ahead and I prepared myself for the encounter. Yaks are the kings of the mountain and we'd been instructed to remain calm and stay out of their way, being careful not to spook them. I scampered up onto the crumbling bank of the trail, giving the scruffy animals plenty of room to amble past, oblivious to the world around them. The 'boss' followed behind hooting and hollering and waving a stick to keep them moving.

We passed through small villages, each with colourful *Lung ta* fluttering between stone buildings plus a couple of small teahouses for tired trekkers to rest, drink tea, and sleep if needed. Lunch was in one of these villages, Phakding, in a dining room that seated only a few more than our small group. We had tea and *dal baht* and gazed out through windows on three sides, at the valley below as other trekkers slowly picked their way along the magical trails on the way to Everest.

The next section of trail incorporated my first suspension bridge spanning the vast valley below. I stopped for a moment to watch as the emerald-hued water smashed and roared its way through twists and turns of the rocky valley below. Clouds of mist rose from the valley creating an image so mystical it's almost impossible to describe. I was in sensory overload.

The bridge was bigger and bouncier than I imagined and I thought of my mum, who hates heights, as I took my first shaky steps across the moving platform. *Lung ta* were draped along the length of the wobbly crossing, and rightly so, I thought.

Just as we reached Monjo, the afternoon clouds rolled in. Our guides had already arrived with our packs, and most of the group retired for a nap before dinner.

The communal dining area of the two-storey teahouse bustled with trekkers from all over the world. One group of about 15 people brought plenty of home comforts up the mountain including cereal, chocolate biscuits, jams, peanut butter, even their own franchise coffee! The teahouse served them burgers and pizza for dinner, but not quite to the standard of home, if their complaints were anything to go by. After dinner, the leader did a health check of his group, including resting heart rate, blood oxygen levels and blood pressure – a sure-fire way, in my mind, to freak people out!

Lindsey earned herself a new nickname in Monjo. Jan tagged her 'Loo' as she seemed to constantly need the bathroom, and in this part of the world, bathrooms were few and far between, so Lindsey was often spotted heading into tiny restaurants, family homes and occasionally into the bushes, taking her husband Scott with her to act as a 'guard wall'.

Jan and I bunked in together in a drafty, unheated room with a narrow single bed each. Within minutes of being horizontal, Jan was out like a light and snoring with enthusiasm. Despite wearing earplugs, I struggled to sleep with the human chainsaw in the room. Over the next few hours I threw a pillow, a couple of t-shirts and a pair of socks at Jan to quieten him down but to no avail. By the time my alarm chirped at 6 a.m. I'd managed only a couple of hours of restless sleep.

I had arranged to meet Ramkumar Bhattari (Ram), one of the Nepalese runners who had trekked with us, for a 30-minute run before breakfast. I got dressed in the faint light of dawn, and we set off along one of the surrounding trails, deserted but for a few goats. Ramesh joined us and we jogged side by side where there was room on the trail, keeping the pace nice and slow. Ram had recently finished on the podium of a 100 kilometre race in Hong Kong, and I studied his technique, and questioned his training and nutritional habits. With his lack of English, and my lack of Nepali, the only information I managed to extract was that he liked *dal baht*, drank water, and ran every day – not exactly the insider tips I was hoping for. Ram's run style was nothing out of the ordinary – relaxed, a slight bend through his knees, and a mid-foot strike. On the climbs, Ram immediately transferred weight to create a forefoot strike and he took small strides all the way to the top of the small hills. He stayed relaxed and let his legs spin through quicker on the descent to a suspension bridge where we turned back for the teahouse.

By the time we got back, I was a little fatigued and out of breathe, not in a horrible way, but something felt different in my body. My standard breakfast for the trek was two boiled eggs, two *chapatis* (local flat bread, warm from a brick oven), black tea, and a bottle of water. The meal gave me a good mix of carbohydrates and fats to keep me fuelled on the climbs, enough protein to help top up my depleted stores, antioxidants in the tea to help fight the free radicals created the previous day, and plenty of fluids to stay well hydrated, which became more important as we gained altitude.

The day's trek would take us to our next overnight stay at Namche Bazaar and before too long we reached our first real climb. We easily managed the incline, winding our way around the dusty switch-backs, passing other trekkers in both directions. At the top, we caught our first glimpse of Mount Everest, a moment I will never forget. The mammoth snow-capped peak was instantly recognisable with Lhotse sitting close by.

The aura of respect around this iconic mountain was awe-inspiring. I couldn't wait to get to the start line to take on the Everest Ultra.

We reached a long flag-draped suspension bridge that marked the start of our final climb up to Namche. It was a hairy ride as the bridge swayed from side to side. It looked hundreds of metres above the valley's floor, and at times I had to stop and wait for the right rhythm – a bit like a high-altitude dance. For me this crossing marked the point of no return. I told myself I would finish the world's highest ultra-marathon, and give it everything I had.

Once we reached Namche at over 3000 metres above sea level, we had a day to acclimatise, then it was on to Tengboche, at nearly 4000 metres and a few days trek away. After that, Gorakshep, and the start line for the Everest Ultra Marathon.

Beyond the bridge, the trail was steep and technical, with winding steps and narrow passages packed with trekkers and herds of yaks. We arrived around lunchtime and being Saturday – market day – it was a hive of activity. Merchants from surrounding villages brought their wares to Namche, and set up along a terrace that circled the small town. Everything from fruit and vegetables to mops, buckets, brooms and all manner of plastic homewares were laid out on mats creating a kaleidoscope of colours and shapes. There were a few random combinations of products including one merchant who offered hard-boiled eggs alongside a mound of fresh ginger. As the last main village before Everest, Namche sells everything imaginable and has a bank, a post office, a police station – even Starbucks coffee and an Irish pub!

The terraces were abuzz with trekkers enjoying the warmth of the afternoon sun and picking up last minute purchases. It was quite amazing to see such a thriving village almost 3500 metres above sea level in a remote area of Nepal. Our accommodation was at a teahouse six or seven terraces further up from the markets, with spectacular views back over the blue and green tin rooftops and beyond to the hills and valleys surrounding Namche.

The next morning, most of our group planned to head out for a morning walk. Lindsey was fully kitted up and ready to run. She could barely contain her excitement and energy, bounding ahead up short inclines and waiting impatiently for the rest of the group to catch up. We reached our highest elevation so far, at 3750 metres, and were rewarded with possibly my favourite view of Everest. With the clear blue sky, no wind, and bright sunshine, it looked deceptively close, and truly majestic, surrounded by the neighbouring summits of Lhoste, Lhoste Shar and Nuptse.

We were mesmerised by the bizarre 'smoking' cloud rising from the summit of Everest which we learned was the extreme winds of the jet stream flowing through the sky, blowing snow and ice off the summit. The photographs we took that day were stunning and we shared crazy ideas of jumping off in flying suits and cruising down through the valley to land at Lukla airport. We laughed at our imagination, but it was one of those incredible moments of experiencing something so utterly breathtaking, it triggers a sense of child-like amazement.

From that point, the group split and headed off in different directions. Ram, Lindsey and I went for a run and Lindsey was so excited, Ram had to remind her to run 'slowly, slowly', as he pointed to the sky (indicating altitude) then bent over with his hands on his knees gasping for breath. Lindsey calmed down and started firing questions about my time in Nepal and I surprised myself with the knowledge I'd picked up training with Aite and Upendra, and observing other local runners.

I had to remind myself I'd only been a runner for 18 months, and here I was running in the Himalayas, at altitude, and in less than a week's time would be competing in the Everest Ultra. My main learning from the Nepalese runners was to listen to my body, especially at altitude. Many of the locals had no high-tech devices to monitor themselves, just their inner clock and intuition. If they felt good they would increase their pace, and when they felt a little tired, they'd slow down. The guys I ran with would speed up approaching a climb, maintain a steady pace up the climb, then cruise along admiring the views once they reached the top. It was inspiring to watch, but extremely hard to keep up with.

We stopped for a brief rest while Lindsey 'Loo' had a bathroom break. We could see Khumjung in the distance, the largest Sherpa village in the area. From where we were standing I could just make out the low stone fences that bordered the identical stone houses people lived in, a rather remarkable construction feat considering the difficulty of the terrain.

We set off again and as we cruised along the trail, Lindsey complained of being short of breath and having a tingling sensation in her arms, and Ram's chest was tight, so we only ran for another 10 minutes before descending to Namche and a more comfortable altitude.

Aite joined the growing group of runners in Namche a day after us, and the following day we began our trek to Tengboche, with Aite and me leading the pack for the first few hours. We reached a point in the trail where it descended rapidly for about a kilometre, with tight twists and several steep rocky steps down under the dark canopy of the trees above us. We stopped for lunch at a small restaurant where the trail flattened out, before the climb began up an almost identical hill to the one we'd descended that morning. Ahead of us, a large group of guides, trekkers and other locals had gathered by the side of the trail, for no particular reason, other than it being a good spot to rest before the final 40 minute climb up into Tengboche – 3867 metres above sea level, and closing in on the top of the world.

Tengboche's famous century-old Buddhist monastery is the village centrepiece and other than a handful of teahouses, a few tents and masses of ruby-flowered rhododendron trees, the village is basically a spectacular viewing platform for the Himalayas, with Tawache, Everest, Nuptse, Lhotse, Ama Dablam, and Thamserku all in clear sight.

Our rooms were far too cold to sit around in so we met back for a few games of cards and plenty of tea in the dining room, warmed by the yak dung-fuelled heating system.

That night, I constantly tossed and turned – it was freezing and I struggled to take a deep breath due to the lack of oxygen in the air. After my alarm sounded, I dragged myself out of bed, hurriedly put on my running gear and headed out for what had become my regular morning run, assuming I'd be warmer running around in the sun than lying in my sleeping bag. I was fooled by the clear blue sky – I think it was warmer in the shade!

As soon as I saw Lindsey's face at breakfast, I could tell there was a problem. 'Scott is sick, he's been puking all night long, and we haven't slept a minute.' Scott was a big part of our Everest Ultra team and he was potentially going to be out of action for the rest of our adventure. I had spent almost three weeks in local villages without running water or toilets, but I drank only bottled water, or used water purification tablets. I kept my anti-bacterial gel handy and did everything I could to stay healthy. For whatever reason, Scott got hit with something bad. Ramesh decided we would wait in Tengboche for two hours, giving Scott extra time to recharge, and see if he felt strong enough to continue.

I went up to his room to check on him, and he looked exhausted, I really felt for the guy. He is fit and lean, but he looked skinny and weak. Lindsey freaked out that her husband was unwell and that his illness may spell the end of their Everest experience.

With a couple of hours to kill before our new departure time, Ramesh wanted some promotional shots of Aite wearing various t-shirts and caps while running in the Himalayas. I'm all for supporting brands who support athletes, but I'd heard from Aite that he never saw any of the money from these companies and received minimal product during training. It was only 8 a.m. and Aite was in a t-shirt shivering for over an hour, with goosebumps and chattering teeth. More than that, he looked like a broken man.

Jan had his professional camera, and took five minutes to take a dozen shots, but Ramesh insisted on taking more and more photos on his own domestic camera, seemingly oblivious to the fact that his star runner's lips were starting to turn blue. When Aite put on a jacket between photos, Ramesh yelled, 'no, you must stand over here, hold this, and do what I say, we need these pictures for sponsors.'

We all saw the tension between Ramesh and Aite, Jan and I tried to diffuse the situation, but without speaking the language or knowing the ins and outs of any sponsorship agreement, it became tricky. The few words (in Nepali) between Aite and Ramesh soon turned into a yelling match, before it settled into a stern conversation, with many pauses between responses. Aite's frustration was at boiling point, and he was telling Ramesh (I found out later) exactly what he thought. He was pissed off at being treated like a puppet, he was concerned that he was standing out in the freezing cold air, and could get sick, only days before the Everest Ultra race. All Ramesh seemed to care about was getting the right promotional shot.

Ramesh saw red when Aite challenged him about the money, and declared he was unhappy with how he was treated. After half an hour of discussion, they decided to end their training agreement. Aite wanted freedom in his life and his training, while Ramesh felt that he was being ungrateful and was happy to find another runner to 'look after'.

At that point, Lindsey arrived, oblivious to what had happened. She told us there was no way Scott could continue with the trek, and he thought it would be best to head back down the mountain. Everyone's attention turned to Scott's welfare, and how this would affect the group's plans. There was little Lindsey could do for her sick husband so she remained with the group and Ramesh instructed Ram to take Scott back down to Lukla.

Poor Ram's race was over before it began, a talented runner who had already tasted international success. But he had no choice – he was part of Ramesh's crew, so he did what he was told, reluctantly.

Aite marched off with strong purpose to put distance between himself and Ramesh, and I followed to see if I could help calm him down. He had a difficult decision to make. Ramesh provided accommodation near the mountains for Aite's training, and his wife cooked his meals.

I caught up with Aite, and we sat by the river and chatted about what he wanted in life, where he saw his career going, and what his options were. He shed a few tears as he explained how much he wanted to be happy where he lived and trained. I was touched that someone I had met only weeks ago, coming from a different background, trusted me enough to share his worries. He pushed his black sunglasses up on his head, looked me in the eye and said in his soft voice, 'thank you brother, you are a good man.'

It was a short walk to Pangboche, 3985 metres above sea level in the Imja Khole valley, a tiny Sherpa village where we would sleep the night. Tiny potato farms spread out around the dozen or so stone buildings in the village, and each farm was boxed in with a stone fence containing symmetrically planted crops that created a patchwork effect across the landscape. Our lodge was small but comfortable, brightened by the afternoon sun through windows in the common dining room. We'd had news that Scott had made it to Namche and was now resting. Lindsey meanwhile struggled with a constant headache, lack of sleep and feeling tired.

The high altitude was noticeable now and any sudden movements triggered a gasp for air when I lay in bed, thinking warm thoughts. I wore my thermal long johns, thick woolly socks and gloves, with the hood of my sleeping bag covering my head. I felt constantly out of breath and tight in the chest.

The next day, we had Mount Everest in all its stunning beauty in our sights until we reached our lunch-break destination, Pheriche. Aite and I discussed our game plans for the race, and he took me through how I should run the race. I told him I would be running by his side until the finish where I would sprint past him up to Lukla. He knew me well enough now to know I was joking, and he laughed before he said, 'maybe, you never know.'

Aite told me about Sudip Kulung, the red-hot favourite who was a two-time defending champ. A phenomenal mountain runner, especially downhill navigating the steepest terrains at a rapid pace, skimming off any rocks before surging up and over the peaks. Sudip was once under the watchful eye of Ramesh, but now that they'd parted ways, his international racing career had evaporated.

We also spoke of Upendra, my other Nepalese brother, a tough runner, and from what I understood Aite to be saying, a competitor you want to shake off well before the final few kilometres, as he will just continue to grind on to the finish line.

Halfway up one of the sparsely covered peaks, we caught a glimpse of a herd of goats, with one goat much bigger than the rest. The Nepalese guides guessed it was at least 100 kilograms, and dreamt of the steaks it could yield. It whetted our appetite, and before long we stopped in the village of Pheriche for lunch.

Pheriche is home to the Himalayan Rescue Association, the main medical assistance centre on Everest. At 4371 metres, the winds were bitterly cold but with glorious views in all directions as we were in a valley, it was easy to forget you could no longer feel your fingers and toes, or even your face!

By now we were all experiencing the effects of being so high up, primarily headaches and shortness of breath. It was quite toasty inside the dining room of the lodge where we stopped for lunch and we had plenty of room to lie down on the long benches that lined the walls. Even the Nepalese guys were a little quiet. Lindsey had a throbbing headache, couldn't eat, and wanted to sleep, so we took a longer lunch break than scheduled to give her time for a nap.

While Lindsey slept, I went to visit the official Everest Memorial, a striking stainless-steel sculpture that pays tribute to the all the guides and adventurers whose dream of standing on top of the world cost them their lives. The two-metre-high cone structure is split down the middle with names, nationalities, dates and expedition name inscribed on the inside. I found it to be a very moving tribute that brought home the dangers that went alongside the thrill of an Everest adventure.

Lindsey, the pocket rocket, was struggling, but she was determined to get to the start line. She wanted to push on to Dughla. The group kept a slow and steady pace and trekked together for most of the afternoon, but after a while, I felt the need to stretch my legs. With Jan and Ramesh staying with Lindsey, Aite and I forged ahead a little, mostly in silence as talking required energy we didn't have. The silence helped us both stay calm and present.

At one point, Aite turned to me and said, 'I'm very happy to be here with you brother.' For me this was a highlight of my trip, a moment

I'd never forget. With the strength of our friendship, I felt confident we could get through anything the Everest Ultra threw at us. I had a Nepalese friend for life.

I could see Dughla in the distance, wedged into the side of a hill, and we soon reached the tiny village where we would rest for the night.

It was much colder, and the air was noticeably thinner in Dughla. I had a tight chest and was short of breath, plus I had an annoying headache. Lindsey was sitting quietly in the corner with Jan, hands wrapped around a mug of tea. Dinner was a potent garlic soup with chunks of garlic and herbs in a salty broth, which Aite explained to me was good for countering the effects of altitude. I followed it up with a hearty *dal baht*.

My room was only 20 metres away but the cold was so intense I felt an immediate drop of my internal temperature. I rugged up in every piece of thermal clothing I had plus hat, gloves and socks and snuggled into my sleeping bag but just couldn't warm up. I imagined the hot desert of Morocco, the scorching sun, a warm Jacuzzi but nothing worked. Sleep refused to come. I was constantly unsettled by shortness of breath and only managed a few hours of rest before my alarm sounded. At altitude when the body is struggling with each breath, it's hard stay asleep and even rolling over will wake you up, at which point, feeling like you can't breathe, it's hard not to freak out. I felt like that most nights from Namche onwards.

My bones felt so cold and brittle I wondered if they'd snap. I am unquestionably a warm climate person. I remember winter mornings as a kid heading out to Proctor Park in Bathurst for a game of soccer, each breath visible as I made the dash from the house to the car. I would have to psych myself up and focus on how I was going to warm up, then exit the car running and not stop until the game got underway.

Another steaming bowl of garlic soup wasn't quite what I had in mind for breakfast, but I was desperate to boost my body temperature. I sipped it slowly and instantly enjoyed a warming sensation down through my chest, into my stomach, then gradually throughout the rest of my body. It was perfect.

Poor Lindsey had another night of little sleep compounded by a throbbing headache – even trying to swallow warm porridge hurt her head, but she needed it to get through a difficult day ahead trekking to Labouche.

It was a far slower pace as we headed straight into a long, gradual climb at close to 5000 metres of altitude. Jan assured us it was the toughest section, and once we reached the top, it was an easy flat trek past some glaciers, and into our final pit stop before the start line. I could see groups of trekkers ahead of us snaking their way around large boulders that lined the trail in the direction we were heading.

Aite and I discussed race tactics; whether I should run down fast or slow, where it was important to take things easy, like coming down loose rocky trails. He told me, 'if you fall and hurt badly, there are no doctors, no officials, no help, you must walk yourself to closest village.'

We took our time along the trail, walking slowly for 10 minutes, then resting for two. When we arrived at the top of this energy zapping-climb, Aite and I lay down on the ground to recover, and waited for the others. It was the first time I felt as if I might struggle to make the start line in one piece.

With the toughest part of the day behind us, we moved on at a leisurely pace over undulating hills. The surrounding landscape was stunning but we stopped only for a moment as the bitterly cold wind pushed us on. We moved in a slow pack, staying close to each other for warmth, offering encouragement to Lindsey who struggled to even shuffle her feet and hold her head up.

Arriving in Labouche, we dumped our bags in our rooms (Jan and I were sharing again) and headed for the warmth of the dining room to play cards, drink tea and wait for dinner. The communal area was full of trekkers from all over the globe chatting and laughing. Jan was feeling OK, a little tight-chested and slightly out of breath, and I felt a lot better now that I was warm and no longer battling up hills. Lindsey, however was in a lot of pain, and with just 48 hours before the start of the race, it was not guaranteed she'd be well enough to compete.

A few hours after dark, my training mate Upendra, Sudip Kulung (the defending Everest Ultra champion) and a couple of other runners arrived at the lodge. They were tired, having trekked from Lukla to Labouche in just two days, but in good spirits and happy to sit down.

Most of the group retired for the night but I stayed behind to catch up with Upendra and a few other trekkers, staying warm around the yak-dung stove. We swapped stories, and shared our reasons for trekking halfway up the highest mountain in the world. I told Upendra he was crazy for taking just two days to get to Labouche, but he laughed and said, 'it was OK, some good, some bad,' which is his way of saying you just do what needs to be done.

Preparing for bed, I thought about how close we were to the start line, just one more day's trek, up to Gorakshep. I was excited to pit my fitness and mountain running skills against the amazing local athletes. I needed as much sleep as possible over the next nine hours, but with Jan already fired up and snoring like a chainsaw, I wasn't at all confident. Little did I know his snoring would be the least of my problems.

Sleep came surprisingly fast, but I was rudely awoken only a few hours later by a sharp, stabbing pain in my stomach, followed by a wave of nausea as I scrambled for my head torch and sandals and raced to the bathroom. I just made it to the damp, smelly, toilet – a hole in the ground with a plastic toilet seat on top and tried to figure out if I needed to throw up or sit down. Turned out I needed both. The pain in my gut was extreme as my body convulsed violently trying to expel anything and everything.

For a split-second I convinced myself it was a terrible nightmare and pleaded with myself to wake up. Then another wave of nausea came over me, and as I knelt on the rancid toilet floor I knew I wasn't dreaming. The timing could not have been worse.

I made the same mad dash down the freezing hallway to the bathroom at least six times throughout the night. I had very little will to get up when my alarm woke me for breakfast. Food was the last thing on my mind.

Jan had already left our room, and I doubted he'd had much sleep with all my comings and goings. Lindsey's condition had worsened and with a severe headache rattling her brain, a decision was made to take her back down to Pheriche to be checked out by the medics. In the morning, she would start her race, alone, from the valley, roughly 50 kilometres from Lukla. She was disappointed, but she knew it was the best decision for her health.

I ordered a single *chapati* for breakfast, which caught the attention of the group – typically I'd order two *chapatis*, garlic soup and two boiled eggs. Nobody else had suffered any type of food poisoning from the previous night. Jan thought it was most likely Giardia, a parasite in the small intestines, often contracted from untreated water. I played down the extent of my illness as I was determined to get to the start line, even though I was severely dehydrated and had the strength of an overcooked piece of spaghetti.

Jan offered some Giardia medication he bought in Namche, and I washed it down with a warm electrolyte-based drink usually given to babies with diarrhoea, while I cautiously nibbled on my *chapati*. Just as we left the breakfast table, I got that '*here she blows*' feeling again and headed straight for the toilet, where I lost everything I'd just ingested, including a small piece of *chapati* through my nose.

Aite and Upendra were concerned for my welfare, despite struggling with the effects of altitude themselves. Unfortunately, we all knew there was nothing anyone could do, but I did get some comfort in knowing they cared.

Today would not be a good day. I'd expelled all food and fluids from my body and now faced several hours' walk up and over small peaks at an altitude of more than 5000 metres. With Aite by my side, I shuffled out the door of the lodge, and slowly made my way to the trail leading up to Everest's Base camp. We followed a glacial moraine to Gorakshep. The moraine's terrain so unusual we could have been on another planet. A mixture of ice, rock, mud, and other debris had the appearance of frozen waves constantly undulating upwards; it was very slow going. At that point, I did wonder why I had chosen this extreme race when I was so new to ultra-marathons.

Aite was feeling the effects of the high altitude more intensely with a throbbing headache and an extremely tight chest, so we were almost at snail's pace. His usually relaxed, happy face was tense, and full of pain.

The moraine transformed from rolling waves into windswept formations of ice that looked like a series of caves. The occasional waves reappeared, their frozen lips curling dramatically over the icy ground, truly remarkable formations.

Gorakshep had only a few stony buildings on flat, barren ground overshadowed by the peak of Kala Patthar – through my eyes it looked peacefully beautiful. I reminded myself of the pain I had endured during the Marathon des Sables only 12 months earlier, and the joy I felt when I eventually staggered over the finishing line. Pretty much how I expected to feel this time tomorrow when I arrived in Lukla.

I was freezing almost to the point of immobility and hurting from head to toe. I could barely feel my extremities. *12 hours to go,* I told myself.

Gorakshep, a frozen lakebed 5164 metres above sea level, was the original base camp for mountaineers hoping to summit Everest. The name Gorakshep translates to 'dead ravens' as there is zero vegetation and the entire area looks like a wasteland – the green, blue and red rooftops providing the only splashes of colour. It's an ideal resting place after a long day trekking up to base camp, then on to Kala Patthar, an ascent to 5644 metres. It's also good spot for helicopters to land in the event of a rescue or medical evacuation.

Warm tea and garlic soup awaited us at our lodge, and I ordered plain rice, the only food I thought I had a hope of keeping down. I took a deep breath and placed a few grains at a time into my mouth. My body felt weak and in need of some macronutrients. Almost immediately, my stomach began to bubble, but I managed to swallow a few more mouthfuls – a promising sign.

Outside, a helicopter hovered, coming in to collect two people with severe mountain sickness after attempting to climb up to Kala Patthar too quickly. The chopper would ferry them back to Kathmandu for treatment. The excitement gave everyone a much-needed distraction from the monotony of eating, sleeping and sitting around. It was also a sobering reminder of how quickly circumstances can change this far above sea level. No one is in complete control, not even the locals who are accustomed to the conditions. Everest is a place where you must respect your body, and pay respect to the mountain.

I wanted some fresh (freezing) air, and thinking I may never again have the chance to stand at the base of Mount Everest, I forced myself out of the warmth of the lodge, and into the mercy of my surroundings. I took tiny mouse-like bites of an energy bar while staring out at the snow-blanketed peaks. It was mesmerising, yet daunting and for a moment, I was lost in the peaceful beauty of the Himalayas.

By 4 p.m. my condition worsened and I was huddled in bed as my stomach churned in nauseous waves. The nibble of *chapati* I had for breakfast, granules of rice with sips of garlic soup for lunch, and crumbs of energy bar a few hours earlier were playing havoc with my gut. I tried to lay still, breathe slowly and imagine I was somewhere warm and comfortable, but I was forced to make a dash for the hole in the ground at the end of the hallway.

Everything I had managed to keep down since that morning came out, I was back on empty – maybe less than empty as liquid kept coming out of me during short convulsive spurts. I had never felt so sick. The combination of Giardia and altitude sickness was close to unbearable. It felt like I was going into physical meltdown. I had no control over my body and no way of making it better. My body was basically saying, '*screw you man, I'm done!*'

I had to find strength from somewhere. I was in for one hell of a fight and the only person who could get me through this, was me. The little man inside my head has helped me many times before, and I needed him to roll up his sleeves and kick me into gear. This was all about mental strength.

I pride myself on being able to mentally pull myself through any situation when my body has decided it has had enough. All endurance athletes have their own way of dealing with pain and fatigue; I simply tell my little man upstairs it's time to work. He is a completely different person to me, detached from my feelings and emotions. He has one objective: to get me through whatever hell I've found myself in.

'It's time to get to work,' I said out loud as I pushed myself up to a sitting position, my heart racing, after another stint in the bathroom.

I got myself to the dining room and ordered plain rice with salt on top, the easiest thing for me to try and ingest. Eating was the last thing on my mind, I had no appetite, but I had to replenish the nutrients I'd lost. I began to slip into a semi-conscious state and felt Aite's hand on my arm. He knew I wasn't doing too well. My headache was a sharp continuous throb, I felt fragile and on edge. Aite and Upendra pulled their white plastic chairs up close on either side of me to try and keep me warm. I struggled to speak and let my head drop to my chest.

With Ramesh on his way to Lukla, so he could greet the winner of tomorrow's race, Jan was now the official leader for the Everest Ultra. Jan told me I had two options; head back down the mountain to a lower altitude, or stick it out and start the race with everyone in the morning. He didn't mollycoddle, he just gave me the facts. He had many years of high-altitude experience and had seen a lot of mountain sickness. I had to suck it up or get out of there. I desperately wanted to be at the start line in the morning, and test myself on the technical descents. A decision was made for me to try and eat dinner, and see how my body reacted.

12 hours before the start of the Everest Ultra, I should have been shovelling in food to fill up my glycogen stores, not scooping five or six grains of rice at a time into my mouth. I tried delaying the inevitable by chewing the tiny grains at least 50 times, in hope that

they would all but dissolve and slide down my throat as a salty bolus. Within minutes I was heading back down the dark, cold corridor to the bathroom. Mini black outs came and went, gaps in time that could have been milliseconds or full minutes – I had no idea what reality I was in.

I opened my eyes to Aite kneeling in front of me, looking concerned.

'Luke, are you OK?'

'No,' I replied.

And that was it. A decision was made and I was to head back to Dughla, roughly 10 kilometres away and begin 'my race' back to Lukla from that point.

It was after 7 p.m., pitch-dark outside and well below freezing. The last two days of trekking up to Gorakshep were bad enough in the daylight with the uneven trails and twisting gradients. Now I had to retrace my steps overnight, feeling like shit.

Aite, Jan and some local guides discussed who would escort me back to Dughla. Several Nepalese runners helped me to me feet. A young guide was instructed to walk me slowly down to Dughla and stay the night with me. In the morning after I had woken up, he could go on his way.

An extra jacket was wrapped around me, and a head torch strapped to my head over two woolly hats. Aite gave my backpack a final check over to make sure all zippers, clips, and buckles were fastened, before giving me a hug and wishing me well. Upendra wrapped his arms around me and whispered to take care, before I shuffled out the door at 8 p.m. into the cold night.

The Everest Ultra was the last thing on my mind. I had to concentrate on getting back down the mountain. A wave of nausea and pain swept across me with each step, my guide always one step ahead of me. I watched where my guide placed his feet, and tried to replicate each step. Every so often I had to stop as my stomach heaved and a trickle of bile dribbled from my mouth.

My guide, who never spoke, put his hand on the middle of my back as my body continued to convulse. I had a feeling of comfort, just like I did many years ago when I was unwell and my mum would put her hand on my back, rubbing it gently to make me feel better. Then he smacked me repeatedly between my shoulders blades with forceful blows. I guess he was trying to help expel whatever it was he thought I was trying to get out, but I felt like he was about to break me in two. I growled at him to stop and pointed in our intended direction to keep moving.

I could see the glow from the lodges of Labouche and wanted nothing more than to stop and rest my body, but my guide didn't even slow down. Labouche didn't exist on his map. My pace slowed and I needed to stop more regularly with my body releasing from both ends. The little man upstairs offered me soft encouragement and assured me I was already past halfway. I remembered that once I got past the slippery glacier, I had a steep, winding descent before I arrived at Dughla. A voice whispered, 'it's OK champ, all downhill from here.' I came to Everest for a challenge, and this was where it began. To say I was humbled would be an understatement, I simply had to play the cards I had been dealt, and preserve my weakened body as best as I could.

I caught a glimpse of colourful *Lung ta* flapping in the night breeze, and realised we had reached the memorial, just before Dughla. I tapped my guide's shoulder as I needed a quick rest before attempting the final descent.

With a deep breath, I began to twist and turn my way down,

grasping at large boulders that lined the trail for support. Occasionally I'd stop and drape my body over one of the boulders to catch my breath. Eventually we reached Dughla where a single window glowed with yellow light. The little guy upstairs said, 'well done mate.'

My guide knocked on the door of the same lodge I'd stayed 48 hours earlier and a local man I recognised showed us to our room.

I took off my shoes and slid into my sleeping bag, still wearing everything I was wrapped in. I glanced at my watch – it was 11 p.m. I was soon up again, summonsed to the toilet, the first of seven or eight trips throughout the night. I managed maybe half an hour's sleep.

At 5 a.m. I rolled onto my back, took a deep breath, and thought – *let's do this!*

For the first time in over 30 hours, I didn't feel nauseous – my exhaustion had stabilised and I had some strength. I was confident today was going to be a good day – it was race-day. I dressed in a clean race kit to spark race day excitement, in the hope adrenaline (my current choice of fuel) would flood my body.

My guide woke as I was tying my laces, smiled and gave me the thumbs up. I nodded and he was out of the room faster than I could put my backpack on. He was heading back up to Gorakshep to take some trekkers to Everest Base Camp. Talkabout seriously fit. These guys are trekking machines.

At 5:30 a.m. I began my journey down the mountain. There was no countdown, no crowd cheering, nobody to wish me luck, not even a designated start line. I just walked down the trail and told myself to get to my first target, Pheriche. My race was underway.

My mood was positive, I had been vertical for nearly an hour with no need for the bathroom. I was on a voluntary nil by mouth diet – worried if I tempted fate with food or water I'd trigger another bout of sickness. But I needed fuel. I nibbled on a small portion of energy bar, and had a few sips of water. Within minutes it reappeared at my feet. Once again, I was hunched over heaving with my hands on my quivering knees. More fluids lost, more energy expelled, but the little guy upstairs kept telling me, 'one step at a time Luke, Pheriche is only a short walk away.'

The sun was out, but it was cold – cold enough to see each breath I exhaled before gasping for another. I was oblivious to the incredible scenery around me as I focused on putting one foot in front of the other across the rocky valley. I needed a plan, something to work towards, and take my mind off my depleted body. I plotted out two hours of walking, to take me the other side of Pheriche, across the river and up the hill. From there, it was a reasonably flat few kilometres and I could possibly run to the next checkpoint at Pangboche. There was no way I wanted to walk the entire 55 kilometres.

The mental planning helped pass the time as I'd made it to Pheriche and the first official checkpoint. The Mountain Rescue team gave me medication for my nausea and asked a few questions about my condition. I sipped some warm water to wash down the pills, thanked them and kept moving. I covered about 100 metres before the warm water and tablets came back up.

I tightened my backpack, took a deep breath and increased my pace from a staggering stroll to an end-of-marathon shuffle. I lasted 30 seconds before I was hunched over a rock, dry retching. I closed my eyes and summoned up another conversation with myself, with the little man upstairs. I took five minutes' rest for a few visualisation exercises, closed my eyes and absorbed the warmth of the sun into my chilled body. I pictured the next checkpoint in Pangboche, 30 minutes away; I imagined running through it, saying 'Hello' to the locals, and climbing further along the trail to Tengboche, and the iconic monastery. I felt the pain of the climb and put my hands on my thighs where I'd feel it most. Finally, I pictured myself hunched over and my body convulsing. I created a mental note of the oncoming pain, then opened my eyes, slowly got to my feet, took a breath, and started jogging.

Another mental strength technique that I've used over the years is something I call my 'you're the best' talk, and it usually starts with me singing the famous song '*You're the best*' from the original *Karate Kid* movie, repeating its chorus over and over.

When I was playing football, just before heading to the match, I would spend five or so minutes alone, and tell myself, 'you are the best, you are the best!' Walking around my house, looking at my reflection in the bathroom mirror, I would constantly say it out loud and explain why. 'You're the best tackler, no one can get by you, the best passer, every single pass you make today with be precise', and so on. By the end of my 'You're the best' talk, my confidence would be overflowing, I was ready to take on anything.

Shuffling along the undulating trail, I said out loud, 'you're the best Australian ultra-runner on Everest today mate, you will get to Lukla because you are strong, stronger than anyone else on this mountain, no scrap that, stronger than anyone on any given day anywhere in the world, you will beat this challenge, YOU WILL get to Lukla today!' And cue theme music.

Deep down, I started to feel my strength ignite. I felt pumped up, and at that moment, my mind was ready for whatever would be thrown its way. With a determined, 'C'MON!', I shut out the stabbing pains in my gut and the throbbing sensation in my head. I continued my run/walk strategy along the trail, and tried to ignore the pain.

'*never give up*', I told myself, '*Never, never, never!*'

The first of the Nepalese Everest Ultra runners sped past, floating up a hill in his raggedy old, and probably borrowed, trainers. I glanced at my watch to check the time, hoping Aite and Upendra would be hot on his heels. A very focused Aite came running alongside soon after with the defending champion Sudip. He didn't see me, so I yelled out, 'go brother go', he slowed a little and moved towards me but I told him I was fine and to keep going, 'three minutes behind', I said and he nodded, then ran off.

Next Upendra flew by, and without breaking his stride asked how I was then disappeared around a bend before I could reply. A constant stream of Nepalese runners overtook me, many I'd never seen before. I held high hopes for my friends to do well. They are both incredible athletes and amazing people, but I wouldn't know the outcome until I arrived at Lukla well after they did.

Pangboche's checkpoint was just how I pictured it during my visualisation session, and I stopped briefly to remove a few layers. The day was warming up and I didn't want to overheat and exacerbate my dehydration. I politely declined any water, and noted there was absolutely no food at the checkpoint, not that I wanted any just yet. I still had just over a marathon before I reached Lukla, so I'd occasionally try and fuel myself but each time, it came straight back up.

Slowly but surely, I pushed myself into a heightened state of pain, 'The Hurt Locker' as some athletes describe it. The combination of running and walking in a highly nutrient-deficient state was not pleasant, but I needed to get to Lukla, at any cost.

The trail grew busier with trekkers starting their day's adventure heading up or down the mountain, and it helped to see other human beings. To keep my spirits high I said 'G'day' to everyone who passed by. My body was building a small tolerance to the pain and I ran for longer periods between walking. I dared to think that if I continued my pace I could be in Lukla in another four hours. I convinced myself that while I felt good, I should cover as much ground as possible.

The plant life surrounding this gully towards Tangboche gave me renewed energy and I took a deep breath, as more plants indicated the air was becoming more oxygen rich. *'Stay relaxed, soft knees, no fear, don't fight the trail'* I whispered to myself as I curled my way around the winding descent. By the time I reached the bridge, I was light headed, dizzy, and felt like I was going to faint. I semi-collapsed over a rock and wept silently. I wanted to be in Lukla, surrounded by my friends. I cursed myself for running, and admonished myself, "*How could you be so stupid to run, you're killing yourself!*

I picked myself up, dusted myself off, and kept on trudging.

'Don't give up', I whispered.

On the other side of the bridge was the long steady ascent to the colourful Monastery of Tengboche, another checkpoint, and one step closer to Lukla. Only 35-kilometres to go. I held onto one side of the cold metal railing and pulled myself along the bridge. My body hated me for what I was doing to it, and punished me with constant tortuous intestinal spasms, and dizzy spells.

Heading up that hill, I reached a new low point. I felt like I had a fridge full of rocks strapped to my back. I was dry-retching on the side of the trail. Passers-by asked if I was all right, but I just gave them the thumbs up and waved them on. I remained positive for as long as I could, I was close to the top – I just needed to hang on a little while longer.

I emerged through a familiar tree-lined passage, and realised I was on the trail to Tengboche. I'd forced myself to run the 200 metres to the next checkpoint. Why, I have no idea, for some reason it marked a significant victory in the day, to show my body that my mind still had some control over its actions. I thought if I can make it this far, I can make it to Lukla. I had to continually reinforce my belief that I was going get there.

A race official asked how I was, and I said OK (a total lie), then I heard something that not only gave me comfort, it made me smile – the distinct twang of an Australian accent. A group had stopped at Tengboche for a tea break and when they heard my accent a loud cheer erupted. It was exactly what I needed. After a brief exchange of the usual questions including, 'Where ya from? I've gotta mate who lives there, you know him?' there were handshakes and pats on the back before I set off with a renewed energy, heading for my next target, Namche Bazaar.

I thought I was out of ear shot when I heard the infamous and uplifting cheer, '*Aussie Aussie Aussie, Oi Oi Oi!*' It gave me a boost of strength, and reminded me of a quality I would never lose, the fighting Aussie spirit.

I took off down the fast and flowing trail from Tengboche, a mix of compressed dirt and loose rocks, with prickly shrubs lining the way. I used the skills and techniques Aite and Upendra had taught me to navigate through as quickly as I could. I was flying, winding down and around each turn, not slowing for anything, I ran with soft spring-like knees, without any fear – I felt energetic, and alive! I was in what many athletes call 'The Zone.'

I passed Lindsey, and was happy to hear she felt much better. Being at a decreased altitude ignited her spark for running. I told her I couldn't stop, gave her a brief outline of what I'd been through, wished her luck and kept motoring down, looking to find that *Zen* state once more. I made it to the bottom feeling good. The trail flattened out, then I slowly crossed the wobbly suspension bridge and emerged to face a tree-lined trail with a challenging climb. Aite told me all Nepalese runners would walk up this path during the race, so there was no way I was attempting to run.

I tried again to get a small amount of energy bar in my stomach with a couple of mouthfuls of water, but same result. Straight out again. I now regretted running down the previous descent, as it took so much more out of me than it was worth.

Lindsey came cruising past and stopped to see if there was anything she could do for me, I said 'Yes, keep running until you reach Lukla and enjoy the experience.' She promised she would, and took off up the trail. I was hurting like I've never hurt before, and in front of me was a steep, one kilometre climb, winding its way up to a destination I couldn't see. Drained and barely able to walk, I grabbed hold of sturdy looking branches in arms-reach and pulled on them like a game of tug-o-war. Every three or four steps I had to stop and catch my breath. Halfway up the climb I was noticeably sweating, and this concerned me. I was already dehydrated, and couldn't afford to use up whatever remaining electrolytes I still had. This could become a serious problem and I was still 30 kilometres from Lukla. I sat and spoke to myself, oblivious to the many trekkers who walked by.

'Luke, you have no other option, you will do this, you're tough, strong, and nothing will stand in your way. Your next target is Namche, get to the top of this hill, then run the flat terrain, I don't care if it hurts. Then at Namche, walk very slowly back down the hill, c'mon mate, you can do it!'

I dipped into my deep mental energy reserves, and encouraged myself to soldier on as I dragged my body up the incline. At the top was a teahouse with panoramic views, but I kept my head down and shuffled past. I was on a mission and not even a spectacular view of the almighty Everest was going to distract me.

I remembered the twists and turns and gentle inclines of the trail into Namche, and felt a sense of comfort to be on such a familiar path. It gave me hope I would make it. I spotted Lindsey about a kilometre ahead of me, running alone, and she seemed to be moving well. It made me smile. I knew she was doing what she came here to do – run some trails in this magical part of the world.

Namche was tantalisingly close. My strategy was move, stop, rest, and it seemed to be working as the next checkpoint edged closer. I managed to distract myself by imagining Aite and Upendra relaxing at the lodge at Lukla, sipping tea and eating a warm *dal baht* to replenish their depleted bodies. I thought of Upendra's laid-back attitude and his catch phrase of, 'some good, some bad', and Aite, the quietly confident professional focused on running and his family. I had learnt so much from these two humble men. I took Aite's focus and drive to get me to each checkpoint, and Upendra's grit and determination, to help me through the tougher times. Then, like waking from a dream, I turned the final bend to see the coloured rooftops of Namche Bazar. I still had just over a half-marathon to go, but now it was time to implement my new mental strategy.

Arriving at the checkpoint in Namche, I was surprised to see once again no food on the table. I knew the Nepalese carried no nutrition with them, but could they run 65 kilometres without eating a thing and only drinking water? The man at the desk checked off my name, and poured me a cup of orange drink. I guessed it was a type of cordial and thought a sip of something sugary and sweet might help. It didn't.

I covered the stone paving with luminous orange splatter, assured the checkpoint man I was OK, then wiped my mouth and continued through the Saturday markets. The smell of the warm raw meat triggered another bout of nausea and I pleaded with myself not to heave where people were buying their weekly groceries.

On the outskirts of Namche, I sat and considered my options.

I was pissed off! I didn't want to feel like this anymore, I wanted to eat and drink, be able to run, and use the fitness I had gained over three weeks training in Nepal. All logic went out the window, '*screw it*' I thought, and stood up as I told myself, 'no more food, no more water until Lukla.' I wanted to punish myself by beating my body up even more, but I knew it would begin to shut down if I was too cavalier. I was concerned I would cause long term damage. I needed a new plan, one I could stick to that was less self-destructive.

Step by painful step I descended from Namche Bazaar, the steep terrain pushing my legs closer to collapse. Next stop was Monjo at 2840 metres, the final checkpoint. Just as I reached the outskirts of the village, a Nepalese official asked to see my trekking pass.

All the foreign runners in the Everest Ultra had permits, but they were with Ramesh – we'd been told showing our race numbers would suffice.

'Permit, permit', the guard demanded, blocking my path. I pulled at my race number, saying, 'Everest Ultra, Everest Ultra', and tugged again at my sweat soaked shirt. In the end, he waved me on but I couldn't make my legs move. I was as stiff as Tin Man from the *Wizard of Oz*. I cranked myself up and got my joints moving but could only manage 30 to 60 second bursts before needing a rest. I'd made it to Monjo – the final checkpoint.

Only 10 more kilometres, I told myself. 10,000 metres to Lukla. It may as well have been to the moon and back. I slumped into a white plastic chair on the terrace of the teahouse we'd stayed the previous week, and was startled from my semi-conscious state by a Nepalese voice. He asked if I was running the Everest Ultra and I gave him the thumbs up. I couldn't manage much more.

Another wave of nausea had me scrambling for a toilet and with a few directions from the teahouse staff, I got myself there but it was occupied and I had no choice but to throw up on the grass, pleading with my bowels to hold tight. I took a tiny sip of water to wash away the acidic taste in my mouth, but it came straight back up. Then my bowel growled and bubbled, and thank god, the toilet was now vacant.

For the next stage of the battle, my plan was to move for five minutes, rest for one. I looked up at the sky hoping for help, and saw I was staggering towards storm clouds. It made total sense to put on warm, protective clothing before I got soaked. It may not sound like a big deal, but that meant I had to stop, remove my backpack, take out the clothing, zip up my bag, put on my trousers and jacket, then my backpack, and begin to walk again. I ran through this sequence of events in my head several times before deciding it had to be done. What should have taken three or four minutes took me 20.

Minutes later, the first drop of rain hit the top of my head.

This had to be a joke, after everything the day had thrown at me now I had to finish the race in a rainstorm. I looked up at the now blackened sky, raised my arms, extended the middle finger on both hands and screamed, 'FUCK YOU!'

I inched my way closer to Lukla.

The rain was torrential and people ran for cover under awnings and trees, and inside tea houses. I thought about stopping, but I was already soaked. Streams of mud flowed over the trails, and the sheer volume of water down the incline made every step like walking on ice.

I slipped constantly, but only fell a couple of times.

'C'mon Luke, you can do this,' I told myself, remembering the tattoo on my right bicep – *fortis*, the Latin word for strength. The constant patter of rain on my shoulders seemed amplified, and was a welcome distraction from how I felt. I looked up and assessed my final destination, Lukla, was on the fifth ridge. I squinted to see through the haze of cloud, rain, and mist.

'Five more climbs Luke,' I shouted.

Back in my footballing days, whenever I was faced with a set of five sprints, or the final five repetitions of a drill, I would break it down using my *Power of Five*:

1. Just get through this one, it simply needs to be done, and you are relatively fresh.
2. Push on this repetition, it will hurt, but hang in there you are tough, keep going.
3. The toughest repetition, after this, only two left. Easy.
4. Just do it, then one to go. Work hard, hang in there.
5. The last one. Anyone, no matter how tired, can do just one more of anything.

I started the first small incline, and could only manage short stints of walking before I'd need a rest. I could see planes flying in and out of Lukla airport in the distance, a much-needed lift for both myself and the little man upstairs. *Just keep going, just keep going* was my mantra, as I tackled the second summit. I thought of another quote that most endurance athletes can relate to, *'It's time to treat your body like a rental car!'*

I had been thrashing my body all day long, not caring about the damage I could potentially cause. 'Push, push, push,' I yelled at myself, as I rested at the top of the second incline.

'Just get through the third, then it's two to go.'

I got halfway up the third incline before I had to sit. This time I took off my backpack and hugged it, searching for inspiration and some simple comfort. I imagined my mum beside me saying, 'Luke, no one can do this for you, you have to do this yourself, I'm proud of you, and know you will make it to the end.' I stood up, ready to finish this day once and for all. Passing trekkers, seeing my legs buckle, offered help but I politely declined.

I saw another plane take off. 'YES!' I yelled. I knew I was close. I could see the green logo of Yeti Airlines. At the penultimate climb, I saw a patch of blue sky. To me it was a sign everything was going to be OK. One more to go.

I wanted to laugh, I wanted to cry. More than anything I wanted to be horizontal. Every 10 steps, I stopped and placed my hands on my knees and took several deep breaths. I repeatedly muttered, 'C'mon mate, you can do this.'

I was at the bottom of the final summit and had to cross a bridge over a bubbling stream before the last uphill battle. My head was so light it could have been filled with helium, my body was numb. I stepped up on to the bridge, and could see my finish line, Lukla.

For me, crossing this bridge marked the end of a heart-breaking, and body-breaking day. It marked a victory, one I gave 100% credit to the little man upstairs. I shuffled up the final stretch of trail and felt a weight lift from my shoulders, every joint seemed to decompress, I may have even managed a smile. Some people get to the end of a testing time, and declare they're sad it's over. Not me. I was absolutely thrilled.

I walked through the gates, and crossed the finish line of the Everest Ultra. And just like a roller coaster soaring upwards, teetering at the peak, I felt my emotions plummet to an all-time low.

There was no loud cheer from spectators, no officials, no other runners. Not a single soul to share my jubilation. It brought home the stark reality of being an endurance athlete. At times, it can be an incredibly lonely existence – even when crossing the finishing line.

I stumbled up the three steps into our lodge, and pushed open the creaky wooden door where several Nepali runners let out a cheer and ushered me to a seat. My mind switched off from survival mode, and the extent of my pain and exhaustion hit me. My stomach grumbled like a cement mixer with rocks in it, slowly turning, with consistent stabbing pain.

A woman looped a gold satin cloth around my neck and gave me a banana and sweet lemon tea but the smell of both gave me the urge to hurl. There was no way I could stomach anything for a while yet, I needed rest.

After making it up the stairs to my room, I wanted nothing more than to lie down but I forced myself to wash and change into dry clothes, a habit drilled into me as a kid. My sister and I were never allowed to walk in the door from school, dump our bags and flop on the couch; we had to unpack our lunch boxes, remove our homework books and change out of our uniforms, before we could do anything else. Even after the day I'd just had, I still followed my parents' house rules! I knew a huge crash was coming, but I needed another layer of clothing to keep as much heat inside my now shivering body.

'Where is he, what's his room number?' said a voice with a Canadian accent.

'In here,' I replied.

The door creaked open to reveal the smiling faces of Scott and Lindsey. We exchanged warm hugs and seeing my Everest family lifted my spirits. The three of us compared notes on our unexpected and very different experiences. We set out with the same goal of completing the 65 kilometre Everest Ultra, and while none of us achieved it in full, we all fought our own unique battles high up in the Himalayas.

Several hours later I had some noodle soup, and the saltiness of the broth seemed to soothe and settle my battered stomach. Talk in the teahouse dining area turned to the race itself.

Aite had been in the lead group for most of the race until he began vomiting from a stomach bug, and finished in eighth position. Sudip, the defending champion, rolled his ankle towards the end of the race, and was forced to walk and jog his way to second place. The champion was my brother Upendra. He kept his own pace the entire day, passing the vomiting Aite and the hobbling Sudip to claim his first victory in the Everest Ultra with a time of 5:04 hours. I was over the moon for Upendra, but in his usual style, he just shrugged it off as no big deal and said, 'Yeah it's good, I just ran and now I win!'

Aite was bitterly disappointed with his performance. His recent run of good form had increased his sense of pride, and his expectations to win all his races. He was still learning about himself as an athlete, and international competitor, and with each race he would continue to learn and move forward – it's the Nepali way.

It was time for me to get horizontal. I dragged myself up the spiral staircase and shuffled to my room. I sank into the mattress and passed out immediately. Several hours later I heard a noise and at first thought I had woken myself up snoring. Then I realised it was Aite. He had come to check on me, then decided to stay and sleep in the spare bed. He told me the next morning that he wasn't feeling well all night, and wanted to be close to his brother. I knew he'd understand that when I threw a pillow at his head during the night to stop his snoring, it was purely because I desperately needed to sleep.

I woke up feeling like I'd been smashed against a concrete wall, but ready for breakfast, and sat down with the entire contingent of Everest runners, locals and foreigners together.

As we prepared to leave Lukla, I walked over to the archway where I'd crossed the finish line the day before, and leant against the cool stone, replaying the final minutes in my head. The Everest Ultra had been a gruelling, and at times horrific experience, but I knew those many hours of pure hell would help shape me as an endurance adventurer.

7.

BLACK HOLE

London was cold, wet and miserable the day I arrived home from Nepal. I knew I'd be walking into an empty house, yet the impact of that emptiness after six weeks away was overwhelming. I can only describe it as a form of shock. I slid my backpack off my shoulder and dropped it onto the lounge room floor. I walked along the hallway to the kitchen which looked pretty much as I'd left it – the cooking utensils, jars of seeds, nuts and coloured powders were all still there, yet the energy in the house was so different. I could feel my chest starting to tighten but I dismissed this feeling of anxiety as the effects of a long flight, and the depleted physical state I was in. I continued down the hallway, glancing sideways into the different rooms and when I reached the bathroom, the finality of the situation hit home. The vanity, once filled with hair and beauty products was empty. Everything, including her toothbrush, was gone.

Floor to ceiling cupboards in the bedroom housed all our clothes, and the silver handles were cold to touch as I took a deep breath and pulled open the heavy doors. My heart sank at the sight of my clothes hanging neatly on their designated side of the wardrobe, and on her side, nothing.

The physicality of my reaction surprised me and I gasped for air. Although technically we were still a couple, and I believed still very much in love, her absence made me feel like she was gone forever. I felt alone and vulnerable. After a long while sitting at the end of our bed, I wandered back to the kitchen.

I found a box of all-natural energy bars, and started eating as I stared out the window. Rain dribbled down the glass, the drops of water racing each other to the bottom. I mechanically worked through the box of bars, chewing, swallowing and opening the next one. I ate at least 10 bars before I realised what I was doing. I had slipped into a zombie-like state and was confused by my behaviour, as I'd never binged on food before. I figured perhaps I was undernourished and my body was still trying to balance itself out after the Everest experience.

Of course, in a pattern that was becoming almost habitual, I didn't talk about how I felt with my girlfriend – why, I do not know. Instead, I moved out and shared a place with friends as a stopgap measure before heading back to Australia later in the year.

Over the coming weeks, the food bingeing continued. I unconsciously gorged again and again. I would eat an entire loaf of homemade bread, huge bowls of muesli, telling myself it was body's way of recovering from the rapid weight loss after my sickness in Nepal.

Yes I was hungry and it had been a while since I had a decent meal, but I wasn't eating for either of those reasons. I was eating to comfort myself.

My girlfriend and I settled into regular correspondence – text messages and short conversations via Skype during the week and longer catch-ups on the weekend, and it seemed to be working well. We missed being with one another, but we had a plan to be together long-term, this is what kept things manageable from a distance.

Unfortunately, the adventure in the Amazon I'd been trying to organise in the August fell through; we had planned to meet up in Brazil afterwards, but now with this off the table, it would be December before the two of us could spend any time together. The end goal had not changed, and we still talked about our life plans but the extended time apart started to put a strain on the relationship.

I focused on planning my next adventure, which was just around the corner – *Luke Learns to Surf.* Growing up in the countryside hundreds of kilometres from the coast, I had never mastered the famous Australian past-time of surfing. I had my fair share of beach holidays, but I never owned a surfboard and never really tried to 'hang ten.' But with my commitment to live life with passion every day, I decided now was as good a time as any!

Newquay is one of the UK's most popular surfing locations so I hooked up with Escape Surf School and explained I was planning to come down to learn how to surf. When I told them I'd be cycling over 400 kilometres from my London house to Newquay, they thought I was joking.

With a departure time planned for 4 a.m., I practiced going to bed around 6 p.m. every night the week before, to get my body used to falling asleep and waking up early. The trip was scheduled for the summer solstice in June and we'd had a week of warm sunny days so I was feeling hopeful for a bright and comfortable day in the saddle; but London weather proved once again how fickle it can be.

I was out of bed at 3 a.m., made some breakfast, and did a final check over my bike before opening my blinds, expecting pre-sunrise darkness, but instead I was met by wild winds and bucketing down rain. I knew I could handle a cold, wet ride in the dark, but the added danger of gale-force winds forced me to seriously consider my options. I would be facing the very real danger of being blown off my bike into traffic.

After several minutes going over the alternatives, I decided to stick to the plan and set off. I messaged my crew (who I would meet later) and told them it was 'game on!'

I chatted briefly with my girlfriend who was excited for me to take on this new challenge, and carried my bike down the stairwell of my apartment building, realising this would be the last time I'd be dry for many hours.

With an internal '3, 2, 1 - GO!' I set off into the stinging rain holding onto my bike for dear life as I battled the force of the wind. Within minutes my toes were soaked and freezing water somehow seeped in and streamed down my back, but in a strange way, I was enjoying the challenge of being battered by the elements. I felt like I was in a game of 'chicken,' taking on Mother Nature to see who would let up first.

After I slight detour (OK, I got lost), I eventually found my crew waiting for me at our pre-determined rendezvous location. Michael (Magic Hands) is a no-nonsense type of guy who simply put his arm around me as I slowed to a stop and said, 'You look like you've had a tough morning mate!' He pretty much summed it up perfectly!

I battled on and finally had a little more daylight which made me slightly more visible to the constant flow of cars, trucks and caravans flying past me on the A303 – a busy stretch of road heading toward England's southwest coast.

For most of the day I felt good, and joked with my crew as they leapfrogged ahead of me in my support vehicle to find the next layby to wait in. The wind was horrendous: at times I felt like I was going backwards, but when a truck squeezed past me and my shoulder brushed the canopy of its trailer, I knew I couldn't switch off and simply ride. This trip was going to need my full concentration at all times.

Along with Magic Hands, Nic and Paul made up the rest of the crew helping me get to Newquay in one piece. I was incredibly appreciative of their support so I made sure the support car they were travelling in was packed with homemade, healthy and delicious loaves, bars and cookies for all of us.

The long, gloomy day eventually gave way to darkness and the wind picked up so I pulled over for a quick stop to change into dry clothes. My hands were so frozen I couldn't manage to do much with them so Magic Hands had to dress me, feed me and re-attach my hands to the handlebars.

After cycling for 16 hours, I was now battling tiredness in my legs, was struggling to keep my bike upright, and for some strange reason could barely keep my eyes open. Moments later, I saw a road sign that read 'Newquay' and I managed a smile – it gave me a much needed lift of spirits and energy.

With my crew now sticking close by until we reached our destination, Belushi's Bar in Newquay, we were relieved to hit the outskirts of town. Still ahead though was a series of climbs that felt like mini mountains as I zig-zagged my way up so slowly I lost momentum and almost crashed.

Finally, after a gruelling 412 kilometres and 18 hours of non-stop cycling, being hammered by the best that nature could throw my way, I made it.

To my surprise, I was welcomed by the cheers of a crowd waiting outside the bar, and then a slightly drunken rendition of Queen's hit, '*Bicycle Race*' – what a welcome!

There were hugs and high fives, even a few kisses, and we hung around for just a short celebration before heading upstairs to bed.

The following morning the four of us dragged ourselves to Towan beach for some dry land surfing tips, before our instructor Will, took us out into the less than favourable conditions.

Somewhat reluctantly, we immersed ourselves into the chilly water and tried to replicate what Will had just taught us on dry land – and on my first wave, I managed to stand up and surf!

Totally stoked and full of confidence, I surfed several more waves, with mixed results including a dramatic wipe out, but after an hour my energy levels were zapped. I rescued myself from the white wash and headed for the shore. My *Luke Learns to Surf* adventure was done – and a success!

* * *

One of my favourite ways to spend a Sunday involves a mix of training and socialising. A week after the Newquay surfing adventure I was back on my bike cycling the 45-minute route from my place to a gorgeous lake for a regular swim with friends around the 750 metre marked route. After an hour or so in the water, we'd cycle home and our chins didn't stop wagging with gossip and pointless dribble before we'd go our separate ways.

After one of these mornings, I was in an upbeat mood – I had recovering well after my long cycle to Newquay, the sun was shining and life was good. I ate a well-earned breakfast and sat down with a cup of tea for the usual weekend chat with my girlfriend. We'd spoken during the week and she'd told me how proud she was of my achievements, and she was excited to hear all about it. After the usual pleasantries, she completely blindsided me. The words 'I can't do this anymore' came through my headphones, and at first I thought she meant the conversation we were having, and then I realised she meant us!

'What do you mean? I don't understand!' I said, in shock. She gave me a list of excuses, not reasons, saying, 'I just don't feel I'm living my life how I want to' and 'I feel we are going in separate directions', followed by, 'we're more like friends.'

My chest tightened, my eyes filled up and I felt sick. *What the hell was going on?* In a confused state, I tried to make sense of her explanations. If she wasn't living her life the way she wanted, then why did she move back to Australia to be closer to friends and family? Why did we set a clear timeframe around my return from London? What about our plans to start a family together?

She had changed careers and was studying again which was something she'd wanted to do for some time, and I totally supported these changes to her life, so what was the issue?

Naturally these were all the questions I asked, but the responses were non-specific along with her comment, 'You had to have seen this coming.'

Well, '*NO*', I did not see this coming. I had made plans to move back to a city that I had no interest in returning to, and had worked hard to keep our relationship on track from the other side of the world. To say I was devastated didn't even come close to how I felt.

After the call, I lay on the bed and stared at the ceiling – no thoughts, no feelings, I was numb. I had no clue that anything like this was on the cards. We chatted often, and (I thought) openly on a regular basis. Whenever one of us was struggling with our situation we voiced it and tried to sort it out.

A mate called Darrell (nicknamed Sheila) who had been a friend of mine since I first moved to London, talked to me about both sides of the story and I did my best to understand, but none of it made any sense.

My ex and I spoke briefly a few times in the weeks after the break up and she was apologetic for the hurt she had caused, but she wouldn't budge on her decision.

I couldn't help thinking there was a missing piece. Was there someone else? I found it hard to get this idea out of my head.

Three weeks slipped by without contact. I felt like I had lost part of me. Every day it was the same cycle of confusion, anger, pain, and back to confusion again. I was sinking deeper into another bout of depression, and it was near impossible to find positive thoughts.

When I finally got back in touch with her, and bluntly told her I didn't buy her explanation, she simply dismissed my concerns. I desperately wanted to know the true reason why I was now single, and with such an intense ache in my chest. All I wanted was honesty so I could accept the situation and move on with my life.

I occasionally messaged her to question her reasoning, and ask if there was someone else involved. Every message was met with silence.

Finally, she replied 'please don't contact me anymore, I only wish you well.' And that was it. After five years, and plans to spend our lives together, it was over.

I tried to move on with my life. I went to Chamonix in the French Alps to help crew for Aite Tamang in the prestigious Ultra-Trail du Mont-Blanc (UTMB) which starts in France and passes through Italy and Switzerland, before finishing back in France. This was to be his first European race, and I thought it would be a great way to take my mind off my broken heart, and to help my friend who I had stayed in touch with since leaving Nepal; running in this race was one of his dreams.

It was great to be around Aite, and Natalia, a Polish woman living in Hong Kong who I had met in Nepal. She was an extremely talented runner who was competing in her own quest to finish the UTMB. Like Aite, she was a positive influence and always had a smile on her face.

The race starts in the afternoon, so even the winner and other elite runners will go without sleep and run through the night while finishing the gruelling 171 kilometres in a time of just over 20 hours. Aite started the race well and continued to be in the top runners through the halfway mark – just outside the top ten. I was following his progress with another elite Nepali runner, Dawa Sherpa, and his wife, who were living in Switzerland at the time.

We stopped at a checkpoint in Switzerland called Champex Lac, at around 4 a.m., and tried to catch an hour's sleep as we didn't expect to see Aite for several more hours. After about 90 minutes I went out for a walk and watched the sun rising over the stunning pine-covered mountains. I sat at the edge of a pristine lake with little wooden huts dotted around its shoreline. I took a few deep breaths and savoured the moment before checking the online tracker to see how far away Aite was.

I continued to post updates on Aite's progress on my Facebook page throughout the race, and as I scrolled through my news feed I saw a picture that had the effect of a punch from a heavy weight boxer in my stomach, followed by a sharp embarrassing slap to my face. Staring back at me was a picture of my ex-girlfriend cosied up to a guy I had asked her about – with her family. It could have been totally innocent, but it wasn't exactly what I needed to see. We'd had no contact for about a month and now she posts this photo on social media, for everyone to see. I messaged her and asked her if she was now with the guy in the photo. No response, but the photo was removed. Two days later she sent another messaging saying, 'you need to cease all contact with me Luke, it is over!'

Aite ended up finishing in 13th position in less than 24 hours, a phenomenal result.

I returned to London happy for Aite but feeling like I had been thrown to the bottom of a deep well. I was lost and dejected and I felt I did not belong in the skin I was in. I had told only Sheila and my immediate family that I had been single for several months now, only because I knew if I told others they would ask why, and I still didn't feel that I knew the answer.

To the outside world, my life looked amazing; I was an adventurer, living the dream I had set out to achieve, seeing the world and challenging my boundaries. But in reality, I was a mess. I had developed severe insomnia and slept less than six hours a week. Several nights a week I didn't even get into bed, as I knew I wouldn't be able to shut down my brain and banish negative thoughts and scenarios of self-harm.

My final adventure for the year was to climb Mount Aspiring on New Zealand's majestic South Island with a client I was training. Other than that, I had no specific reason to train, so I trained aimlessly, but with increased intensity. I'd do midnight marathons, 12 hour cycles on the weekend and gym sessions lasting however long it took to completely exhaust myself. I knew what I was doing was detrimental to my health but it was only when I trained I felt anything. The rest of

the time, I was living a numb and paralysed life.

On one occasion, I found myself running down the middle of Oxford Street in central London at 3:30 on a Wednesday morning with not a soul in sight, other than a street sweeper passing in the opposite direction. I was lost in the beautiful silence of one of London's busiest streets. As I rounded the main square at Covent Garden and headed home the sky began to lighten. It was a rare moment of magic.

I arrived home after covering more than 30 kilometres in less than three hours, had a shower, ate breakfast and began my day of work. I would put on a happy face and somehow produce the energy needed to help motivate my clients through the tough sessions I had prepared for them, but it was completely fabricated. On the inside, I battled a severe state of unhappiness. It seemed I was trying to fill a void with crazy amount of exercise, but it only made matters worse as I increased the amount of fatigue I was carrying. My self-confidence was at an all-time low.

Back in Australia, my parents knew I was struggling, but I found it too painful to open up to them. My Mum offered to visit London for a couple of weeks, but I didn't feel it would help, so I asked her not to come. What I needed from her was what she and Dad had always given me – just to be there when I am ready to talk, and I knew they would be. My sister lived only two hours away, but I still felt lost and alone. Adding to my destructive habit of excess exercise and getting very little sleep, I started binge eating again – on a more regular basis.

After months of this behaviour, I finally acknowledged that I was heading towards an eating disorder. The highs of feeling completely full after eating were soon followed by shame and disgust. I was angry with myself for being unable to stop eating until I physically couldn't eat anymore. I felt like I was living a massive lie, I felt like a complete fraud.

I trained and worked with other athletes and people to help understand nutrition as a way to perform better, lose weight and feel healthier; and here I was bingeing on the unhealthy food I had stopped eating more than a decade ago.

It was a strange experience. I never consciously decided to go out and buy a tub of ice cream, a loaf of bread or a bar of chocolate, it was like I zoned out and grabbed whatever caught my eye while I trolled the aisles of the grocery store I was in. I would then scamper home and gorge myself on whatever had found its way into my shopping basket. There were times I didn't even make it home, I'd stop in a park, or a café, or eat as I walked. I didn't enjoy the food I shovelled into my mouth – it was as if I was trying to get rid of it as quickly as possible. I needed help, but the shame and embarrassment of admitting to my secret far outweighed my ability to ask for help.

Following a binge session, my stomach would bulge and ache. I would swear to myself this was the final time, but it never was. I struggled for a long time to understand why I had lost all the willpower and discipline I had developed throughout my teenage years. I hated my thoughts and I hated myself, and that hate fuelled more bingeing.

It wasn't always processed junk food, often it was foods from my usual highly nutritious diet, but the serving sizes were ridiculous. I'd make a vegetable stir-fry, with some organic chicken, but I'd cook enough for two or three people and I'd eat all of it myself, and then consume a whole packet of nuts to top off the meal. To counteract the constant bingeing, I'd then eat nothing for 18-24 hours. I'd continue my intense long training sessions, using the energy consumed during my binge.

On the outside, I stayed lean and looked fit, so nobody had any idea what was going on. I would dismiss my typical afternoon sugar slumps as fatigue from the 20 plus hours of training I was doing each week. When I was alone during these slumps I would be wracked with dark thoughts, which would trigger the next violent binge.

The shame I felt was overwhelming but I was now trapped in a nasty cycle and couldn't find a way out. I joked with Sheila about eating the *occasional* tub of Ben and Jerry's, and we laughed about it, but he had no clue this behaviour was beginning to control my life. My self-worth was at an all-time low, and thoughts of suicide were becoming more frequent.

8.

LOST IN TRANSLATION

Around this time, a group of elite runners, including Aite, who I had lived and trained with in Nepal, planned to run a 100 kilometre ultramarathon in Hong Kong. He asked if I would fly over and be part of the support crew. I was keen to help and figured it might be just what I needed to drag myself out of the slump I was in.

My finances were patchy but I managed to scrape together enough for the flight, and as I looked at a map of the area, I decided on a mini-adventure of my own before I met up with Aite.

I found an island off the south coast of mainland China with a mountainous backbone, pristine beaches, and rugged coastline. It looked like the perfect location for a bit of soul searching, so I booked a side trip to Hainan.

The plan was fairly loose. I did a little research and decided to head into the middle of the island, around 90 kilometres from the airport, and use that as my starting point to run through the mountains for several days, sleep under the stars, and let my legs take me wherever they wanted.

It was a sticky November evening when I arrived in Hong Kong and a powerful typhoon was hovering off the coast of Micronesia. Many Asian countries including Hong Kong and southern China were on high alert. Two days before my scheduled flight, Typhoon Haiyan ripped through the Philippines causing catastrophic loss of life and continued its destructive path through the centre of Hainan. My flight was delayed until they reopened the local airport, which for most people would have been a warning sign to reconsider.

When I arrived in Hainan two days later, it looked like a war zone. Uprooted coconut trees, debris and power lines were scattered everywhere. Many roads were blocked and there were no buses to take me to the centre of the island.

I convinced a reluctant cab driver to drive me to Wuzhishan City up in the mountains for the start of my adventure. The driver pulled up in the middle of town, took his fare and drove off with smoke spluttering from his cab's rusty exhaust pipe. Wuzhishan City has around 115,000 residents, and I was sure I would find someone who could understand me, but no one spoke English and I spoke zero Hainanese.

The original plan was to leave a backpack full of clean clothes in the city, before heading to the hills for a few days, but as soon as I surveyed the area I knew the adventure I had in mind was impossible. Chunks of the landscape were sliding away and a mess of vegetation surrounded me. At that moment, I thought of my mother. She always said, 'Luke you might be crazy, but you're not stupid.'

The hills were sodden and unstable from the recent typhoon, and to run through the area would be outright stupid. I decided to base myself in Wuzhishan City for a couple of nights and head out and back for day trips. I wandered across to a hotel overlooking a murky brown river and booked a room. The receptionist tried to charge my credit card but the payment was declined.

We tried again – nothing.

The language barrier was rock solid – neither of us spoke a word of the other's language. The receptionist used an app on her phone to translate her questions. *'Card not working, you have another?'* I went to the ATM in the foyer, but there were no English options on the screen. After 20 minutes, I was still unable to withdraw any funds. I had the equivalent of six British pounds in local currency after paying the taxi fare. The receptionist typed out a message on her app asking if I would like to be taken to a bank. Great idea! After trying the ATMs at two different banks I came back empty-handed. I could feel the anxiety building.

My last meal was in Hong Kong about 10 hours earlier and I was hungry but I had no food, no water, and very little money. The airport at Sanya was 90 kilometres away and I had a seat booked on a flight leaving in three days' time. I closed my eyes and calmly thought through the options. Via her phone app, the receptionist suggested getting a bus back to Sanya to sort out my finances. She took me to the bus stop but the buses were not running – the road through the middle of the island was still closed after the typhoon.

My new friend then took me across the road to a small budget hotel and spoke with the receptionist there, and in an act of total kindness, she paid for my room. She had only just met me, I was just another foreigner in her country, and she could have easily disregarded me when I asked for help. But she showed compassion to a stranger in need. It gave me hope that kindness still existed in the world. She waved and smiled as I took my bags up to my room.

Without cash, plan B was no longer an option. My thoughts of adventure took a back seat while I tried to solve the more pressing challenge. How would I get out of here? I decided the best solution was to run the 90 kilometres back to the airport.

First priority was to find a supermarket and buy whatever food I could with my miniscule cash reserve. I would boil water using the kettle in my room and leave it to cool overnight before filling up my backpack's bladder, and guzzling down whatever was left in the morning. Hainan is hot and humid and after a day without water, I was feeling dehydrated.

After jogging through the streets for around half an hour, I found a local supermarket. I browsed the aisles in search of cheap, high-calorie fuel, passing over the dehydrated chicken's feet and salty animal crackers. The colourful fruit display in the fresh produce area was tempting but well outside my budget. I worked out what would give me the most bang for my buck and settled on 200 grams of oats, 100 grams of green tea flavoured pumpkin seeds, and a two-litre bottle of water. My cash was spent, and I have to be honest, I was feeling slightly vulnerable. I went to Hainan looking for adventure, and I sure got it!

I needed a good night's sleep so I could leave at first light to cover the distance between Wuzhishan City and the airport. My plan was to complete the distance over two days.

When I woke before sunrise the clock had started ticking in the race to catch my flight. It was already 30 degrees Celsius and very humid when I set off along the same debris-covered road I'd travelled the day before by taxi. The first road sign I saw indicated 87 kilometres to Sanya. My breakfast of a mouthful of oats washed down with a gulp of water had served me well.

And the first few hours ticked by. I was out of the built-up city and running through the countryside, past coconut plantations and beekeepers selling fresh honey. The rice fields were a patchwork of green on the mountain terraces and my mind drifted back to London. I was a world away from the familiar sights of home and my senses were zinging.

A shopkeeper with a tiny roadside stall waved me over and gave me one of his oranges. I pulled out the few coins I had left, but he refused to take any. It was the juiciest, best damn orange I had ever eaten.

To the few passers-by on the road I must have looked like I was doing it tough. The sweat poured off my shaved head as I shuffled along with two packs strapped together on my back. Every few hours I stopped for a mouthful of oats and a gulp of water. The day was heating up, and when I made my second pit stop, in the shade of a patch of coconut trees, I realised my water supply was running low. It was just after midday, the sun was beating down and I still had the afternoon heat to deal with.

I rationed my sips of water to 30 minute intervals and was starting to feel the effects of dehydration. I had a headache and was lethargic and dizzy. The last time I peed I noticed it was a dark amber colour, a concerning sign. I was on the lookout for anything to drink, anything to keep me hydrated.

I ran past a resort and could see cabins scatted across the hillside, but I had no chance of getting beyond the stern looking guard in full military uniform outside the iron gates. I could see a water cooler inside the gatehouse so I removed the bladder from my backpack and approached the guard. I tried to explain I needed water, hoping he would let me fill up. He must have understood, as he let me take what I needed. He pushed a chair in my direction reminding me once again what a kind and helpful community I had found on this beautiful island. After a brief rest, I strapped on my packs and got my kit in order. I smiled and bowed, then gave him a thumbs-up. What a top bloke.

The heat of the day was unforgiving and I could feel my energy waning. I tried to stick to a rule of one small sip of water every 30 minutes, but I broke it countless times trying to quench my parched throat – I was so thirsty.

I began to see familiar shapes by the side of the road. Coconuts!

I figured there must be a village up ahead selling them, and once the juice was drained they were thrown from passing cars. I hoped there might be some moist flesh inside – but I had to find a way to crack them open.

I picked one up, held it tightly in both hands and smashed the thick green husk against a large rock. After a dozen or so strikes, it split open. I scooped out the white slimy flesh with my fingers and crammed it into my mouth. The flesh was lukewarm but it was soft and gooey and slid down my dry throat. The sweetness soon began to recharge my batteries. Judging by their taste and smell, the coconuts had been lying by the roadside for more than a few hours, possibly a few days, but I needed the fuel. They were lifesavers. I cracked open two more to top up my depleted energy stores. It was all I had to get me through the rest of the day.

After more than eight hours running, just as my body started to seize up, a shopkeeper waved me over to her roadside stall. She invited me to sit down with her friends and enjoy a fresh coconut. I gestured I had no money, but she indicated she wanted me to rest. She hacked the top off a fresh coconut with her machete, stuck in a straw and handed it over with a toothy smile. The coconut water was sweet and full of electrolytes, perfect for replacing the minerals I had lost through sweat. Once I finished drinking, I asked her to crack open the fruit so I could devour some fresh coconut flesh. It was almost luminous and had no hint of sourness, so much nicer than the off-white, road-kill coconuts I had eaten earlier. After a moment of rest, I heaved myself out of the green plastic chair and with cheers from my new friends, jogged off for my final push of the day. They gave me renewed energy to continue my journey.

The last stretch began with a winding incline up the mountain. I planned to make camp on the other side and settle for the evening. After nine and a half hours covering 65 kilometres, I was ready to stop. On the other side of the mountain, I came across an elderly woman sitting at a table filled with mini bananas, coconuts and bottles of water. I desperately hoped she would consider exchanging the few coins I had left for bananas and water. She had the crinkled face of a loving grandmother and with a smile she pushed a bottle of water and six bananas across the table. I let out a sigh and nodded with gratitude. I remembered everyone I had met along my journey on this long, hot day and mentally thanked them all with much gratitude.

As I sat on an upturned milk crate eating some bananas I felt a gentle pat on my back. I looked up to see a shirtless man with a friendly smile giving me the thumbs-up. He gestured to the old woman to give me a coconut. Once again I tried to explain I had no money, but he insisted and paid for me. I tried to explain I was running to Sanya and I think he understood as he twirled his index finger in a circular motion near his head – the universal symbol for crazy! I took a photo of the two of us, and he jumped onto his motorbike and sped off.

It was time to find somewhere to sleep and I needed two trees to hang up my hammock. I looked for a spot close to one of the storm drains funnelling water from the mountains above. The water was muddy and had a foul stench to it, but if I boiled it over a fire and left it to cool overnight, I would have fresh drinking water. I had already downed the bottle I bought from the old woman so I had no water for tomorrow's trek to Sanya. I eventually found a small clearing next to the road at the edge of a coconut farm. After negotiating my way over the waist-high barbed wire fence I removed my packs and the relief was instant. I tied my hammock between the trees, and set out to collect wood for the fire. I arranged twigs and sticks ready to light, and then went in search of water. A kilometre or so further up the road I found a storm-water drain trickling brown liquid, filled two empty bottles I'd picked up from the side of the road, and headed back to camp.

The combination of dusk and the dampness of the forest after the typhoon meant the mosquitoes were out in droves. I used the cotton wool I had packed to help light the fire, and eventually got it going, but the bigger sticks were too wet. I tried everything I could think of, even scraping layers of bark off with my knife, but the fire wouldn't burn long enough to boil the dirty water. I rummaged under fallen trees to find drier wood, but to no avail. After more than an hour, I gave up. I let the fire smoulder to keep the mosquitos at bay, and climbed into the hammock.

Gazing at the stars, I wondered what dramas tomorrow would bring. I was alone in a forest in the middle of a remote Chinese island, hungry, thirsty and at least 25 kilometres from my destination. I drifted off to sleep for a couple of hours but hunger and other pains kept waking me. All I had left to eat were the two tiny bananas I was saving for breakfast. I had absolutely no water.

Just as I figured the situation couldn't possibly get any worse, it started to rain. Before long it was torrential. This was true tropical rain, each drop felt like a tiny marble smashing against my head. With only a thin waterproof jacket to protect me from the elements, it was going to be a rough night. I was caught off guard by the sudden downpour and began to question my sanity.

How did I end up in this ridiculous situation? I thought about my family, my friends and the journey ahead and I felt like crying, but I knew that was pointless. Around midnight, two hours into the downpour, I was getting seriously cold. The air temperature still felt in the low twenties, but my body temperature was dropping and my skin was covered in goose bumps. I began to shiver.

I mentally flipped through my options. Do I search for better shelter? Go back to the village where I had the fresh coconut? Stand on the side of the road and hope someone pulls over? I tried to come up with alternatives, but nothing struck me as a better option than staying put and hoping the storm would soon be over. After another two hours the downpour slowed, then stopped. I lay shivering until first light appeared.

My body felt beaten up from the previous day's running, and the lack of food and water. As soon as I stood up, I vomited bright yellow bile from the pit of my stomach. I was concerned I had reached a state of extreme dehydration or I had contracted something from those road-kill coconuts. I packed up my wet hammock, put on my waterlogged shoes, and climbed back over the barbed wire fence.

With no fuel on board I couldn't find the energy to run so I walked for the first hour. I threw up twice more. After a while, I managed a slow shuffling jog, knowing each step took me closer to Sanya.

I had been in this state once before, while running the Marathon des Sables through the Sahara Desert. I had become incoherent and was wobbly on my feet. When I reached the checkpoint in that gruelling seven-day race, the medics gave me an ultimatum – have an intravenous drip, or drop out of the race. I took the option of the drip and had three litres of fluid pumped into me. But in Hainan, I had no checkpoint with a medical team, nor was anyone standing on the side of the road with an IV drip.

I recognised the signs of dehydration and knew I was in serious trouble.

I can barely recall the first 15 kilometres I covered that morning. I remember a dog chasing me and with a burst of adrenaline I ran faster, worried the scruffy mutt would sink its teeth into me and give me rabies.

When I reached the main road leading to Sanya I still had 10 kilometres to go but my body refused to cooperate. I ached all over, inside and out, and had nothing to fuel me. The high humidity was draining my body of any fluids it had managed to retain. I needed help, and fast.

Traffic whizzed by me in a blur on the four-lane highway as I tried to flag down a driver, but what were the chances someone would stop? A six-foot-one-inch-bald Westerner carrying two backpacks, sweating profusely, looking sick and filthy – not the ideal passenger.

A couple in an old farm truck carrying hay bales eventually pulled over. As they slowed to a stop, I began to shout out 'Sanya, Sanya', pointing in the direction I wished to go. Right on cue, as the words came out of my mouth, so did a stream of bile. I could not believe the timing. The couple shook their heads and drove off.

Moments later, a new model black BMW X5 pulled over and the driver signalled to get in. 'Hang on,' I thought to myself, 'is this real, or am I hallucinating again?'

Earlier in the day I had seen a stick on the side of the road, convinced myself it was a bottle of water and bent down to pick it up.

I touched the door handle and the cold metal reassured me this was no dream. The driver gave me a bottle of water and a pat on my shoulder. His kindness was more than I could have hoped for. I was so grateful to rest my cramping body. He spoke no English, just gave me a smile, the universal gesture of happiness. I said 'Sanya', and with outstretched arms tried to mimic a plane. He nodded and turned his attention to the road ahead.

As we drove along I thought I could hear a song in English playing on the car radio. I was confused and doubted my hearing as I still felt totally out of it. I must have been staring intently at the console, as he turned up the volume. It was Cat Stevens singing 'Morning has Broken' on the radio in a remote Chinese island. I thought of my Mum – a Cat Stevens fan – and remembered her insistence that I was not stupid, just crazy!

With little warning, the nausea overwhelmed me and I threw up out the window as we sped along a busy inner city road. I expected the car to come an abrupt stop. Instead, the driver gave me another bottle of water and a wet wipe. I wished I could speak his language so I could tell him how much I appreciated his compassion.

We pulled off the main road and into the parking lot of a youth hostel. He came inside with me and after a short conversation with the receptionist, gave me a smile and a wave before heading out the door. I was hunched over struggling to stay upright and could do little more than lift my arm to wave goodbye, but I will never forget his kindness.

The staff at the youth hostel let me sleep for a few hours in one of their dormitory style rooms, for free. As with all the locals I had met on Hainan, they went out of their way to help me. I stumbled up the stairs to a dusty room with timber bunk beds. I felt completely depleted and fell asleep on the plastic covered mattress for two hours before it was time to face the world once more.

The short nap invigorated me but I still hadn't eaten and was feeling extremely dehydrated. I needed cash. The receptionist spoke just enough English to understand I wanted to find a bank and go to the airport. She gave me a piece of paper with the number six followed by Chinese characters, then the number eight with more Chinese characters. She explained the note translated to 'bus six to the bank', then 'bus eight to the airport.' I smiled my thanks, and before I could explain I had no money, she passed me a few notes. 'Bus money to bank,' she said with a friendly smile. She walked me to the bus stop down the road and did her best to explain when to get off the bus for the bank, and where to board the bus to the airport.

I showed my note to the driver, he nodded and I found a seat. After about 15 minutes we stopped, the driver looked at me and flicked his head in the direction of the door. We had arrived at the bank. A well-dressed bank employee greeted me and I asked if he spoke any English. 'Yes Sir,' he replied with perfect pronunciation. He asked if I would like to exchange some cash, ushered me to the machine, helped me through the process and pointed me in the direction of the number eight bus. As I stepped out onto the street I shook my head and thought *what a bizarre experience.* The man at the bank seemed to be expecting me and didn't appear to think it strange someone in my condition stumbled into his bank.

The directions from the young woman at the hostel were perfect, and my journey continued without incident. The number eight bus wound its way through the bustling city, then along a road that hugged the coastline, reaching Sanya airport an hour later.

I made a beeline for the only hotel in the area to book a room for the night, have a shower, and eat. The cash I exchanged fell marginally short of their nightly tariff so I tried my card and held my breath as it was swiped through the machine. The man behind the desk shook his head and showed me the failed transaction. I tried the ATM in the foyer, and when that didn't work, I explained I was going across the road to the terminal to withdraw cash. No one had any idea what I was saying, so I just left.

Surely I had exhausted the setbacks by now! I tried to withdraw cash from several machines in the small airport but each attempt ended in disappointment.

Then I spotted an ATM tucked away under an escalator and figured it was worth a try. I inserted my card, guessed which buttons to press, and was presented with a page I figured was asking how much cash I'd like to withdraw. I typed in enough for the hotel room and waited. Nothing happened at first, then I heard a flicking noise, and money appeared. It was like winning the jackpot!

I grabbed the cash and headed back to the hotel. I was absolutely buzzing, but when I placed my passport and cash on the counter I was met with blank faces. I struggled to understand what the girls behind the desk were trying to tell me. Finally, a man who spoke some English approached and confirmed my fears – there were no rooms left.

At this point I remembered a piece of advice from an old Irish friend. He said 'Luke, if you don't laugh, you will cry.' This was one of those moments. I took his advice and let out a roar of laughter.

Back at the terminal I searched for someone who spoke a little English to ask about nearby hotels. A woman from the Sanya Holiday Centre wrote something on a piece of paper. I had no idea what she wrote but I was past caring. I jumped in a cab and gave the driver the note. After a short trip, he pulled into the driveway of a hotel. I paid the fare with a large tip, gave him a high five and approached the check-in desk.

Again, no one spoke English, but my passport and cash did the talking for me. I was handed a keycard and shown to my room. At long last, my sanctuary! I unpacked my gear, showered and collapsed on the bed for 13 hours of undisturbed sleep.

When I woke up I was bursting with energy and had the afternoon free so I jogged down to Sanya Bay for a swim in the ocean. The water was cool and calm as I lay back and floated, feeling my body rejuvenate. I re-lived the previous 48 hours in my head, remembering the people and their remarkable friendliness.

The spirit of adventure was still with me. Rather than take a bus back to the terminal, I hailed a motorbike. The rider looked around 15 years old and his spluttering Honda would be my final mode of transport before flying out later that evening. The coastal air felt fresh and clean against my face as we cruised along.

Hainan challenged me in unexpected ways but I had only positive memories of the beautiful island and its generous community. They were dealing with their own crisis, cleaning up after the destructive typhoon, but still extended a helping hand to a stranger. As the plane left the tarmac, I promised myself I would return. The experience gave me a new perspective and I pledged to always find a way to help someone who was down on their luck. A fresh coconut or a simple pat on the back could be all they need to harness their inner strength and take that next step.

9.

FIND YOUR TRIBE

I had about three weeks before heading out to New Zealand to fulfil my final goal for the year, helping long-time client and friend Nic attempt to summit Mount Aspiring. I spent most of this time recovering from my whirlwind Asian adventure, and then an email popped into my inbox.

It had been around two months since I'd heard from my ex-girlfriend and she wanted to meet up while I was in Australia 'to talk through things.' This request annoyed me, as she hadn't wanted to talk or explain anything so I sent off a slightly abrupt reply. After a few more email exchanges, we organised a time to meet up after she finished work one afternoon in December. I was slightly hopeful that after six months of battling the inner turmoil, I might get closer to understanding why we had split up and be able to move on with my life.

Nic arrived in Queenstown a few days before me and we both felt the sense of adventure in the air. Unfortunately, due to bad weather up on the Southern Alps, we were told to stay put in the beautiful lakeside town of Wanaka. There were worse places to be stuck that's for sure. We were surrounded by mountainous peaks, a stunning lake and numerous trails for hiking, running, and mountain biking – truly an adventurer's dream location for fun. We spent a day practising our climbing and belaying techniques on a rock wall, and a few days cycling and running around the lake, before the weather further up the mountain cleared.

We helicoptered up to the edge of a glacier, then spent three or four hours traversing this treacherous terrain, following the very serious instructions to stay away from the crevasses as we followed our guides to the base camp hut.

Visibility was poor the afternoon we arrived and we couldn't see the summit, so we bunkered down and waited it out with several other hopeful mountaineers – all wanting their own shot at a summit push in the next day or two.

But the bad weather stuck around for several days and our time ran out (we had a plane to catch) so we made the tough call to walk back down the mountain. There was no helicopter ride this time, just 10 hours of hiking through some of the most spectacular scenery, and a dangerous river crossing – even our seasoned guides looked a little concerned – but it was all part of the adventure. We stopped for the night in a communal hut and grabbed a few hours' sleep while drying out our kit. A short 10 kilometre hike got us back to the outskirts of Wanaka the following day.

We didn't achieve our goal of summiting New Zealand's second highest peak, but Nic and I still had a fantastic time. I was ready to head to Australia for some much-needed time with my family.

I spent a few days in Bathurst and caught up with some of my best mates who still lived in our hometown. Then it was on to the Central

Coast, north of Sydney where my friend Paul now lives with his wife and two kids. I stayed at Paul's house for a few nights, with Dayno, Raz, and Baz (yep, quality Aussie nicknames) who came to hang out with me. It was nice having a few of the boys back together. This was my extended family and I felt extremely comfortable, and safe being around them. It was the perfect place to relax and gather myself up before heading back to Sydney to meet my ex.

My phone beeped, it was a message from my ex. It read 'I will not be meeting you tomorrow, take care.' So after months with no contact, then out of the blue asking to meet up, she cancels. I had no idea what to think.

I wrote several messages again asking for an explanation but got no response. My mates were a little dumbfounded but told me that it was the end of it and to move on with life. I'm sure if they understood the extent of my distress, they may have tried to console me a little more, but to be fair, no one knew what I was going through.

I thought the only way for me to move on was to gain some closure. I had things I needed to say to her, things I had to get out of my head once and for all. After another sleepless night, I wrote and sent an email that explained how I saw the situation and how it made me feel, and I still did not know why we broke up. I didn't expect a reply. A week went by and I was back in Bathurst on Christmas Eve when her response landed in my inbox, 'I only wish you well, take care.' And that was the end of that!

I tried to relax and enjoy the final 10 days I had left, spending time with my extended family, and old friends – but the undertones of my life back in London were seeping into my time in Australia and I began to binge again. I would unconsciously graze on chocolates, fruit, nuts and cake until I was so stuffed my eyes were about to pop out of my head. Then in the morning, I would go for a two to three hour run.

I felt sick and ashamed, and wanted to be swallowed up in the deepest hole imaginable. I wanted to be released from the constant pain. More concerning was the fact I was surrounded by family and friends who knew I was going through a rough time and were amazingly supportive yet it had no positive effect on my mental state. It was sunny, I was lying on a beautiful beach celebrating the New Year, and I felt more depressed than I'd even been.

A little while after returning to the UK I began swimming once a week with a triathlon swim squad I had previously trained with. I wanted to increase my speed and fitness, as well as meet some triathletes to learn what it's like to swim, cycle, and run all in one day! I mentioned the Ultimate Triathlon to my coach, so she understood what I was training for, and she pointed me in the direction of the fast lane to a bloke by the name of Graham.

Graham, a fellow Australian, was an Ironman triathlete already, and training for another crack at this gruelling event. We hit it off from the first time we chatted. He had organised a Saturday morning cycle group with a few of the guys from the swim squad. I was excited, as I had never been involved in any sort of formal or informal training group associated with endurance sports. I'd always been a bit of a lone ranger.

We met at Richmond Park in London's south west, and from there cycled through the outskirts of the city, into the lush hills of the Surrey countryside. Alongside Graham, our cycling crew was Alistair, Marwin, and Kevin. These guys became an important part of my weekly training routine with a few laughs on the pool deck every Friday night, and then out together cycling for many hours on Saturday morning.

As the months went by, we saw less of Alistair due to work and family commitments, but the rest of us pushed each other to new levels of fitness, while having plenty of fun on two wheels. Then the nicknames came. Graham was referred to as Dad because he was a little older than the rest of us, and because he would organise the route each week. Marwin became Twinkle (which he hated), as without a doubt he would need to stop two or three times during the ride to pee. I was tagged GPS, as I simply had no sense of direction, I would put my head down and cycle, constantly taking the wrong turn on a route we cycled along many times.

And then there was Kevin, with his constant tardiness and a magnetic force for something to go wrong whenever he was around. He was (and still is) known as Disaster!

During one Saturday ride, Disaster somehow ran over a fork on the road (not a fork *in* the road) in the middle of nowhere, and the silverware managed to flick up and stab into his elbow, leaving a puncture wound with a trickle of blood. How does this even happen?

That's classic Disaster. The four of us became quite close throughout the year, and these guys made my life more enjoyable and gave me a sense of stability during a very turbulent time.

It might have been good times in the pool, and out on the bike, but 2014 grabbed me by the scruff of the neck and tried to drown me. I still felt quite lost in my life, although I had some big goals for the next 18 months, like competing in my first 100 mile ultra-marathon, The Double Brutal Extreme Triathlon (my first official triathlon) before attempting the Ultimate Triathlon 12 months later. It was shaping up to be a big year physically, but I simply could not switch off my brain and stop the constant noise and negative thoughts in my head.

At the height of my insomnia I was surviving on just five to six hours of sleep a week, despite 25 hours of training on top of full-time work. I should have been exhausted. I would fall into bed shattered at around 11 p.m. then lie there wide-awake. By 3 or 4 a.m. without having slept a wink, I would get up and start the next day's work emailing, researching, or preparing for clients. Some nights when I just couldn't fall asleep, I would take myself out for another midnight run.

With the vast and beautiful Richmond Park only a short distance away, I'd often find myself navigating the dark trails for hours with my head torch lighting the way. Deer roam freely through the park, and at times I'd catch their eyes glowing in my light beam as they crossed the path in front of me, scaring me out of my wits.

One overcast evening, the park was shrouded in thick fog covering the tree line, and all I could see was my feet in front of me on the compacted dirt trail. I heard a rustle from the bushes, and turned to shine my torch towards the noise. A dark furry animal scampered across my path at about knee height. My guess is it was a badger, but to this day I've no clue. I almost needed a change of underwear after that encounter!

Training became my salvation.

Whenever I was pounding the trails I was free of the mental torment. I felt alive, but at the same time, I was well aware the intensity and frequency of my training on my sleep-deprived body could be detrimental to my long-term health. But the alternative was unbearable. When I wasn't pushing myself to my physical limits, I constantly critiqued my actions and behaviour over the past four years – my former relationship, how I was living my life, I constantly questioned if it was all worth it. I was in a very dark place, I felt emotionally alone and withdrawn from the world.

Most days I dragged myself out of the house to motivate, inspire and train others, prescribing advice I was a long way from following myself. I was not walking the talk, not even close. Each session I would take a deep breath before entering the training studio, put on a fake smile, produce some artificial energy, and throw myself into the next hour-long session. Once we finished I would transform back into the miserable bastard I'd become, hiding behind my glasses, or hood over my head. With my self-belief at rock bottom, I'd seek out comfort in food, bingeing without control.

To quote Fat Bastard in *Austin Powers: The Spy Who Shagged Me*, 'I eat because I'm unhappy, and I'm unhappy because I eat.' I was a long way off being a fat bastard, but I could truly relate to his sentiments. I was caught in a vicious cycle without the will power, courage, or strength to turn things around. My self-esteem had not bounced back since my relationship ended and although hate is a strong word, I cannot think of a more accurate description of how I felt about myself at that point.

Somehow, I kept myself on track, ticking off training sessions, researching and planning the Ultimate Triathlon routes, and looking at funding options. There were plenty of tasks to distract me each day. To the outside world, including my family and closest friends, I was living a 'normal' but busy life, working towards achieving my dream adventure. Such is the hidden danger of depression – it's too easy to fool people you're doing OK.

This was an extremely difficult time for my parents back in Australia, and much as they knew I could conquer just about any physical challenge, they also knew enough about depression to understand it's not always something you can deal with on your own. They said to me, 'You must tell us everything even if it's not what we want to hear, we must know, we must be part of it.' Mum has since told me they felt they had failed me as parents.

The few people who knew my depression had returned tried to reach out to me, but I simply lied to their faces. This made me feel physically ill. I hated not being able to open up to the people I loved, the people who loved me and wanted to help.

It was around this time my parents flew to the UK to visit all of us – me, my sister Moo and her son Max – their first grandchild. I'm sure Mum realised I was having a rough time when I picked them up at Heathrow airport, but I doubt she could have imagined just how bad things were.

I was in the early stages of revealing my battle with depression, but only to those in my inner circle. Beyond that, it was still very much hidden. I was also trying to talk about my frustration with not knowing why my relationship fell apart. I'd been single for a year now and desperately wanted to move on. My inability to cope had crippled me emotionally for too long, and was getting in the way of any future relationships and happiness.

Although my parents were not sure how to help beyond simply being with me, I was incredibly grateful to have them close by. I was also happy to have them in the UK to crew for my attempt to tackle the North Downs Way 100 mile ultra-marathon.

As I waited at the start line with my parents cheering me on I felt happier than I could remember being all year. They were my childhood heroes, they'd been with me at the beginning of this journey, and had always supported me through all the ups and down along the way. With my sister, nephew, and brother-in-law as part of my crew, I felt the love and support of family.

I was alive and running well, inhaling the fresh air and enjoying the August sunshine on the Downs. At the half way mark, I remember seeing my Dad by the roadside wearing one of my trademark propeller caps (worn by all my crew so I could easily find them at the checkpoints). He waved me in from the course and around to the back of the town hall, the official checkpoint base.

I sat on the tailgate of my sister's car, with my family huddled around, helping me through this 100 mile journey. My Dad massaged my calves as they were a little tight, and as I had a minute to stop and think, I realised this was exactly what I'd needed – to have my family rally around and support me to reach my goal. Team Tyburski.

My crew asked me to be honest about how I was feeling throughout the day, and I was. They did everything they could to get me to the finish line, even my nephew gave me high fives and yelled 'go Uncle Boof' as I ran by.

But beyond the race, I didn't know how to ask for their help. I knew I only had to be honest and they'd all do whatever they could to help me live a more balanced and less self-harming existence, but I just couldn't build up the courage to say three little words: *I need help.*

Just past the 60 mile (100 kilometre) mark I developed severe knee pain. I battled on for another seven or eight miles, but the pain worsened, so I called it quits on my 100 mile dream, knowing in six weeks I'd take on my first triathlon. We all headed back to my sister's place in good spirits as we all had done everything we could to get me to the finishing line, but it was just not my day.

My parents returned to Australia, and with my sister living several hours' drive from London my loneliness and dark thoughts soon returned. On the surface I was oozing confidence, pumped up, excited and not phased at all about my looming double Ironman distance triathlon, but deep down I was struggling big time.

The Double Brutal Extreme Triathlon takes place in the mountains of Snowdonia National Park in northern Wales. Most people laugh when they hear the name of the race, but it's called that for good reason – it's the distance of two Ironman triathlons – double swim, double cycle, double marathon – through steep, winding roads, narrow valleys, with freezing temperatures in and out of the water. But the scenery is nothing short of spectacular.

The weather in Snowdonia is the biggest 'X' factor for competitors – it's bright and sunny one minute, then with a chilly puff of wind from the Irish Sea, the sky grows dark and menacing, and visibility plummets as fog rolls into the valleys.

I discovered this event by searching for *the world's hardest triathlon* and it popped up on the first page of results. I remember thinking 'what a cool name', and with that, I signed up for my first ever triathlon.

First up is a 7.8 kilometre lake swim, followed by a 375 kilometre cycle with over 5000 metres of climbing, before running up Mount Snowdon, which has 1000 metres of vertical gain across 15 kilometres. Next is a 65 kilometre run with well over 1000 metres worth of climbing. To me it sounded like fun, and great training for the Ultimate Triathlon, which was fast approaching.

One of the mandatory conditions of the Double Brutal Extreme Triathlon is to be accompanied by another runner while summiting Mount Snowdon. This is a safety measure as competitors have already completed more than half a day of extreme output in the lake and on the bike.

I put together a crew of good mates to help me get through this mammoth task but as they were all training for their own events in the weeks to follow, running a double marathon up a mountain in the early hours of the morning was not ideal. I still had no one to chaperone me up and down Mount Snowdon, so I asked on Twitter if anyone was interested. Hannah replied. She had recently completed her first 100 kilometre ultra-marathon. She seemed normal enough, so I thought, 'she'll do!'

The rest of my crew included Graham, a.k.a 'Dad' and Tarsh – Little Miss Organised – both multiple Ironman triathletes. They already knew I was crazy, so I guess they thought it could be an entertaining weekend of watching me push myself further into the dark pit of self-inflicted physical and mental pain! These three will always be amongst my closest friends; it's funny what a weekend together helping someone achieve a tough goal can do to create a close bond.

The dive into the chilly lake at 7 a.m. on a clear Saturday morning literally took my breath away. I felt strong and confident and was excited about the weekend of racing ahead, in and around the town of Llanberis. Swimming is my weakest of the three disciplines, but I felt like I was in my element and kept thinking, 'I could stay in here and swim all day long.'

I exited the water after nearly three hours, peeled off my wetsuit and got ready to head off on the bike. I chatted with my crew, and joked around like a kid, happy to be doing what I loved, and hanging out with some close friends. After about half an hour of me talking rubbish, Graham finally said, 'Will you shut up and get on the bike!' I could hear them laughing as I took off on the first lap of eight.

The hours and kilometres ticked by and the day became a little overcast, then dark and cold. My energy levels began to decline. The eighth and final lap of the 45 kilometre course was a test of survival due to the conditions. Graham had to drive slowly behind with his headlights on high beam for most of the lap as the lights on my bike had failed. As we approached the start of the penultimate climb at around 3 a.m., I was struggling on two fronts – keeping my eyes open and keeping the pedals spinning.

Graham pulled up beside me and suggested a quick break and I did not argue. We set an alarm to go off in five minutes, turned the car heating up to full boil, cranked up the volume on the stereo and listened to Bono from U2 scream his lungs out.

In the blink of an eye, the alarm sounded and I was back on the bike tackling the final climbs. Before I knew it, I was flying down a steep descent and arriving into Llanberis to finish the bike leg.

Hannah was all kitted up and ready to run. She looked cold and very nervous. I changed into my running gear and we took off together, ready to summit Mount Snowdon.

We passed through the large wooden gates that signalled the starting point of the official climb to the summit. Our head torches lit up the trail and the sky was full of stars – it was a beautiful time to run. But after just a couple of kilometres, I had a feeling we were heading the wrong way, as the trail we were following still hadn't started to climb up the mountain.

I said to Hannah, 'I think we are on the wrong path, I think this is someone's driveway.' She assured me we were on the right track, but just after she said this we ended up at a dead end, on someone's doorstep. We backtracked for several kilometres, and with the help of early morning light, scrambled up the side of the mountain to find the trail we were supposed to be following.

After the slight diversion, I gave Hannah the nickname 'Tom Tom' as she *clearly* had the sense of direction only a satellite navigation system could offer!

We reached the summit in glorious Welsh sunshine, with a clear sky and visibility for miles, but with nearly two marathons still to run, we quickly ran back down to where our crew waited.

The next section was eight laps running around the lake I'd swum in at the start of the race. I looped around twice before Graham joined me for a lap three; it was nice to have some company as I battled the steep winding climbs throughout the second half of the run course.

Tarsh and Hannah joined in for some fun for the next couple of laps, all wearing the official Team Tyburski spinning propeller caps! What can I say? I think they're cool!

I had been moving continuously for more than 34 hours and now had just one lap remaining – there were just eight kilometres between me and the finish line. Graham, Tarsh and Hannah wanted to run with me to cap off what had been an amazing weekend of swimming, cycling, running, eating and laughing, but I wanted to complete this lap solo. It was important to me that I achieve my goal for 2014 on my terms. I wanted to exterminate any leftover feelings of negativity, so I put my head down and ran hard.

My legs immediately filled with lactic acid from the increased pace and the pain was excruciating. I reached the hilly section of the course and sprinted up every hill, gasping to absorb any oxygen I could into to my deprived lungs. I zoned out and was physically hurting, but the memories and feelings I conjured up as I covered the final four kilometres of the Double Brutal Extreme Triathlon became an emotional war between my ears. I tried to push out all the negativity, frustration, and anguish of the past two years and tears streamed down my face.

The final stretch was about 400 metres along a flat dirt track through a paddock. I felt energised and strong, ready to not only finish my first triathlon, but more importantly, start living the rest of my life.

I crossed the finish line, fell to the ground, and my crew followed suit. We lay on the cold grass as the sun descended behind the hills and were all smiles and thumbs up for the finisher's photo. A little over 35 hours of swimming, cycling and running and I was now officially a triathlete, for ever grateful to my amazing crew.

* * *

For a week afterwards I was buzzing. I was proud of my effort – and dare I say it, feeling happy. I was rested, enjoyed time with friends, and most importantly, I was kind to myself. Of course, the positive feelings didn't last long.

Two weeks after Snowdonia as I sat at home alone, negative thoughts started to creep into my head. 'You could have cycled faster, why did you walk most of the hills?' My mind's chatter became increasingly destructive, 'you're putting on weight because you haven't trained.'

It sounds ludicrous after what I had achieved in the space of only six short weeks; running 110 kilometres, and completing a double Ironman distance triathlon but still I wasn't satisfied. I hated myself for putting on a kilo or two so I ordered enough Thai takeaway to feed four people and ate the lot.

I compulsively signed up for two more ultra-marathons in the space of three weeks – a hilly 75 kilometre race, and a relatively flat 100 kilometre event. I began training the following week, as the first race was only five weeks away.

As I smashed out fast run sessions and hill repeats around my stop-start binge eating, my weight remained relatively stable. I was running faster over longer distances, and with my harmful eating habits seemingly not having any effect on my performance, I never urged myself to get help to change this destructive behaviour.

I pushed my body hard during this period of my training, then like a light switch flicking off, roughly 10 days out from my first race, I woke up completely exhausted. When I opened my eyes I knew immediately from the sun coming through my blinds it was late morning. I felt like someone had sucked the life out of me.

Extreme fatigue had set in, and my weary body said enough is enough. It was another 30 minutes before I could get myself upright. My arms felt like they were full of cement, I could barely sit up and when I tried to stand, my knees buckled. I shuffled to the bathroom like a nursing home resident.

I sat on the couch for an hour before admitting I'd have to withdraw from both ultra-marathons.

I took stock of my year. My goal had been to compete in a 100 mile ultra-marathon, and although I didn't finish, I was still happy with what I achieved. More importantly, I wanted to become a triathlete and complete one of the toughest triathlons in the world, to serve as an apprenticeship for the Ultimate Triathlon. I had definitely ticked that box.

I felt content I made the right call for my long-term health. I was in a confident frame of mind, and finally making decisions that looked after my body rather than trying to destroy it. But the roller-coaster ride was far from over and soon I was heading back down that emotional trajectory I knew only too well.

In just two months I would officially launch my plans to attempt the Ultimate Triathlon, a self-created epic challenge, now only 10 months away. First though I had to get myself through the next 10 days, and try to find a way to start loving myself, so I could start living.

Something in my life needed to change, I just had no idea what!

10.

THE GIRL WITH THE FULL SLEEVE TATTOO

For months I had been promoting the imminent announcement of my next big challenge, with a plan to reveal details at one of the UK's largest triathlon trade events. I had a speaking slot at the 220 Triathlon Show and had assumed, as 220 Triathlon is the most read triathlon magazine in the country, I'd be speaking to a reasonably large crowd. As it turned out, other than staff, a handful of friends and a few ring-ins, there was not nearly as much interest as I had hoped. With only nine months until the event, it was a kick in the guts I did not need.

The trade show was over a few days, so wearing my trademark multi-coloured propeller cap, I wandered the halls of the pavillion at Sandown Park, just outside London, trying to find sponsors for the Ultimate Triathlon. I was hopeful of securing at least two brands to help cover the cost of the event, and potentially provide in-kind product.

A number of global sporting companies had stands at the show, displaying their products, one of which was a well-known compression wear and wetsuit brand. I noticed one of their sales reps was free so I took the opportunity to introduce myself and pitch my event.

I had pre-loaded a promotional video onto my iPad to provide a glimpse of my background and the planned challenge – a 2000 kilometre ultra-triathlon over 12 days from Morocco to Monaco. I took a deep breath, mentally cued my well-rehearsed pitch, and walked over to the staffer who was busy organising a rack of garments.

'Hi, I'm Luke Tyburski the Endurance Adventurer' I said. 'Nice to meet you Luke Tyburski the Endurance Adventurer, I'm Vanda!' she replied, looking me in the eye.

Her Australian accent and overly confident response threw me at first, but I regained focus and began my pitch. Afterwards she asked where I was from in Australia. As is so often the case many miles from home, it turned out I had randomly bumped into someone who grew up in Orange, the neighbouring town to my hometown of Bathurst.

We went through the obligatory 'do you know so-and-so' trying to figure out if we had any mutual friends, but as Vanda was a few years younger than me, and I'd left home at 16 to play soccer in Sydney, we couldn't find any connections we had in common.

She was studying Osteopathy and impressed me with her knowledge of the human body (she'd already graduated with a degree in Exercise Physiology) and with her outlook on injury treatment. We shared a passion to learn more about how the body works, how it functions, and how it can be treated.

She was diminutive, but self assured with an unexpected edge. She had blonde and light brown hair, a nose ring through the right nostril, red lip stick on, and her left arm covered in a sleeve of tattoos, alongside a large Manta ray inked on the inside of her right forearm.

My initial thoughts of Vanda were that she was direct, with a straight to the point attitude, but I sensed an underlying softer side to her. I was intrigued.

We wrapped up the conversation and I handed her a couple of my business cards to pass onto her boss, in the hope he might sponsor my challenge.

At the end of the show a couple of days later, I popped back to the stand where Vanda was working to say goodbye, and ask her to get in touch if she ever wanted to catch up for a coffee.

Early the next morning, totally unexpected, my phone beeped. It was a text from Vanda asking if I wanted to catch up for that coffee. The first thought that went through my head was 'this girl knows what she wants!'

Meanwhile, trying to find sponsors was proving frustrating. I had sent out hundreds of emails, made dozens of phone calls and progress was slow. I pushed on, determined to find a way to get myself to the shores of Morocco later in the year and plunge into the choppy waters of The Strait of Gibraltar – just me and a few dozen shipping tankers – for the first leg of my crazy challenge.

* * *

In March I flew to Malta for an 'Ocean Walker' open water swim camp. The training retreat is designed for people looking to complete a qualifying swim for the English Channel or similar long-distance swim.

The Ocean Walker camps are run over five days by Adam Walker, the first British swimmer to complete the 'Oceans Seven' swim series, seven of the toughest open water swims around the world. The list includes the North Channel between Ireland and Scotland, the Cook

Strait between the North and South Islands of New Zealand, the Moloka'i Channel in Hawaii, the English Channel between England and France, the Catalina Channel in Southern California, the Tsugaru Channel in Japan, and the Strait of Gibraltar between Europe and Africa.

When I decided the Strait of Gibraltar swim would be part of the Ultimate Triathlon, my research led me to Adam Walker. He is the fastest Brit to swim the two-way – Spain to Morocco and back again – his knowledge and experience would be priceless.

I had already done some stroke technique work with him in the UK, and wanted to expand on that with a week of practice in the ocean under his supervision.

One of my preferred means of transport is on foot, and I always travel light, so when I landed at Malta International Airport I changed into my running kit, put on my propeller cap and hit 'start route' on my phone's GPS. The hotel was 12 kilometres away and other than a couple of dual carriageways, I mostly travelled through old villages and down back streets dotted with buildings with white-washed walls and timber shutters. In the distance were rolling hills and beyond that, the Mediterranean Sea.

I knew next to nothing about open water swimming, and thought I could handle the 15 degree Celsius waters without a wetsuit – and perhaps with a little more body fat I'd have been OK! After the first 50-minute swim I was so cold, I have limited memory of the van ride afterwards back to the hotel. The following day I had to be fished out of the ocean after an hour when my arms and hands stopped working.

'Ocean Walker' co-founder, and Adam's partner Gemma Clarke, was also in Malta with Adam. She had crewed several of the Oceans Seven swims, so I knew I was in safe hands.

Our next few sessions were in a heated pool that everyone (except me) complained was too hot. Then it was back into the ocean for a six-hour swim. My plan was to break up the six hours into three 45-minute swims, with an hour's recovery and defrosting in between. My fellow swimmers thought I was crazy, swimming out and back from the shore several times, but I knew I wouldn't last the cold water for the entire six-hour swim. I pictured myself freezing into a block of ice and floating out to sea!

It was a long and tough day. I would stumble out of the surf after each swim and Gemma would warm me up with cups of tea. After 45 minutes, the alarm on her watch would sound telling me I had 15 minutes to find my cap and goggles and get back into the water.

For many people, ocean swimming means confronting a range of fears – fear of deep water, big waves, strong currents, sharks, jellyfish, and passing ships. I felt my mental framework was strong, thanks to past endurance events using techniques like visualisation, focusing on positive thoughts and keeping my motives clear. No one forced me out of a warm bed into the freezing water, I was very clear on why I was there. When I am struggling during an event, I dip into this mental strength. Over the five days, I did more open water swimming than I'd ever done and that practical experience was the key benefit for me. The amount of swimming we did over the week at the Ocean Walker camp buoyed my confidence.

Malta is famous for its natural beauty and is a favourite spot for divers who travel from all over the world to explore the depths of the Mediterranean around the three main islands in the archipelago. The water was remarkably clear and it always fascinated me to see the ocean floor many metres below, changing colour with the changing depth and at different times of the day, from bright aqua to turquoise to the deepest blue. Small schools of fish skimmed the sandy bottom and darted around barnacle-covered rocks. The massive sheer rock face along the coast of the Maltese islands created an almost spooky series of shadows underwater. When I swam through these sections, and the light dropped suddenly, it was like the master light switch above had been dimmed.

Each swim took place in a different part of the island which provided a range of deep water experiences for both mental and physical training. The rocky shoreline added a level of difficulty swimming in and out of the horseshoe-shaped bays.

One of the psychological tips Adam taught at the Ocean Walker camp was to eliminate the 'c' word – he told swimmers he has removed the word 'cold' from his vocabulary and instructed them to imagine they were wrapped in a blanket or soaking in a warm bath. A great tip – I can also highly recommend wearing a wetsuit.

When I wasn't in the water, I was out exploring. I had done a bit of research on the natural trails criss-crossing the main island, and set off on what turned out to be a 50 kilometre run with no map and initially no timeframe. It was adventure time. I wound my way along dusty tracks until I reached the summit of a hill, then I looked for a different trail down the other side. The natural pathways hugged the clifftop, scarily close to the edge in some sections, with hundred metre sheer drops below. I stayed focused on foot placement as I didn't fancy an unplanned swim.

The vista was stunning, and distracting. At one point, I was looking out at the view rather than at the rocky terrain beneath my feet and I stacked it. I crashed hard, clipped a rock, and punctured my elbow, which bled immediately. I searched my backpack for some type of bandage and found a sock. That would have to do. I wrapped it around my elbow and ran for another 20 kilometres. It was a magic five-and-a-half-hours of exploring, before I eventually ending up at the multi-story hotel where the Ocean Walker group was staying. I finished off the session by dunking myself, propeller cap and sock-bandaged-elbow, chest-deep in the water, noticing many a bewildered look from the lunch-goers in cafes along the foreshore.

Vanda and I still hadn't managed to coordinate our schedules for the coffee we'd talked about, so I hadn't seen her since the triathlon show several months earlier. We had been keeping in touch via text messages during the swim camp in Malta, and I asked her plenty of questions as she had plenty of ocean swimming experience having completed the English Channel crossing as both an individual and part of a relay. Seeing her name pop up as a notification on my mobile made me smile. We were slowly getting to know one another.

After Malta, I had an ultra-marathon scheduled – 64 kilometres on the edge of the Peak District in the north of England. Training felt tougher than usual and I struggled with my energy levels. I felt lethargic, was suffering headaches and didn't have much of an appetite.

I started the race well, running with a group of four just behind the two leaders. But with 15 kilometres to go, the wheels fell off. I had eaten but had no energy and was battling a pounding headache. My legs simply stopped running. I kept going, at times staggering across the trail, desperate to lie down – I was in a bad way. At the final checkpoint, with just five kilometres to go, but with one final climb, I pulled out of the race.

I booked myself in for medical tests when I got back to London and was diagnosed with the flu. In hindsight considering the symptoms, it's more likely I had a bout of glandular fever. I dubbed it my 'super virus' as it took five weeks of complete rest from training and life to feel my usual healthy self again.

For the next four months, I worked long days promoting the Ultimate Triathlon with little help. I would set my alarm clock to nudge me awake with mellow chimes around five, get a few minutes of guided meditation using my Headspace app, or do some focused deep breathing to reset my system.

I found time to enjoy simple pleasures like the ceremony of brewing a morning cup of tea and watching the leaves unfurl in the hot water. It brought back childhood memories sitting with my Grandma in her house sipping tea as we chatted about the world.

Switching on my laptop and adjusting to the bright screen in pre-dawn darkness was my 'starting siren' for the day's battle ahead. A typical workday involved planning and research, sending emails, making phone calls and creating and posting promotional content online to gain exposure and funding for the Ultimate Triathlon.

That would fill up several hours of my morning, before it was time to train.

Most days I'd grab my running shoes, propeller cap and swim kit and run the six kilometres to Hampton pool. After a couple of hours following the black line up and down the 36 metre outdoor pool, I would run back home, often extending the trip for an extra hour or two by following the tow path of the River Thames.

Historically, the Thames Path was used to tow boats and barges from the shore and is now a stunning National Trail that stretches almost 300 kilometres along the river. It's widely used by runners, walkers and in parts, cyclists. The mostly dirt track from Hampton Pool weaves around and through small outer suburbs in southwest London and there is plenty to see along the way. Colourful houseboats moored to jetties are a unique reflection of their owners, covered with bric-à-brac and all manner of household items including deck chairs, firewood, bikes, flags and fake flowers. One even has a large talking head sculpture, which caused me to do a double-take as I ran past.

Other days I would run straight home, grab a few handfuls of seeds and nuts or a couple of avocados and jump on my bike for a ride, with no planned route or destination. I liked the sense of adventure of ending up somewhere unexpected. The remainder of my day would involve meetings with potential sponsors, doing media interviews, and generally getting the word out about the Ultimate Triathlon.

Every spare moment was filled with thoughts and plans on how to fund the Ultimate Triathlon. I still had no idea how I would cover the cost of the 12 day challenge.

For my other day job, I had regular clients I was training to help achieve their own health and fitness goals, and was also doing motivational speaking at various seminars, businesses, schools or health clubs.

Throughout the year, I needed to break up the monotony of training 25-30 hours a week on the same roads and trails, and following the same black line in the pool. I had planned to cycle around the Spanish island of Majorca in the annual 312 kilometre event, but as I had only recently recovered from my 'super virus,' I opted for the shorter 167 kilometre route. I arranged to meet up with friends on the opposite side of the island from the airport, but rather than drive the 90 kilometres, I thought it might be fun to cycle. I left my bike travel box at a long-term luggage storage near the airport and took off with a backpack filled with all the kit I'd need for the three day stay.

I cycled out of Palma, riding on the back roads through the Spanish old town until I reached a wide single-lane road, surrounded by open fields. I had basic directions to the villa where I was staying, at the foot of the hills not too far from the coastal town of Port de Pollença.

During the day, I was more interested in exploring the surrounding countryside than sitting around relaxing, and once I realised we were staying near a trail head, I took myself off for a loosely-planned run – an hour out and an hour back. The track wound its way through pine trees with plenty of switch-backs, and at times steep enough to make my quads burn and my chest pound. I shot out of the covered terrain and into a National Park rest area briefly, before heading back into the enclosed trail once again. The dense forest gradually opened up and I descended into a valley and followed a narrow creek bed, mesmerised by the water, before the trail began to shoot straight up. I checked my watch and realised I'd been running for just over 90 minutes. My friends were expecting me back two hours after I left and I had no phone to make contact. I also had no water and no food, but I wanted to get to the summit of the trail I was on.

It turned out to be a false summit that took me over the top of the main road I'd cycled on the day before. The view was incredible and I could see a ridgeline that swept to the right with a dirt track covered in loose rocks and pebbles. After around two and a half hours I stopped, and turned around. It was late afternoon and it had been a hot day, over 30 degrees Celsius. I'd removed my shirt and tucked it into the back of my shorts. I needed to get back on the trail I'd come from and find the creek to get some water. I eventually found it and immersed my head and chest to cool down my body temperature. I figured I was only about three kilometres from the house at this point, but I'd been gone for three and a half hours and I knew my friend Jo would be worried.

After a brief rest, I gunned it down the hill, spinning around trees on the many switchbacks. About a kilometre from the villa, deep in the forest where the sunlight barely penetrated, I spun around a hairpin and the earth gave way beneath me, sending me toppling down a two-metre drop, where I bounced a couple of times. I did a head to toe check, noted the blood coming from my shoulder and hip, took a deep breath and finished my fun. I arrived back bloodied, sweaty, covered in dirt and emerged into the back garden where my friends watched the sunset, drinks in hand. I was grinning like an idiot and told them it was one of the best runs of my life. They told me they were giving me another 15 minutes before they sent out a search party. Jo wasn't too concerned, she figured it was just another day of Luke out running.

Back in the UK, I struggled to get much publicity or funding for the Ultimate Triathlon. Many of the sporting brands and media outlets responded with messages like, 'We covered someone who did an Ironman last month, this is too similar', or 'This doesn't fit with what we stand for, or our message.' It was frustrating. How is covering 2000 kilometres in 12 days like covering 226 kilometres in one day? How is it not adventurous enough to be the first to cross two continents and three countries swimming, cycling, and running from Morocco to Monaco?

In the US, it was a different story. I'd had a few offers to appear on different podcasts with US fitness and motivational experts. It seemed the US market understood the enormity of what I planned to conquer, and celebrated the fact that I was 'going for it.'

The voice in my head kept telling me I only needed one person to believe in my idea, and that person was me. Ever since my coach Joe Judge instilled the near limitless self-belief in me all those years ago, I knew the Ultimate Triathlon would happen!

Meanwhile Vanda and I were still trying to find time together.

We had finally had our first coffee date and the conversation flowed freely. We sat outside in the spring sunshine and sipped our drinks as we talked and laughed about life. While we chatted, I tried not to stare at the intricate detail of Vanda's full sleeve tattoo. A mesmerising pattern of small symmetrical shapes and long flowing fern like designs wrapped around her forearm, and up to her shoulder. A mandala flower encompassed her entire left elbow, looking like it was strategically placed.

I felt relaxed around Vanda, and for the first time in a very long while, thought about the possibility of being in a relationship again.

Between my preparation for the Ultimate Triathlon and Vanda's study commitments, it was another few weeks before we saw each other again. We met at the Natural History Museum in London to catch a wildlife photography exhibition, and in the quiet space lit by tiny spotlights, standing alongside one another, our shoulders touched. We looked at each other, and with a smile I knew there was something special about this woman. The day continued with lunch and a walk around central London, sharing our own journeys up until this point. Time seemed to fly as I began to see a softer caring side of Vanda. I made her laugh several times during the afternoon, each time a broad smile spread across her face, a smile that was beginning to warm my heart. It was now the evening, and we shared dinner in Covent Garden, making it a 12-hour date – I must have done something right...

Around the same time, I accepted an offer to travel to California to appear on several prominent US podcasts, and to do some media interviews. I had close friends living in Los Angeles who were happy to put me up for a few nights and I wanted to add some variety to my swim and run training. The only problem was finding the cash to cover flights and car rental. Every spare dollar I had was earmarked for my big event – I literally was going all in!

A few of my UK friends felt the publicity was too good an opportunity to pass up and generously lent me cash to cover the cost of a flight. It was difficult to accept but they insisted, so I thanked them and booked my flight.

My first podcast was with Rich Roll, an elite ultra-athlete with a fascinating life story, overcoming addiction and changing his diet to become one of the world's most famous plant-powered athletes. Rich is a superstar in the ultra-endurance scene and has built a remarkable second career (he was previously an LA lawyer) inspiring people with the story of his physical and life transformation.

Rich's office and studio was in the stunning Calabasas area north west of central LA, near Malibu Creek State Park. We had an afternoon interview scheduled so I had the morning free. I set off on a three-hour trail run through the park, planning to run out and back and see where it took me. I grabbed a backpack with water and fuel, picked a hill to run towards and off I went, on what looked like an old miner's trail with, nice switchbacks and a few potholes. On the latter parts of the run, the landscape became more desert-like with knee-high shrubbery and rocks scattered around. Above me, the vapour trails from planes created a patchwork of white lines across the blue sky. On the way to the summit I didn't pass a single person, and when I got to the peak I took some photos and spun back down. By the time I got to the creek at the bottom I'd been running for three hours. It was a hot and cloudless Californian day, probably over 30 degrees Celsius. I bathed in the cold water and ran back to the trailhead where I'd parked my car. I had some food in the cooler (cold stir-fry from the night before) and refuelled before heading over to record the podcast.

Rich dug into some of the emotions I'd struggled with throughout my journey to becoming an extreme endurance athlete. He understood a lot of the challenges I'd faced and we talked for hours. I felt extremely relaxed in his company, but the stonewalls I rigorously laid still guarded my true emotional state, and I wasn't letting them down to reveal the exact depth of what I was battling with mentally. He was intrigued with my plans for the Ultimate Triathlon and I left his studio feeling positive and inspired for the rest of my American trip.

11.

PEAR SHAPED

For the most part, life seemed to be going well, but I found myself slipping into a deep hole and I didn't feel at all confident I could find my way out. Whenever I stopped for a breather between training and travelling, my depression would reappear on my shoulder pestering me. It was a dark beast that sapped my energy and controlled my moods.

The walls of my bedroom were like the confines of a jail cell, I knew every inch of the space, and it was a safe place I did not want to venture beyond – who knew what could happen out there? I upped the ante on my training to try and escape the beast – I wanted to outrun my depression. But more time training meant less time to promoting the Ultimate Triathlon, which caused me to worry I couldn't pull off the whole ridiculous idea. It was destined to fail – I was destined to fail.

So once again, I was trapped in the cycle – incapacitated by the negative thoughts of my depression, trying to counter the emotions with binge eating sessions, which led to increased training to ensure I maintained my optimum weight. All these factors compounded to create a frustration that paralysed me. I felt no self-worth and wanted to end it all, but still I told no one the full extent of my inner turmoil.

Around this time, a good friend asked if I would like to join him on a four-day cycling adventure through France. Warren co-owns a real food sports nutrition company called 33Shake whose products I have been using for years, and I am a proud ambassador. The ride sounded perfect – time on the bike with a mate, someone to keep me accountable to myself to stay positive, and a new cycling adventure through another beautiful country.

We planned to meet in Paris then set off along the famous 'Paris to Roubaix' race route. There are many sections of cobblestones along this 257-kilometre-single-day classic, through several small villages – it is certainly not *smooth* riding. The actual start line is just under 100 kilometres from central Paris, and the finish line is in Roubaix, 150 kilometres from Calais. After completing the actual race route, we would then cycle to Calais and catch the train back to London. We had a fun 500 kilometres of cycling ahead and I was excited to get started.

We woke to the smell of freshly brewed coffee, and the delicious aroma of baked bread somewhere not far from our rented Parisian apartment. We negotiated our way through central Paris on our bikes using the GPS device attached to Warren's bike, keeping our wits about us in the morning peak hour traffic. He had pre-loaded our route but there was no underlying map of any roads, just a line to follow. When we had to turn, the line would simply divert at right angles in either direction.

Outside of Paris, we spun the legs out along the canal system, chatting about life, cycling, and motorbikes (Warren was previously a journalist for a motorcycling magazine). The GPS indicated we should head through a park. With Warren on my right, a wheel length ahead, and neither of us paying enough attention we rolled through the park gates and approached a four-directional intersection. Mid-sentence, and with no warning, Warren turned left.

He cut across my front wheel and I was about to T-bone him so naturally my instincts kicked in. I grabbed a handful of brakes and my new brake pads worked extremely well, forcing my rear tyre up off the road and sending me crashing to the ground. I felt the full force of the pavement on my left side, mostly on my hip and elbow.

After a few moments to compose myself I performed a quick head to toe check. I was a little dazed and confused, and had blood oozing from my left elbow, but it was the severe dull ache in my left hip I was concerned about. The bike wasn't too bad, apart from the rear derailleur that shifts the gears being noticeably bent.

Warren was in more shock than I was, and extremely apologetic, but I assured him I was fine and wanted to carry on. My hip hurt with every revolution of the pedals, forcing us to stop several times along the way so I could lay on the side of the road to wait for the sharp pain pulsating through my hip to pass.

I was determined to 'ride it out', right up until we hit a stretch of small cobbles in Compiègne, the official start line for the Paris to Roubaix race. The vibration from these uneven scattered cobbles intensified my agony. I knew there was something seriously wrong with my hip, and after several hours riding in pain (and with just over three months until the Ultimate Triathlon), I needed to get back to London for treatment. The Paris to Roubaix trip was all over for me.

Warren rode on and I caught a train back to Paris, then another train to Calais for an overnight stay before travelling on to London the next morning. My head was all over the place. I was in a lot of pain and struggling to walk. My state of mind deteriorated rapidly throughout the afternoon in Calais, so I turned to food for comfort. I shovelled cheese-filled croissants into my mouth, washed down with a tub of ice cream, and wallowed in a pool of self-pity – destructive behaviour that only compounded my self-loathing.

My mind wandered, and the words 'Why am I doing this to myself?' bounced around in my head. I started repeating it aloud, berating myself as I stared at my bare torso, my stomach bulging and full of food. I felt lost, confused, and alone.

Back in the UK I put on a brave face to everyone I spoke with about my little mishap in France. I went back to see my old friend Dr Lorenzo Masci, so he could survey the extent of the damage caused by the accident.

Lorenzo could tell using the ultrasound machine in his office nothing was severely broken (a positive), but he wasn't sure what was going on inside my hip joint. He suspected damage to some of the connective tissue, so he sent me off for an MRI scan and said he'd be in touch with the results.

Two days later I woke at 6 a.m. to see my phone blinking with a message.

It read 'You have a fracture in your femur with cartilage damage, make an appointment to see me today.' Shit!

What a way to start the day, I tried to stay positive and not freak out, but in all honesty, I found it very difficult to remain upbeat. I met Lorenzo and he confirmed there was a fracture in my femur (upper leg bone) but thankfully, it wasn't too serious. I also had significant cartilage damage in the hip joint as well.

The doctor's advice was to rest, give the injuries some time to heal, and then see my physiotherapist Mo 'Magic Hands' to begin rehab. I was thrown back to the painful memories of the years when I was a broken-down footballer and was seeing Mo and Lorenzo on a regular basis.

Since the bike crash I also had a significant amount of shoulder pain, and it seemed to be worsening. Stupidly, I ignored the pain and did the only form of exercise I was capable of – swimming! All the while the little niggle in my shoulder continued. My two-hour swim sessions stretched to three hours, two-three times a week, then five-six times a week of varying lengths of time. I was unable to run or cycle to the pool so I would drive there and force myself to swim extra laps to maintain my fitness.

I knew what I was doing was stupid. Total nonsense.

My behaviour went against everything I believed in when it comes to listening to the body, and how it speaks to us. But I was stuck in a mindset that told me to train my arms more because I was unable to train my legs at all. Madness and dangerous.

I needed someone to slap me out of it, someone to say, 'Wake up and look at what you are doing to yourself!' My problems weren't life threatening, they were trivial in the grand scheme of things, but I was at the mercy of my ego and a selfish desire to achieve the goal I had set for myself – to swim, cycle, and run from Morocco to Monaco.

I was making childish errors in my judgment when it came to the one thing I knew best – how to train my own body. The physical battles and the mental torment were deeply intertwined, feeding off one another, but nobody really knew what was going on. Something had to give, or everything I had been working for over the last four years would begin to crumble.

My one haven was with Vanda, who I now happily called my girlfriend. She had plenty going on in her own life but we both found time to see each other. When I was with Vanda I was totally present, I was at ease. She brought a sense of calm to my out-of-control life.

2015 should have been an extremely exciting time. It was the year my crazy dream of the Ultimate Triathlon would become a reality. Sadly, I felt totally out of control and worried my life was about to be derailed. I knew I needed help and wanted desperately to confide in my closest friends, my family, or Vanda, who was so supportive, but I was too ashamed. I was a far cry from the guy who believed he could tackle anything. I tried for months to overcome the negativity and self-sabotaging behaviour, but to no avail. I had the number of a therapist stored in my phone, and after another week of inner turmoil and staring at the number, I finally built up the courage to make the call.

For nearly a month I kept the weekly therapy sessions to myself, until one day during a quiet moment sitting with Vanda on my couch, I started talking. I told her I felt my life was totally out of control and I was an emotional breakdown waiting to happen. I immediately assured her I had taken measures to get on top of my life once more through therapy. Vanda listened and said nothing, but the look of concern on her face told me she understood. We sat facing each other while I talked and I could tell she knew I had been dealing with the pressures of life.

Once I stated talking, I felt the release of a huge amount of self-imposed pressure to create and deliver the Ultimate Triathlon, pressure to be the all-inspiring, all-conquering Luke Tyburski – it was all internally driven. Vanda's comforting words stabilised my immediate anxious state. She held my hand and told me she was there to support and help me however she could. I could feel tears welling up in my eyes, then down my cheeks – I knew I had found a partner for life.

I had asked many people for help with many different aspects of organising my event but I was constantly let down. People put their hand up to do what they could, but then pulled out. This dumped more pressure on me and I was drowning in my own expectations. After many hours talking with my therapist, I gradually got life back into perspective. I needed to cut myself some slack. The expectations I had put on myself were nothing but a delusion I had created for myself.

I began to understand that being extremely busy does not necessarily make you productive. Doing more tasks at a faster rate does not guarantee you will achieve a high-quality outcome. I lowered my expectations of myself and focused on what I could control. I tried to be less self-critical. Throughout my entire life, right back to the days as a kid playing soccer in Bathurst, I was always my own harshest critic, beating myself up for missing a tackle, even if I had a cracking game and made one tiny mistake, I'd focus on the mistake. My coach and my parents would tell me not to be so tough on myself, but I simply did not know any other way.

So now, with the Ultimate Triathlon looming and being unable to properly train due to injury, I was supposed to change a mindset I'd had since I was a child! It was a tough time, but I had no other option.

Financially, things were dire. I had taken out a second personal loan despite struggling to pay off the original loan. I had been living at the limit of my overdraft, and often went over the limit at which point the bank would immediately put a stop to any transactions. More than once I found myself at the supermarket checkout unable to pay for my vegetables, at an ATM unable withdraw cash, or trying to pay my rent, only to have the transaction reversed. There were times when I questioned if going completely *all in* to simply get to the Ultimate

Triathlon start line was worth it, while digging an emotional and financial hole for myself was something I needed to do.

I just kept thinking to myself that if it were easy, everyone would be doing it!

I have so much love and gratitude for the people who helped me get through this tough time. On a few occasions, I had no choice but to ask for money, which I struggled with – it dented my pride. I would always ask for less than I needed and rarely asked the same person twice as didn't want to be a burden on anyone else's life. Having these special people believe in what I was doing gave me enough confidence to keep my up, and head above the water.

Just.

I tried everything I could think of to raise cash for my event from Morocco to Monaco. I had to pay for accommodation for 14 nights, buy enough food to fuel myself and my crew through the swim, the ride and the run legs, plus cover the cost of van hire and petrol for the 2000 kilometre trip. I was out of ideas, and out of time. As a last resort, just a few weeks before the planned start of the Ultimate Triathlon, I launched a crowd funding campaign. I knew nothing about crowd funding, but one thing was for sure, if it wasn't successful, the Ultimate Triathlon would not be happening.

It was now eight weeks until the designated start date of what would be the most intense journey of my life, but I still had many hurdles to overcome.

The logistics of the event were a nightmare, mainly due to the start date. Swimming the Strait of Gibraltar can only be done when the conditions allow – so we would be given a 'window' of one or two weeks. Once we knew the swim date it would be a mad scramble to line up all the other arrangements including accommodation.

I had planned the 2000 kilometre journey over 12 days, several days shorter than many people believed was needed. I did this intentionally. If it was easy, anybody could do it. This is probably what scared off potential sponsors and investors. They didn't want to take a chance on a relative 'unknown' on the world endurance stage. All I could think was they clearly had no idea who they were dealing with!

The crowd funding campaign was my number one priority. I set a target of £6000 and had no choice but to believe I could pull it off. Even if I did, it was still slightly under the bare minimum I needed to make the event a reality.

My budget was for the pure necessities, food, travel, and accommodation.

Most pledges made in a crowd funding campaign come in the first few days, so it was critical I primed my network of contacts, prepared promotional content and had a solid marketing plan. The campaign attracted a few big donations off the bat and the pot was looking in reasonable shape.

So-far-so-good.

But with each day, the pledge numbers dwindled and soon stopped. I extended the campaign and continued to promote in any way I could but I was running out of time. I am truly thankful for the amazing bunch of people who got behind me and contributed their own hard-earned cash, but I fell short of my goal, raising 65% of my target.

Of course, any funding is better than none but it wasn't enough to cover even the tightest of budgets. I had no choice but to continue looking for sponsors. I was working harder than ever to pull all the moving pieces together.

I questioned everything about the messaging of the Ultimate Triathlon. I thought it ticked all the boxes – it was a pioneering ultra-endurance triathlon full of extreme challenges, there would even be a film crew following this journey making a documentary, providing opportunities for product placement and branding within spectacular countryside. I was at my wit's end. Then I got a phone call.

'I'm really sorry Luke, but I have some paid work I've just been asked to do during the Ultimate Triathlon's timeframe, I need to take it.'

Six weeks out from the start of the challenge, and my filmmaker pulled out. The news hit me like a ton of bricks. I had been working crazy hours to raise funding, keep up my training and promote the challenge – and now this. The mountain I had been scaling for more than a year had suddenly become too big to climb.

There were no hard feelings towards Chris, the filmmaker. He was doing the job pro-bono with a share of revenue down the track. It was a huge ask to take three weeks out of his business, capture a vision of my swim, cycle and run across the 2000 kilometres, and produce a captivating story on the smell of an oily rag.

My head felt like it was about to explode. I was overwhelmed by all the things on my to do list, and it seemed every time I ticked an item as 'done' another two would be added. By the time I fell into bed in the wee hours I would be so wound up, sleep was impossible. How the hell was I going to make this come together?

All the while, I pushed my body through consistent 25 to 30 hour training weeks, maintained my personal training business, and fulfilled speaking engagements across the country. One thing I made sure of, was finding time to be with Vanda, the one person who helped me find some measure of calm.

From my perspective, life had lurched from 'out of control' to freewheeling into a deep abyss of survival. Everyone said I needed to slow down – my therapist, Vanda, family members, and close friends all expressed concern.

I couldn't see the point in slowing down. If I pulled back on anything, the event would not go ahead, and what would be the point of that? It's not like I had a team ready and waiting to help ease the workload. Slowing down was not an option, so I continued to drain my energy reserves and erode my psychological wellbeing. I was hanging on by a thread.

Thankfully, the wisdom of my parents was ringing through my head during this intense period: 'Do everything you can to achieve your dream, work hard and give yourself the best chance of success.' So I listened. I stayed positive, I did all I could, and I tried not to react to the other voice in my head, the one that said 'Just because you put your heart, your soul and every waking moment into this project, doesn't guarantee it will happen.'

12.

THE LAST MILE

After my interview on The Rich Roll Podcast, I was getting regular emails, and messages from people wishing me luck. Rich has a legion of fans all over the world and one of his listeners is a British guy by the name of Jay Cox. Unbeknownst to me, Jay heard my interview with Rich and had been following my journey ever since.

It was mid-week and I had just returned home after a long training ride. I was doing some stretching while I cooked a meal and in my usual multi-tasking way, picked up my phone to check my email. I laughed out loud as I read Jay's message. I could not believe what I was reading. Jay owns a video production company called Fizzeek Media and he wondered if I needed any help with promotional material or editing. Jay wanted to be part of my crazy challenge!

I clicked through to his website, saw some of his work and was impressed. I gave the garlic, onion and turmeric a quick stir in the coconut oil sizzling in the frying pan and wrote back.

'Thanks for your offer Jay, would you like to come along for the 12 days and film the documentary yourself?'

He replied 'YES,' and we arranged a time for a call the following day. As it turned out we spoke while I was out on my four hour training run, as I had no other free time during the day, but he didn't seem to mind.

Jay talked while I ran along the compacted trail that circles the beautiful Richmond Park, near where I live. He told me he finally 'worked up the courage' to make contact after hearing me on Rich's podcast, and his enthusiasm was contagious. He had been looking to collaborate on a big documentary project, and was waiting for the universe to give him direction! He wanted to start right away but I had to slow him down slightly, being careful not to kill his energetic buzz, and explain I had no budget to pay for his services up front. Hearing this didn't seem to faze Jay, but I wanted him to run it by his wife Katie first, as they had a family to take care of.

The following day he sent a message saying, 'I'm in,' and with six weeks to go, the Ultimate Triathlon documentary was back on!

I was now in my final training block. I wanted to give my mind and body one final test before I threw it into what I knew would be the toughest physical challenge of my life. I tried to mimic how my body would move, and what it would go through during the 12 days, but on a smaller and shorter scale. The final training plan looked like this:

Day One: 200 kilometre cycle, 3 kilometre ocean swim

Day Two: 6 kilometre ocean swim, 200 kilometre cycle

Day Three: 200 kilometre cycle

Day Four: 6 kilometre pool swim, 65 kilometre run

Day Five: 60 kilometre run

Day Six: 60 kilometre run

I wanted to replicate consecutive long days on the bike, followed by running, and throw in a few swims to keep me ticking along. I tried not to load up too much in the water, as I had ongoing pain deep in my shoulder joint from over-compensating with swim training after the bike crash in France.

Jay lives near the south coast of England, roughly 200 kilometres away – the perfect distance for my Saturday ride to kick off the final block of training. It would be the only chance I'd have to meet him before heading to our basecamp in Tarifa, Spain.

As I approached the coastal town of Boscombe, I shared my location with Jay using an app on my phone. My first encounter with him was on a busy dual carriageway as I was cycling into a head wind. I sensed a car moving at a similar speed I was travelling at on my bike. I assumed it was a random driver trying to get close enough to say hi or yell abuse, so I was alert to what might happen next.

'Hi Luke, having a good cycle?'

I looked over and saw a bald guy shouting out from the driver's seat with a camera mounted on the passenger side window, pointing right at me.

'You must be Jay,' I replied.

We laughed and he sped off up the road.

Vanda caught the train down from London, and met me at the apartment I'd rented for the night. The three of us arrived at the apartment simultaneously, not bad timing considering I cycled 200 kilometres, and Vanda caught three different trains to get there. We had a quick chat, before I grabbed my wetsuit and headed for the ocean. I gave Vanda a kiss before heading out on a three kilometre swim and whispered, 'Suss him out!' Even though I immediately liked Jay from our brief conversations, I wanted to be sure he was serious about the project. By the time I came back out of the water, Jay had the camera on me again as he was capturing some footage we could use in promotional video of my final training block.

We watched the sun set behind the resort town of Bournemouth as Jay asked me about the Ultimate Triathlon, about my background and my training as he filmed. I had a good feeling about the bloke.

Once the shoot was over Vanda and I walked back to the apartment to get ready for dinner.

'Jay is a winner, he's perfect,' said Vanda.

That was enough intel for me, Jay passed his Ultimate Triathlon job interview with flying colours.

The following morning Vanda and I were back at the beach at sunrise so I could squeeze a six kilometre swim in before breakfast, and start my 200 kilometre cycle back home. Vanda would reverse her trip back to London, catching several trains and carrying my swim kit plus the previous day's cycling kit with her.

The final leg of the cycling portion of my big training block was extremely important. I was sleep deprived and physically tired, with 400 kilometres worth of cycling in my legs – which was as close as I was going to get to replicate the Ultimate Triathlon. The major difference was, I also had a couple of clients to train after the day's cycle before collapsing into bed.

Over the next three days, I had only 185 kilometres left to run, and six kilometres of swimming to wrap up my block. Knowing I was so close to getting it done brought a smile to my face as I drifted off to sleep.

The long day ahead called for some mental preparation. I began my day visualising the next 18 hours, playing over in my head all I hoped to achieve throughout the day, then finished with some deep breathing.

I had two morning clients and a meeting with a potential sponsor before training. I got to the pool around midday and it took a while for me to switch off the negativity clouding my mind as I followed the black line below me. Each lap got easier as I absorbed the energy of the swimmers around me and before long, my watch had ticked over six kilometres, With the sun radiating off my bare back, I didn't want to leave the pool – now almost empty after the lunchtime swimmers disappeared. But it was time to run, and I was excited!

I hadn't been vertical for two hours, and now with very little blood supply flowing through to my legs they were a little shaky, and I looked like I'd had a few beers. But with each stride, I found a consistent rhythm and maintained it for the next seven hours.

I imagined shuffling along roads in the south of France, smelling the salty sea on the breeze with the sun warm on my neck – quite a stretch from the muddy waters of the Thames I was running alongside.

Following the trail that hugged the winding path along the river gave me some positive visual stimulus. I passed rowers making their way up and down the river, kayakers out for an afternoon paddle, and many other runners. My run was uneventful – I simply focused on putting one foot in front of the other. I was a little tired as I rounded the corner leading to my house, just as the numbers on my watch ticked over 65 kilometres. I was quite happy to walk the final 50 metres to my front door – my day was done!

The legs were a little stiff the next day and I followed the tow path once more, but in the opposite direction, heading into central London. As the landscape changed from a tree-lined dirt trail to high-rise apartment blocks, I had plenty of sights to take my mind off my sore and heavy legs.

But just over halfway into the run, my energy levels dropped and my legs began to throb, sending pulsating pain through my lower extremities. I slowed to a walk, dragging my feet as I tried to reset my mind. Endurance sports can be a fickle character, one minute you're riding the endorphins, the next, you could be close to tears, asking yourself 'Why?' In my experience, when it's the latter, self-doubt rises to the surface, compounding negative thoughts and you ask yourself, 'Should I give up?'

It's usually a rhetorical question (for me at least), and I remind myself to be clear on my 'why'. It is an essential part of endurance competition, and has helped me out of many 'I want to give up' moments.

'Clarity is the eternal energy that fuels our dreams.'

I came up with this mantra after a hard training session, and I bring it into my thoughts during difficult times. It has helped me through some pretty tough situations, training sessions, and times when I've lacked direction. It has also made me realise at times I do need to stop and focus on something completely different. It's a true leveller of what you want.

'The Ultimate Triathlon run leg isn't going to be easy mate, so suck this moment up, and let's move on,' I told myself. My 'why' for this run was to prepare my body and mind to run the equivalent of 14 marathons in seven days along the south of France.

I was very glad to get home that afternoon, and as I sat down after my usual recovery routine and started to refuel my body with some food, it suddenly dawned on me; I had an hour before I needed to make my way to the gym, for two clients I had scheduled.

The final day of the mammoth training block arrived, and with it, some sunshine to keep me in good spirits. I ran through Richmond Park and spoke to some of the smaller deer that roam freely across the park. Their spotted backs caught my eye and I remember thinking, 'I wonder how many spots each deer has on its back.'

A random thought by someone who was about to complete 50 hours of training in just six days – I was clearly getting tired. But after seven hours of running and some one-sided conversations with wildlife throughout Richmond Park, I was done. Not just finished for the day, or the week; I had completed my training for the Ultimate Triathlon. I was excited, anxious and tired, but I had done it. Best of all, I remained injury free throughout the biggest training week of my life. Apart from sore muscles, I felt great … clearly still riding that endorphin wave!

With only three weeks remaining, I still needed to finalise my crew. I had been in contact with numerous people to help me over the 12 days, and knew it wouldn't be easy going for those who chose to come along. I needed a mix of people to do the jobs of navigator, chef, motivator, medical officer, drill sergeant, comforter, logistics officer and so on. Vanda had offered to be my medical officer, and I accepted before she even finished asking. She had been treating my body for several months now, combining her skills of massage and dry needling with the knowledge she had gained during her Osteopathy and Exercise Physiology degrees.

Jay had been offered the job of cameraman, director and producer for the documentary, so I just had to find the rest of the crew.

Many months earlier, I had asked all my close friends, but asking busy people to give up three weeks of their time was a tall order. Six people said they could help out to some degree, but three said they could only do weekends. Another friend's work became busy, and the time she thought she could get off disappeared, so she was out.

Then, just as I was running out of people to ask, my phone rang and the name 'Warren Pole' displayed on my screen.

To say I was 'on edge' at this point would have been a huge understatement, I was freaking out. I tried to keep a cool and calm demeanour, but my head and heart were being pulled in every direction. My out-of-control existence was well and truly taking its toll on my physical, emotional, and psychological wellbeing. I tried to focus on what I could control and not dwell on the rest. I answered Warren's call.

'Hello mate, how're you doing today?' he asked.

'Good thanks mate,' I replied, a lie. But this phone call wasn't to check on my welfare, it was to tell me some news.

He and his lovely wife Erica wanted to be part of the Ultimate Triathlon support crew and offered to drive their 33Shake van down from the UK and use it as the official crew vehicle. That was the moment I knew for sure this crazy challenge was going to happen!

My crew was *finally* complete. Warren would be driver, navigator, and in charge of logistics. Erica would handle food preparation, and help navigate. Along with Vanda and Jay, I had four incredible people for the Ultimate Triathlon All-Star crew.

I now had less than three weeks until my adventure began, and physically, I was struggling. I was barely sleeping and my bones felt like they were full of lead. I was exhausted. I also felt I lacked time in the ocean, as I'd only had about six swims in salt water throughout the year. I thought I needed one more swim, so Vanda and I drove to the south coast of England to the seaside town of Brighton. The plan was to get there late morning, swim for 90 minutes, then jog together for half an hour along the cliff tops overlooking the English Channel.

The trip took about an hour from London and conversation was weirdly absent as we listened to the gentle hum of the tyres gripping the motorway. There was no tension between us, we were both excited for our future together and enjoying our relationship, but there was definitely a fog in the air.

We got out of the car and sat on a bench, gazing at the ocean in silence for what seemed like an eternity. With our eyes fixed on the horizon, and the ocean sparkling in the autumn sunshine, I felt nothing. My mind was blank, my body drained, and my energy tank had only a whiff of fuel.

'I can't do this!' I said to Vanda, 'I'm done.'

Without giving her the chance to respond, I followed up with my explanation.

It had nothing to do with the late September water temperature, or the fact that swimming was my weakest discipline, or that my motivation was at an all-time low. After stopping and letting my mind slow down, I realised I wasn't just burning the candle from both ends, but there was no candle left. I needed complete rest and recuperation to rebuild my mind and body in the three weeks before I would tackle the Ultimate Triathlon.

I was physically and emotionally exhausted, completely burnt out.

We walked together through the maze-like lanes in and around Brighton, past the touristy gift shops, edgy clothing stores, and tattoo shops scattered amongst the quirky restaurants. We found a place to sit and eat, and have our first real conversation of the day, even though it was now well into the afternoon.

Eventually, after a long meal, chatting about anything but training and the Ultimate Triathlon, we headed back up to London, and had an early night. For the first time in months, I had a full night's sleep.

Two weeks before heading to Morocco, I received a call from a marathon runner I'd trained with earlier on in the year. He wondered if there was still time to get on board and have his company sponsor the Ultimate Triathlon.

He liked my message and work ethic, and he knew how hard I was pushing to make this dream of mine come true, so he offered some cash, just enough to fuel the 33Shake van and help with food and accommodation costs.

It was a much-needed contribution at the absolute eleventh hour. Now all I had to do was to swim, cycle, and run 2000 kilometres in 12 days from Morocco to Monaco.

13.

THE ULTIMATE TRIATHLON: JUST KEEP SWIMMING

The Strait of Gibraltar swim window was due to open in a few days so I settled into our Tarifa apartment with Jay, Warren and Erica. Vanda had work and study commitments back in London, and would meet us later in the week.

There was a sense of calm before the storm, both metaphorically and literally, as we watched dark, menacing clouds gather overhead.

Over the next few days we sorted out my kit for the swim and the rest of the trip. We packed and re-packed the plastic containers that would fill the crew's van and be my lifeline throughout the event; the medical supplies, food and utensils, a spare bike, and Jay's camera equipment. The crew's personal bags were strewn across the open-plan living room of our southern Spanish base.

The rental apartment had a rooftop area where we would practise yoga, meditate, or simply sit and gaze at the view, whenever there was a break in the weather.

TV aerials dotted the terracotta-tiled roofs of the whitewashed buildings, and, in the distance across the Strait of Gibraltar, was a clear view of the landmass that was Morocco.

Seeing Africa as I sat in Spain made the adventure come to life in my head. I was here, it was happening, and any sense of emotional exhaustion was quickly replaced with excitement. Mentally, I was ready, and nothing would stop me from completing the swim from Morocco to Spain. Or so I thought.

I walked with the crew down to the old part of town along the uneven cobblestone streets. Above us, timber shutters framed the windows and planter boxes hung from window ledges. Old wooden signs advertising restaurants and cafes added to the rustic feel of this old fort town. Eventually, after taking several wrong turns down the narrow and crooked streets, we found the building we were looking for.

Anybody wishing to swim across the Strait of Gibraltar will get to know Rafael Gutiérrez Mesa, the President of Associación Cruce a Nado Estrecho de Gibraltar or ACNEG. The swim briefing would take place at his office in Tarifa.

I had been in contact with Rafael for over two years, and had been clear about my desire to swim across the Strait in the non-traditional direction, starting in Morocco. My friend and coach, world-class open water swimmer Adam Walker swam from Morocco to Spain on the return leg of his two-way Strait of Gibraltar crossing. He had reassured Rafael that I would be fine with the more difficult direction of the swim.

'I understand you prefer to start in Morocco?' said the burly

Spanish man in his heavily accented English.

This shocked me for a split second, and a rapid fire 'Yes' came straight back as Jay filmed us gathered around a nautical map.

'Why?' Rafael asked.

What the hell is this guy talking about? We've spoken for years about this, and now he suddenly has amnesia …

But I kept my thoughts to myself and tried to stay calm. I replied to Rafael with a cool but serious tone, explaining that, as discussed, my challenge is from Morocco to Monaco, not the other way around.

He told me that the swim would be more difficult, which I already knew, then hit me with new information that felt like a punch in the gut.

He drew a squiggly line on the plastic covered map on his office wall, highlighting the usual route from Spain to Morocco, explaining the swim could be 17 or 18 kilometres in distance.

Then in a forceful manner, he drew a straight line, starting from the northwestern coastline side of the Moroccan Peninsula, just east of Tangier, and firmly stated, 'It is a double! I can count on this, it's more difficult, and you have the probability of not finishing.'

Due to the extreme currents, he was advising me to start closer to the western Moroccan coastline to give myself a better chance of getting further into the Strait before its invisible forces dragged me into the Mediterranean. The current could potentially push me beyond the designated finishing area of the southern Spanish coastline, and I'd fail in my attempt to swim the Strait of Gibraltar.

My stomach clenched on hearing this critical piece of information. I was shocked, and if I'm honest, a little angry. In all the years of communication about the swim, I was never told the reverse direction would be double the distance.

The news sunk in immediately and I had to decide; do I start in Morocco to keep the Morocco to Monaco name alive, and risk not completing the swim? The chance of failure was high, as I hadn't prepared to be in the water for that length of time. Or the flip side of this coin, do I do the swim distance I had prepared for, just in the opposite direction – from Spain to Morocco?

I had around 30 seconds to decide. The conversation was going around in circles and emotions were starting to bubble up. I reminded myself of the goal for Day One: swim across the Strait of Gibraltar *and* cycle 100 kilometres from Tarifa to Marbella. If I spent most of the day swimming followed by four to five hours cycling over the hilly region beyond Tarifa, how much time would I have left for sleep before Day Two started?

All these thoughts were flying through my mind, along with the fact that I had been planning and organising this challenge for years, and now a large chunk of it was being flipped on its head. It was all a bit hard to take in.

Externally, I stayed calm. Despite the chaotic discussion inside my head, I made a decision. I confidently pointed to the map on the wall and said, 'let's move forward, we do the normal route from Spain to Morocco.' It was done!

With that out of the way, I sat down with Rafael to discuss the logistics of the swim, including the danger posed by the hundreds of large tankers crossing the ocean passage during my swim. Then there was the weather. Over the coming days, horrible wet and windy conditions had been forecast.

'I'll call you at 4 p.m. the day before we plan to try and swim, if you don't hear from me by 4 p.m., then we don't go the following day.' Each of us shook hands with Rafael and said our goodbyes, hoping the weather would soon clear. I only had a week-long window before the next athlete came into town to attempt their crossing. Jay was also on a limited timeframe, as he had taken leave from his full-time job. If I didn't start the clock for the 12 day Ultimate Triathlon by the week's end, he would be forced to fly back to the UK, and I'd be left without a cameraman, director and producer.

I had bottled up a lot during the discussion with Rafael, and once we emerged from his office I needed to release the emotional pressure. We found a quiet side street where Jay set up a tripod, began recording and slowly backed away from me, not knowing what would happen next.

I didn't yell or scream, there was no rage – that's not my style. I didn't see the point in wasting what little energy I had in my weary body. But frustration boiled over and I was upset. Upset that the Ultimate Triathlon wouldn't be perfect. I had researched and planned meticulously. It was a difficult project to get up and running, and now a major part of it had changed. In my eyes this was a setback, one that I needed a few minutes to deal with.

We make plans in life and things change. We get hit with setbacks all the time. I find it helpful to accept what has happened, then adapt in a way to give yourself the best possible chance to achieve your initial goal. So, this is what I did, in a quiet street in Tarifa, moments after hearing news that was difficult to swallow, I looked directly at the camera and expressed how I was feeling. To me, swimming from Spain to Morocco, not the reverse, was a huge deal, but to the world out there, it was nothing.

With a few tears, I released the emotional weight and expressed my frustration that my challenge may not be perfect – but few things in life are perfect. I looked at the obstacle with a clear mind, processed the information and adapted to the setback. With that, I was ready to move forward. I wanted to focus only on the things I could control; something I constantly strive to do every day.

We now had a new plan and I wanted all of us to get prepared as best we could, physically and mentally, for several days of waiting for the weather to clear, so the 2000 kilometre adventure could begin!

Back at the apartment, Jay and I were sorting through a bag of numerous electrical appliances. We had them spread across the floral sofa that doubled as Jay's bed when my mobile phone rang; it was my mum calling from Bathurst.

'Hi Mate, how are you?'

I knew instantly something was wrong, and she knew I knew something was wrong. Mum and I usually Skype. We never communicate the traditional way by calling each other on the phone.

'Fine, what's wrong Mum?' I cautiously asked.

'Your Uncle Phil had a heart attack, he is OK, but he's in hospital and having surgery tomorrow.'

The news took the wind out of me. I walked onto the small balcony with distant views of the ocean. I grabbed the cold, wet railing as the rain pelted down, the words not quite sinking in. This was my Uncle Phil who spent endless hours kicking a football with me in my Gran's backyard all those years ago. The man I looked up to, who in my eyes, was invincible.

Mum did her best to downplay the situation, as she knew what I was facing. But she also knew I would want to know about Uncle Phil and promised she'd keep me updated with any developments. Warren, Erica, and Jay were anxiously waiting inside to hear what the phone call was all about, looking concerned. My body language must have said it all.

My crew were very much my family for this trip, and like any close family who care deeply for one another, we sat down and talked. They kept me in good spirits, but we also had to focus on what we'd come here to do. I knew, as did my family back in Australia, that if Uncle Phil was here with me in Tarifa, he would simply tell me to 'get on with it.' So, that was my plan.

The next day, between the torrential rainstorms blowing in from the North Atlantic, I went out for a short run. It was my first bit of exercise in nearly a month. I ran out along the costal path hugging the sandy beaches of Tarifa for 10 minutes, spun around and made my way back to the apartment.

The 20 minutes I spent shuffling along the sand-covered concrete pathway confirmed how I felt – completely drained. I needed a few minutes to stop and think so I sat down on a wooden bench to rest my legs. My entire body was exhausted. It was going to be a mental slog for 12 days once I got started.

The next few days were spent waiting, while we watched the rain come down. Our rooftop yoga sessions switched to the lounge room after we pushed the furniture to the edge of the room.

I knew the crew would be taking care of me over the next few weeks, so I took this opportunity to look after them, and spent the afternoon preparing and cooking dinner.

Spending time in the kitchen has always bought me a sense of calm – it's a form of mindfulness training for me. I'm 100% present, thinking about cooking methods, ingredients and timing, allowing my mind to drift into neutral. Right now, I needed some calm, as Uncle Phil was having surgery, the swim window had opened, but the weather wasn't looking like it would ease anytime soon. While my crew bent, twisted and breathed into each yoga pose, I was in my happy place, switched off from the world.

Each afternoon as 4 p.m. came and went without a call from Rafael, we realised we would be bunkered down together for at least another 36 hours.

One evening, after nearly a week in Spain with no news of a swim start, we washed a load of towels, and went out to find a laundromat to dry them, before heading to a supermarket to buy dinner. It was 7:30 p.m. We couldn't find anywhere to spin dry the towels, and as I daydreamed about recipes using the plump, red tomatoes sitting in front of me at the supermarket, my phone rang.

'So, the weather looks not so good, and not so bad in the morning, I think we will try to go then. Please come to the port at 8 a.m., if it's OK, we go at 8:30,' said Rafael so nonchalantly, he could have been inviting me to breakfast in the morning.

This is it … the Ultimate Triathlon may *soon be starting!*

That night was a bit of a blur, sorting out last minute preparations for both the swim and cycle legs of Day 1, while we cooked and ate dinner, in typical Spanish style at around 10:30 p.m.

I showered and laid out my swim trunks, wetsuit, Dryrobe and shoes, ready for the morning. At 1 a.m. I said 'goodnight' to the crew knowing when I woke up from a few hours' sleep, I would be swimming to Africa!

'Go to sleep Luke' my mind kept telling me, but to no effect. I was excited for the swim and couldn't shut my brain off as I visualised going through the process I'd been practising for years, feeling the water against my skin, and mentally checking my technique.

In reality, I was rugged up and feeling the warmth of my blankets, but my brain imagined this heat was coming from the sun's rays beaming down onto my neoprene-covered body gliding through the water.

No matter what I did, I couldn't shut off my thoughts about swimming. The excitement that I was about to begin the Ultimate Triathlon was overwhelming. So instead of fighting it, I went along with the fantasies my brain was producing.

I did not sleep a wink. My alarm buzzed loudly at 6 a.m. to signify it was 'game day' and not surprisingly, I felt a little groggy when I stood up.

DAY ONE

PLANNED SWIM:
TARIFA TO MOROCCO
16-18 KILOMETRES

There was a real sense of *this is happening* for us all in the apartment and our energy quickly shifted as a result. Erica began preparing my swim bag with the nutrition I would use to get me from Spain to Africa. Several 33Shake chia energy gels, and a bottle of water mixed with maca, a Peruvian root I've used for many years. It has a malty flavour that sits easily in my stomach while exercising, as well as being nutrient dense and full of vitamins and minerals to help keep my body functioning efficiently. My choice for getting vital nutrients I'd need for the entire challenge was by eating only real, non-processed food.

I prepared my own breakfast – one I eat most days back home in London, an avo mash. It goes something like this: mash up an avocado (or two if you're doing an endurance event) add loads of seeds, nuts, and superfood powders like maca, raw cacao, spirulina and cinnamon, mix in fresh citrus juice, followed by coconut cream for a big green bowl of creamy, crunchy, chocolatey goodness – yum!

Jay was sorting out his camera kit, while Warren was taking the bags full of kit and food down to the van. There wasn't a lot of chatter other than a few bad jokes from me trying to make light of what was about to go down. I don't like things too serious.

Mostly we were focused on having everything we needed to get me across the Strait of Gibraltar to Morocco.

The crew took the short drive down to the port together, as I wrapped myself in a Dryrobe for a pre-dawn walk through the old town where I would meet the crew, and Rafael.

The air was crisp against my cleanly shaven face as I strolled through the ancient town. The whispering I could hear in my head was my mind readying itself.

I enjoyed a moment of quiet solitude, just as I would have before I left for a game during my footballing days. I'd focus on positive reinforcement and remind myself I had done all I could to prepare for what lay ahead. I ticked off a mental checklist as

I weaved my way alongside the mural-covered walls that made up the labyrinth of Tarifa's old town.

As I strolled through an arched walkway I was reminded of the hundreds of nights I walked through dark tunnels in the stadiums I played at around the world. I thought of those damp, cold concrete walls and running out into the blinding floodlights, which lit up the field where I would do battle for the next 90 minutes.

But, as I approached the end of this tunnel, there were no lights, there was no cheering crowd, or grassy covered stage; all I could see as I lifted my head, was an endless space stretching out to the horizon. The dark mass of water stared back at me, waiting, inviting the challenge. I was about to be as far out of my comfort zone as I had ever been.

The crew waited at the port with the few bags I'd packed with essential kit. Then a figure appeared out of the pre-dawn darkness, it was Rafael.

'The weather is better than expected,' he said.

A shot of adrenaline pulsed through my body and my heart pounded against my ribcage. Rafael confirmed the swim was on.

Erica boarded the small support boat that would cruise beside me, giving directional or speed-related instructions. She would also feed me every hour from this vessel, signalled by a loud blow of a whistle.

Warren wrapped his arms around me and gave me a strong and confident pat on my back, then stood back as Jay and I boarded the larger lead boat. The lead boat would communicate with the huge shipping tankers coming through the Strait of Gibraltar, as well as any domestic watercraft in the area.

We left the harbour with the morning's sun trying to pull itself up and over the horizon, from the opposite end of the Mediterranean Sea.

I was concerned about the swim. I was nervous, I didn't know what to expect. I wanted to get going but I just wasn't confident in my physical ability. Mentally, I was good.

The official start line of the Ultimate Triathlon would be from a rocky plateau at the edge of the southern most point in Tarifa, only approachable via boat.

It was a 15 minute boat trip out of the port and through the choppy swell, and I could feel the intense beating of my heart through my tight-fitting wetsuit. Another shot of adrenaline burst into my bloodstream with each bump of the boat's hull against the waves. We were now well beyond the secluded waters of Tarifa's harbour and exposed to the might of the ocean.

I looked to my right, watching the salty whitewash roll up to where I would soon begin my swim, then 180 degrees to my left, looking out at the route I would be following, and searching for the distant land with lights glittering in the pre-dawn darkness. My head turned slowly back and I gazed straight ahead, peering deep into Jay's camera lens.

Without thinking I sang, 'I'm so excited and I just can't hide it,' in an unexpected nervous outburst, before my mood returned to a more focused approach.

I was ready to begin; ready to see what I was capable of, and find out who Luke Tyburski The Adventurer really is.

I slipped off the edge of the boat and into the surprisingly warm water, and began rolling my arms over, past the small red dingy Erica was in and towards the start line.

After a 20 metre warm up, I reached out and held a chunk of rock on the shoreline. I noticed a rocky perch protruding off the island under the waterline – the starting block for my swim.

Within seconds, a whistle sounded, then all I heard was a mix of accents yelling, 'Go, go, go!' But I wouldn't be rushed setting off; I would begin when I was ready. I adjusted my goggles, took a deep breath, and internally screamed *'Let's do this,'* before I pushed away from Spain, and set off in an adrenaline-fuelled frantic state, swimming into the unknown.

I felt like I was in a washing machine. I was in a state of panic, I was exhilarated, I was freaking out, I was excited.

The adrenaline rush was intense. My stroke rate was rapid and my heart rate powerful. I had no self-belief at that moment but I kept swimming and swimming and swimming as the waves lifted me up and dropped me on the other side, lifted me up again and dropped me. Getting a rhythm was tough.

The thought *'What are you doing Luke?* rang through my head as my arms spun out of control up and out of the choppy water. My body was being thrown around as I focused on my current negative mindset that was trying to convince me to stop.

You cannot do this, you shouldn't do this, and you will never make it. How are you going to swim in these conditions for five, six, or even seven hours? What's the point of all this?

The little man of negativity was running around in my head screaming like the world was about to end.

My stroke rate was extremely high as was the amount of effort I put into each arm movement. This elevated my heart rate to a point where I gasped for air every time I turned towards the red support boat. The only comfort at that point was having Erica in my line of sight for each breath.

During these distressing 45 minutes, my confidence played hide and seek; I searched for a glimpse of this invisible power, but it did an amazing job of evading me. I tried to settle my nerves and heart rate by focusing on my training and preparation but to no avail. I was left to battle through the waves at an unsustainable pace, using what felt like a foreign technique.

At times, I had plenty of water underneath me to pull myself through, but other times when riding the crest of these waves, there was very little water to grab hold of to propel me forward. After a while I realised my heart rate had dropped, my inner turmoil had resolved itself, and I settled into a familiar technique following my swimming mantra: *don't waste a stroke!*

The whistle sounded rounding off the first hour of the swim and Erica threw out a 33Shake chia energy gel attached to a carabineer and rope. At that point, my body had become accustomed to the unsteady conditions, and I had finally discharged four years' worth of built up nerves. The Ultimate Triathlon was underway!

My mind had calmed, I was now 100% in the moment.

I can do this.

After a quick feed, I focused on getting back into a rhythm, with my mantra murmuring in the background. I was feeling comfortable.

The second hour flew by while I gazed into the deep blue abyss below me. My body continued to swim on autopilot, I was completely lost in the rhythm. The whistle for my second feed startled me.

I was now relaxed enough to notice the Strait coming to life around me. Giant shipping tankers moved slowly through the headlands bookending Europe and Africa, some exiting the Mediterranean Sea and out into the open ocean, others looking to unload at a designated port.

At a glance, some of the ships carried more than 50 containers. I tried to count as I swam; 10, 11, 12 across, and stacked four or five on top of one another.

Erica grabbed my attention with her whistle and I figured I was at the three-hour mark, and my next feed.

After a brief stop and a few mouthfuls of chia energy gel while floating on my back like an otter, I rolled back over and set off to find my rhythm.

I had never swum for more than three hours in one stretch, so I was about to head into unchartered territory. The water was still quite choppy and I struggled to maintain my rhythm. I focused on putting one arm in front of the other, nothing else.

I was feeling positive so I let my mind wander.

I can do this, I feel good, if this is how difficult it's going to be, then this swim is in the bag!

I should have known better than to get too confident. Endurance sports can be volatile – you get caught up in the good moments only to be sucked way down when things take a turn for the worse, as they invariably do.

The water for some strange reason had become like thick, sticky treacle. My arms felt like they were full of concrete, and there was an invisible force trying to hold me back and drag me under the oncoming waves. I was initially confused and had no idea why I felt so physically drained – I'd eaten enough and was in relatively good spirits, but it was like someone had flicked a switch and I was out of power. Could I possibly be that tired so suddenly?

Erica and the captain of the small boat started yelling but I couldn't make out what they were saying. I swam closer to the boat, and heard clearly, 'Swim faster, go, go, go! The currents are picking up and are strong, go, go, go Luke!'

I knew at some point in the swim, the currents would interfere and I would hear these words, but that didn't make things any easier.

So, I focused on my mantra, and swam with more energy and purpose; this was getting serious.

I was swimming 95% flat out, intentionally saving a little in my tank for later, knowing I'd need it.

The currents and swell pushed and pulled me in several directions and sprinting was awkward and difficult. My energy dropped and my stroke efficiency plummeted, but there was no holding back now.

Crunch!

My right shoulder pinched and I felt a twinge deep inside the joint. Pain ricocheted with every movement of my right arm. I slowed down and immediately heard louder screams from Erica telling me to swim faster. I needed to figure out a way of managing the intense pain, while maintaining my speed.

I changed the angle of my arm and skimmed it along the water, which helped somewhat, but overall, nothing affected the pain levels – this was my new normal.

I thought about the endless hours swimming up and down pools and around lakes in my training, preparing for this very moment. I knew I'd done the work – physically and mentally.

Many times, during my training swims, I visualised being deep into my cross-continental swim, exhausted and battling the elements, thinking of different scenarios, including injuring my shoulder.

You've been here before and won I told myself, to help boost my confidence.

I replayed many of the scenarios I had practised, and experimented with varying techniques to minimise the pain. I tried to focus on the one thing I had control over – the self-talk between my ears.

The conditions and the shoulder pain were both out of my control, so I had to call on my own personal cheer squad, *you can do this Luke.*

At the centre of my mind was that I had swum longer than ever before, and that the Moroccan coastline was getting closer. I focused on these two facts with each individual stroke and it helped keep me calm and positive. I slipped back into an almost comatose state and reached into my reserves to give 100% effort. I was experiencing the pain of my shoulder and the exhaustion of my body, but I could mentally block out the sensation of discomfort and urged myself to focus only on positives. The whistle blew loudly and pulled my mind back to reality.

I flipped over on my back and sucked down another chia energy gel in between deep, heavy breaths while Erica yelled at me to swim faster as the currents were getting even stronger.

Although I could clearly see the Moroccan shore, I knew it was further than my brain was telling me – but it did give me a much-needed lift knowing with each stroke I was getting closer.

With my mantra of *don't waste a stroke* still playing in my head, I blocked out my shoulder pain and fatigue with positive talk as I accelerated through the water.

Filling my head with uplifting thoughts definitely helped to keep me in the present moment as I struggled to get enough oxygen into my lungs and gasped for air every two strokes. My wetsuit felt like it was crushing my lungs and a burning sensation spread through my chest. I realised this was it – this was the challenge I had been looking for.

With what felt like miniature fireballs shooting into my shoulder joint with each stroke, I willed my arms to keep moving as I remembered the many hours of training I'd completed over the past three years. I refused to give in. I knew if I remained positive and embraced the pain rather than fight it, I would open up a new realm of possibility. So, I gritted my teeth, focused on not wasting a stroke, and zoned out again into a meditative state.

A change in my immediate surroundings broke me from my trance. I was half expecting a whistle to signify another feed, but the lead boat I had been trailing behind, like a lure at the end of a fishing line, peeled off to reveal the rocky coastline and emerald green hills of northern Morocco.

I was now through the worst stage of the swim, and on the home straight. For the first time, I felt a sense of relief. All that was left to do was to get across the bay to complete a swim I'd always thought was a little crazy – across the Strait of Gibraltar!

I smiled at Erica, as the support boat drifted closer to me. I have no idea if she saw me, or had any clue how important her presence had been for me, hearing her encouragement while stopping briefly for a feed and simply seeing her familiar face continually kept me calm and focused.

This was a moment to celebrate and without making a conscious decision, I casually rolled onto my back and started to swim backstroke. Being playful in that very moment was my way of congratulating myself and celebrating what I had just achieved.

I tried to shout out to Erica 'we did it', but my words sounded more like a gurgle, as water spilled into my mouth each time I opened it.

In her thick Italian accent, she yelled at me for a final time, 'you did it, this is Morocco!'

Right at that moment, for the first time in over five hours, I could see the ocean floor. It looked like it was scampering up towards me from the depths so I reached out with both hands and grabbed on to a solid piece of earth.

I had done it!

My legs were shaking as I stood up, and I nearly fell back into the sea. I bellowed 'WOO WOO WOO' while spinning both arms around like a windmill, totally ignoring the sharp pain piercing through my right shoulder.

I bent down to kiss the ground of Morocco, my lips touching a soft, but slightly slimy substance covering the rocks – seaweed. For some strange reason I thought, 'eat some of it!' I knew that many types of seaweed contained vital minerals like potassium, iron, and magnesium, and I could use some of those now! I chuckled to myself, before pausing and taking in a panoramic, 360 degree mental photograph of my surroundings.

A huge wave of self-accomplishment washed over me, and I was grinning from ear to ear. I worried more about completing the swim than anything else related to the Ultimate Triathlon. This was a massive achievement for me, and there was no hiding my pride – I was beaming with joy from the inside out!

My spirits were high as I paddled back to the lead boat for the 45 minute trip back to Tarifa – I couldn't contain my happiness. After giving Erica and Jay massive hugs I found out just how far I had swum – almost 25 kilometres! I nearly fell overboard.

I reflected on what I had just achieved as we all made our way back across the Strait of Gibraltar to Spain.

Warren was there to greet us at the port and tell us lunch was ready and the van packed. After more than five hours in the water, I had an hour to shower, eat, and get on the bike to finish Day One of the Ultimate Triathlon.

Completed Swim: Tarifa to Morocco (Point Leona) | 25 kilometres | 5 hours 11 minutes.

DAY ONE (AFTERNOON)

PLANNED CYCLE: TARIFA TO MARBELLA | 97 KILOMETRES

Replacing a wetsuit with my Teenage Mutant Ninja Turtle cycling jersey was like putting on a different superhero cape, I felt invincible!

My confidence was sky high, with plenty of positive adrenaline running through my body to help get me up and over the surrounding hills of Tarifa.

The afternoon was perfect for a cycle, with temperatures of around 27 degrees Celsius as I hugged the winding Mediterranean coastline.

It was beautiful out on the road as I negotiated my trusty two-wheeled steed past wind turbines nestled up in the hills. I repeatedly glanced to my right, seeing the sun's rays sparkling on the surface of the Mediterranean. Morocco was clearly visible.

'I swam there!' I said out loud, before throwing my head back in laughter. My tongue had swelled to almost twice its size from the salty water during the five-hour swim, which made for an interesting noise when I laughed.

The sun was slowly setting behind me and its afternoon warmth felt like a hug from my mum when I was a child. I smiled as I thought about riding my bike down the laneway of our Bathurst house all those years ago … I was a long way from home now though.

The Ultimate Triathlon was intended to be shared with friends, family and followers worldwide via social media, but as we were operating on a tight budget and minimal crew, updating social media fell on the shoulders of yours truly!

I tweeted and shared messages on Facebook and Instagram, and updated all those who were following me live via the interactive tracking app on my phone as I cycled.

The crew managed as much as they could, but updating social media was the last thing on their mind – their main concerns were getting me fed and safely to the end of each day.

Both shoulders ached, my right one to the point I could barely hold onto the handlebars as I cycled. But aside from the pain, I was loving life, so for the remaining time I was on the bike on this 'warm up' day I tried to remind myself I was living my dream!

* * *

In the six months leading up to the Ultimate Triathlon, I mostly trained alone, and it was the same now, apart from the occasional sighting of the crew when they pulled over to cheer me on, or provide directions. So, when a group of 15 or so cyclists flew past, I tagged onto the back of the group.

It was great to be in a pack and be part of a large working organism, all striving for the same goal; to get down the road as quickly and efficiently as possible.

But it didn't last long; my legs started to prickle while sustaining the increased pace and I could see the group starting to stretch out – the pace had quickened. I toyed with the idea to stick on the back of the pack for the final stretch into Marbella, but soon reality hit home – they were too fast, so I watched them race one another into the distance.

When I saw a sign saying MARBELLA, I let out a cheer – Day One was all but over!

I followed the crew to the outskirts of town before they disappeared into the distance. Shortly after, they waved me into a parking area, I assumed for the place we'd be staying that night – and I was more than ready to stop for the day. At the hotel check-in desk, we were told the address was correct, but hotel we'd reserved had moved two kilometres up the road – back in the direction I had just cycled. Talk about confusing, and frustrating!

In hindsight, this was probably a sign of how the Ultimate Triathlon was going to play out, but at that moment, late into the first evening of our journey we couldn't do anything but laugh. We eventually found our place of rest, and wrapped up the first day of the challenge I'd dreamt of creating all those years ago.

Completed Cycle: Tarifa to Marbella | 97 kilometres | 4 hours 12 minutes

DAY TWO

PLANNED CYCLE: MARBELLA TO CARBONERAS 350 KILOMETRES

A blinding light woke me up from my four-hour slumber, and I opened my eyes to see Jay's camera lens, only centimetres from my face.

'How do you feel?' Jay whispered from the darkness.

'A bit tired, I feel rough!' I croaked.

My shoulder was stiff and I struggled to move it without pain. My body, well it wanted to stay in bed, but my mind was primed and ready to jump on the bike and cycle *all day!*

After wolfing down my bowl of avo mash, I was keen to get going. While I was out on the bike, the crew would detour to the airport to collect Vanda. Having my caring girlfriend around was an emotional bonus – she had been with me in the trenches over the past few months – plus the added benefit of her professional expertise; as an exercise physiologist, massage therapist, and on the final leg of an intense four-year Masters of Osteopathy, I knew at the very least she could patch me up!

The day began well, the horizon of the Costa del Sol glowed with such intensity I pulled my bike over to the side of the road to watch the sun rise. Beams of light created an aura that shot up into the sky and across the sea. It was both spectacular and humbling, and a moment I will never forget.

The pristine water running parallel to the road kept me company, reminding me why my body felt stiff and tired, and why I had pain shooting up into my shoulder. Yesterday's swim had left its mark on me physically, but I still smiled when I glanced over and locked eyes with Morocco.

The first few hours passed quickly; the small coastal towns began to wake up around mid-morning, shopkeepers rolled up their shutters and the streets filled with traffic and pedestrians heading to work. Spain was coming alive.

At times, I cycled only centimetres from the white sandy beaches and could feel the crisp coastal breeze coming off the salty Mediterranean, hitting my face as I spun my legs and pushed down onto the pedals. It was a magical morning.

I restocked my jersey pocket with almonds, my mix of sunflower seed and cacao nibs and a few 33Shake chia energy gels, and waved the crew off to collect Vanda.

It would be a few hours before I saw them again and I was fine with that – all I had to do was stay on one road, and with plenty of miles ahead I was enjoying being lost in my surroundings. And then – my first flat tyre.

Luckily, I've had plenty of practice changing flats – usually dodging cars along narrow English roads in mid-winter, so I had no problem using a footpath in the Spanish sunshine.

The day was perfect for cycling; the sun warmed my bones and bronzed the exposed skin on my legs, arms, and neck. I wound my way around the idyllic coastline, sweeping in and out of horseshoe-shaped bays, and through small villages. I was grateful to be completing this mammoth challenge, and grateful to be alive.

The coastal road would take me inland briefly, up small, but punchy climbs to the top of the opposite side of the sparkling bays. The spectacular views were energising and encouraged me to keep pushing myself. Once I negotiated the narrow winding roads, I could look back and see my morning's effort – the coastline stood out remarkably well against the glistening turquoise of the sea.

I noticed two cyclists coming towards me, their loaded pannier bags hanging over their rear wheel suggesting they were on an adventure themselves, so I waved them down.

They made up half of a group of friends cycling from France to the bottom of Spain, finishing in Tarifa. I told them I was doing the same route in the opposite direction.

It had taken them 'four long weeks' they told me, and then laughed when I told them it would take me 'four long days'. They realised I was serious when I explained a little more about the Ultimate Triathlon. It was a brief and chance encounter but we found a connection through our chosen cycling routes. After a few high fives, and a quick photo, I was off!

A little further on, I spotted the crew's van parked in a lookout area, and with the team was Vanda. As soon as I saw her I felt an injection of love, hope and energy flood through me. I pulled over and gave her a huge, lingering hug.

The Ultimate Triathlon crew was complete! I filled my water bottles, topped up food supplies, and gave the guys my sob story about having to change the tyre without them. We had a laugh before I was on my way.

Next stop, lunch!

Another hour or so up the road and I met the crew in a supermarket car park (luxury right!) and munched on a family sized salad bulked out with seeds, chickpeas, and generous glugs of olive oil. It was tasty and nutrient-dense, exactly what my body needed. I used my phone to update social media of the morning's activities, and took off down thc road again.

The views kept getting better – hilltop villages overlooking the coast with its sandy beaches and rugged shoreline. I buzzed with excitement – this was me feeling truly alive.

I could see clearly where I was headed. Each mini peninsula was my next target as I continued to take in the beauty around me. Passing Almeria, I needed to head slightly inland, and as I approached the junction, contrary to my research, it turned out to be a motorway. Although *technically* illegal, cycling on the motorway was the best way to get me up the coast without having to navigate narrow winding roads, and head further inland. Day Two was already a 350 kilometre session, but without the help of the A-7 it could have easily passed 400 kilometres.

I battled constant honks as disapproving motorists sped by, and as day transitioned into night, I passed the exit where my crew was waiting. I didn't want to pull into the service bay, I just wanted to get off the busy motorway and finish for the day.

It's a true test of your wits to cycle on a long straight road at night with cars zooming by your ears at roughly 130 kilometres per hour. Further complicating this stretch was all the debris of vehicles, stones and chunks of tar – it's like cycling through landmines, waiting for one to go off and pop a tyre. So, I guess it was only a matter of time before I had that sinking feeling of the wheel rim rolling along the road's hard surface – puncture two of the day!

It was pitch black, and whilst I wore a glowing safety vest and had flashing lights on my bike, it's never a good idea to be on the side of a motorway changing a tyre. Luckily the crew wasn't far behind and pulled over to help.

They wanted to move me to the other side of the guardrail where it was safer, but I put my foot down. I asked someone to grab the spare wheel from the van to quickly change it over, and I would be off in a few minutes. I didn't want to hang about on the motorway, and getting me over the guardrail and back again was a waste of time. No one argued with my request, and we quickly swapped over the wheel to keep me moving.

We arranged to have dinner around 9 p.m., and the crew found a service station just off a motorway exit. I sat on the van's tailgate and munched down another 'bucket' of vegetables, seeds, nuts and legumes.

The next stretch was tough – it was dark, the roads were straight and boring and I struggled to stay awake. The crew continued to leap frog ahead as I put more kilometres behind me.

The road became undulating and most of the vehicles alongside me were large trucks. I pushed my weary body up and over the climbs, before tucking into an aero position to cut through the wind during the descents to preserve energy any way I could.

The moon was brilliant and lit up the rocky hills exposing their rawness. It was my guiding light and I smiled up at it many times – I felt at times, it smiled right back. It was approaching midnight as I edged my way up and over another long climbing section of motorway. As I flew down the other side I realised there was an increasing amount of vibration coming through my seat – I had a rear flat, my third flat in one day!

At midnight on a motorway, I reacted the only way I thought might help; I threw back my head and laughed. It was my way of focusing my energy on things I could control, and right now, that was to keep my spirits high!

I didn't bother calling the crew, as I knew I could have it changed by the time they arrived, plus the activity would keep me warm. I jumped over the guardrail and with the help of my bike lights and phone torch, got the job done.

The crew was waiting for me at exit 520, and seeing the silver VW van as I peeled off the motorway onto a small country road bought a huge smile to my face; it was time for today to end.

The remaining 15 kilometres took me along relatively flat but winding roads, and when the crew asked if I wanted to stop and rest I replied with an emphatic, 'No!' I was in a state of flow and felt energised coming off the motorway. I may have come across angry or upset, but I was just in the zone so many athletes aspire to be in. I opened my throttle to finish off Day Two.

The early morning air was cool against my skin as I ground away on the pedals. I had a surreal feeling of flying. Warren tried to lead the way, but his mechanical beast was no match for the speed my legs produced on my two-wheeled machine. I continually passed him on the inside and eventually he got the hint and hung back, lighting the way with the van's headlights on high beam shooting past me.

Leaning into the long sweeping bends, I gently squeezed the brakes when the road took a ninety-degree turn, then let go, rose out of the saddle, and crunched my way back up through the gears.

When approaching roundabouts, I'd hear from the van, 'go straight' or 'turn right', until they pulled up alongside me and I heard the words

I'd been waiting for all day; 'We're here, well done mate, you smashed it!'

I felt a massive release of pressure, I was exhausted, but happy. Time to eat and sleep! I munched down another avocado mash, swallowed a 33Shake and other superfoods to help my body deal with copious amounts of inflammation it had produced, before I showered and collapsed into bed. Day Two ended a little after 2 a.m.

Vanda massaged my cramping hands that were so curled up they looked like they were still gripping the handlebars. She then turned her attention to my feet, which felt bruised from an entire day of driving into the pedals. I winced when she touched them but soon began drifting off. For the next hour, she massaged my back and my legs and I slept through the entire treatment. I was completely out for the count.

Completed Cycle: Marbella to Puerto Rey | 360 kilometres | 17 hours 11 minutes

DAY THREE

PLANNED CYCLE: PUERTO REY TO DÉNIA 340 KILOMETRES

My alarm beeped, and I opened my eyes to see Vanda moving around the room organising my kit – I could tell by her sombre greeting she'd had little, if any, sleep.

'Your breakfast is ready, and your cycling kit is there,' she said pointing at a chair in the corner of the room. It was time to eat, cycle, eat and cycle all day once again!

As I attempted to move, I realised my sheets were wet – initially I thought from the massage oil, or perhaps I'd had an 'accident,' but then I realised my body was radiating heat like a furnace. The soaked sheets were a result of my intense sweating throughout the night. The previous day's 17 hours of non-stop cycling had increased my metabolic function, and my body was simply doing its job of trying to cool itself down while I was asleep.

The mood throughout the crew mirrored Vanda's – it seemed the enormity of the challenge ahead had suddenly become apparent to all of us.

I left the hotel with my jersey pockets full of food and bottles of water while the crew stayed behind to pack the van and book some accommodation for the next couple of nights.

One of the biggest realisations about the Ultimate Triathlon was just how much of a logistical nightmare it truly was. For starters, we hadn't been able to predict when the swim would begin, as it was dependent on the weather. As soon as the swim was underway, we could start booking accommodation within our budget for the subsequent nights. Typically, we were booking hotels the same day of travel.

We also had unexpected mapping issues with the route itself. We often discovered only when we arrived, the roads I'd planned to ride on, clearly stated, 'No Cyclists'.

It took several hours for my body to feel completely awake, my legs were spinning and I was upright, but my reaction time was slow – I was simply going through the motions.

By 8 a.m. I was yawning, by nine, my eyes were heavy and I was still yawning. At 10 a.m. with the sun blazing, I struggled to keep my head up and began to yell out loud.

'Just keep pedalling Luke, just keep pedalling, and look up! Check out the scenery!'

The morning's ride took me inland slightly, navigating through a canyon surrounded by barren hills. I could have been riding through a desert, it was completely different to yesterday's landscape, but just as beautiful. I rode for hours and saw no one as I snaked my way through the prickly surroundings of cactus and what looked like palm trees.

I could already feel the warmth of the Spanish sun on my neck, it promised to be another hot day. In the distance, I saw a large wall of mountains I figured I had to cycle up and over.

As I edged closer, I realised the motorway cut through the middle of the mountains and as I came around a sharp bend, I saw toll gates, and guards who looked at me strangely, before waving their fingers at me rather sternly. There was no way they would let me through, so I turned around and headed back to find my crew.

After weighing up all the options, we decided the best course of action was to hide me in the back of the van under a pile of clothes to get me through the toll booths. As soon as I was out of the guards' view, we made a quick pit stop and I got back on my bike, ready to cycle through the tunnel and continue up the coastline.

Our plan was going perfectly until I reached the tunnel entrance. I heard a siren, glanced over my shoulder and saw flashing blue lights. *Oh crap!*

There must have been cameras leading up to the tunnel as a security guard drove right up behind me, got out of his car, and expressed his disapproval.

I speak no Spanish, so it wasn't exactly a conversation. I tried to explain that I just wanted to get to the other side, but he wasn't having any of it. He didn't seem to understand any of my hand gestures, but I could read his gestures loud and clear.

He crossed his arms at the wrist and with steely eyes glaring directly into mine, shouted, '*Polićia!*'

I knew what that word meant, and based on his gesture, I guessed I was about to be put in handcuffs. I wasn't going to argue.

I hobbled across the dual carriageway in my cycle shoes, carrying my bike, and negotiated the large barrier separating this major road – it was no easy feat.

I was now back at the exact place our stowaway operation began. We decided I would ride, as a passenger this time, through the tunnel to the other side of mountains – around five kilometres. I was back on the bike in no time, bumbling along a flat road, heading through more smaller undulating hills, back in the desert-like landscape.

I was feeling quite tired, but put it down to the large spike in adrenaline I'd just come down from during the whole tunnel fiasco. The crew overtook me and gave me a 'thumbs up', which I returned. There had been enough fun and games, it was time to put my head down and make up some lost time.

The road began to get steeper, which meant more weight through my butt on the saddle as my front wheel began to rise. After 25 hours of cycling in less than two days, my bum was sore.

Winding around tight switchbacks, the road was getting interesting – exactly what I needed – a no-way-out pain cave to focus on. As I ground down on the pedals I had an impulse to attack the climb as if I was leading the peloton in the Tour de France. Not one to second-guess my thoughts, I went with it!

I yelled at the shooting pain in my bum to 'shut up' as I spun the pedals faster, shifted up through my gears, and watched my legs pump up and down like pistons.

With three switchbacks to go, the climb increased and I continued to push. I may have been grimacing on the outside, but inside I was laughing and having fun. To me, life and adventures are all about being playful in the moment – I felt like a kid racing his imaginary friends.

Cars passed in both directions and honked with approval at my efforts, several drivers gave me the thumbs up.

Approaching the final switchback, I increased my efforts once again as the road became even steeper. I shifted up two gears, got out of the saddle and danced on the pedals. OK, two gears might have been too much – I down-shifted and found a rhythm and laughed at getting caught up in the moment. I knew I was finally awake and ready for an afternoon of riding.

At the summit, I pulled off to the side of the road for a quick photo, let out an adrenaline-fuelled roar, and then started my descent.

The ride downhill was a little too quick in parts and I felt my rear tyre slide out from behind me as I squeezed the brake, at times too late and a little hard. I shot out the bottom of the winding bitumen trail and onto a long straight road, heading for the opposite side of the plain it dissected.

The crew had pulled over to the side of road with lunch ready to eat. Erica and Vanda once again created 'the best salad I'd ever had', and I could see Warren meditating in a nearby field. He had been working around the clock finalising the route, and driving hundreds of kilometres, so taking some time to be calm and mindful would serve us all well.

By mid-afternoon, I was cruising along the esplanades of San

Javier, Torrevieja and Santa Pola, heading north towards Alicante, up against a nasty headwind. The sun was just beginning to drop over my left shoulder when I saw Jay filming from an overpass, with the rest of the crew only a few hundred metres up the road waiting in a small side street. I ate, put on my high visibility vest, packed some food into my jersey pockets, and off I went. Little did I know the next time I'd see the crew things would have changed rather drastically.

After nearly two hours cycling into a headwind, my left hamstring started to tighten. Being attuned to the biomechanics of how my body produces power, I could feel it change to accommodate the niggle in the back of my upper left leg.

During any endurance event, there are ups and downs, and moments, which at the time seem small, but can make a huge impact at a later stage. It could be not eating enough or eating too much, your fluid intake, or a choice you make with your kit. These are the moments where you learn what you are truly made of – and test your ability to adapt when faced with setbacks.

One of these moments for me came as I approached Alicante.

The sun had set, my lights were on and the reflective strips on my high visibility vest shone brightly. I was hunched over, gripping the handlebars and my upper body was shivering. During the last crew stop, I wasn't given a jacket or arm warmers and with night approaching, this was a mistake. Granted, neither the crew nor I expected to be apart for more than two hours, but I was now cold and pissed off!

'Where are they?' I shouted.

Yes, I'm a grown man, and I could have thought of it myself, but as an endurance athlete on a massive adventure, it's the crew's responsibility to make sure I'm fed and safe, and have all the kit I need, when I need it.

When I finally spotted the crew pulled over just outside Alicante, hazard lights flashing in the dark, a wave of relief spread over me. I couldn't feel my hands or toes, my teeth were chattering, and I was shivering like I'd spent the night naked in the Arctic. To add insult to injury, all four crew members were snug in their thick, down jackets – this pissed me right off!

There were no pleasantries on my behalf.

'Are those jackets warm?' I asked. 'I'm freezing!'

I directed my disapproval at Warren, looked him in the eye and said, 'Don't leave me alone for that long again!'

The dinner stop was as icy as the air I'd just cycled through and no one said much. After a few minutes filming, Jay backed away, leaving me to finish my dinner.

I was shown the route, said 'Thanks' and 'Bye' in the same sentence, and pedalled off – this time wrapped in warm clothing.

I negotiated my way through the vibrant city of Alicante and was back on a dark dual carriageway feeling tired – really tired.

The crew popped up occasionally over the next hour or so, my grumpiness dissipated, and it was all-good in the Ultimate Triathlon camp once again. But exhaustion was setting in and I still had 100 kilometres to cover before today's finish line in Dénia.

Over the next 10 kilometres, I struggled to keep my eyes open – my bike seemed to have a mind of its own and was steering itself, but not exactly in a straight line.

I had cycled the best part of 14 hours, it was almost 10 p.m., and my eyelids were heavy. Each time I widened my eyes to try and keep them open, I felt my helmet shift as my eyebrows raised and scrunched my forehead upwards. I was trying everything to stay awake.

After battling up what felt like a huge summit, I decided to stop for a minute. I propped my bike against the guardrail, sat on a rock and contemplated the job ahead – another 85 kilometres of cycling.

I desperately wanted to sleep, and my speed had slowed to a snail's pace. I was concerned I would close my eyes for a fraction too long, and …

'You have 85 ks to go Luke!' I said with as much vigour as I could muster. I ate, drank and slapped my face a few times.

'C'mon' I whispered to myself, with little effect.

I pulled out my phone and filmed myself micro-sleeping before thinking, 'SCREW IT! Whatever happens, happens!'

After the unscheduled break, my left leg had stiffened from the tightening hamstring. I struggled to lift it over the bike's frame, and had no idea how I was going to get through the final few hours.

The micro sleeps came more regularly and I felt like I had little control of my bike. I tried to lift my head and look ahead. The last thing I remember is seeing lights in the distance …

'As we approached we started to get that uncomfortable feeling when you know something isn't quite right but you're not sure what it is. Had he been hit?'

Vanda

'He was moving so slowly, zombie slow. We saw him ghost past us – he did not stop, he did not look, but we were able to run and catch up with him. When Vanda and I put our hands on him it was like watching someone being hypnotised when the hypnotist says 'Sleep' and the person just collapses. That was Luke.'

Warren

'We placed Luke in a barely conscious state in the back of the van, I checked his vitals and everything was normal, he was just exhausted. We stood there for a moment staring at his limp body.'

Vanda

I woke up with a massive headache, still in my cycling kit, in an unfamiliar hotel room. Vanda was standing over me with a look of grave concern on her face.

What the hell had happened?

Completed Cycle: Puerto Rey to Dénia | 303 kilometres | 16 hours 50 minutes

14.

THE ULTIMATE TRIATHLON: MIND AND BODY DISCONNECT

DAY FOUR

PLANNED CYCLE:
DÉNIA – MIAMI PLATJA
325 KILOMETRES

How often do you hear people say they feel like they've been hit by a truck? Well, I can honestly say, that's exactly how I felt. Not just hit, annihilated.

'What happened?' I asked Vanda.

Before she had a chance to answer, I fired off more questions about my pounding brain.

'My head, did I hit my head? Did I crash?'

You'd think I'd be a little more concerned, but all I could think of was the day ahead. As soon as I realised it was almost 9 a.m., I had a sudden urge to get up and get going. A late start to the day's 300 plus kilometre cycle would lead to a late finish – and that meant less sleep, and less energy the following day.

My mind clicked into 'athlete mode'; eat, get on the bike, and pedal. I asked Vanda to make my breakfast, and tell the crew we would leave in one hour. I dragged myself out of bed and stumbled the first few steps as my legs wanted to give way.

I had to lean on Vanda and the wall to keep my balance. By the time Warren, Erica and Jay turned up, I had collapsed onto the lounge.

'One hour and let's go Wazza!' I said.

'Yes mate, yep one hour we are on it!' he replied. 'Get some rest now and we will get going.'

I sat wrapped in a blanket with the look of someone who'd just been airlifted out of a near-disastrous situation. I could barely eat my avo mash. Mentally, I wasn't feeling any after-effects from my ordeal, other than memory loss. My mind was strong and willing, and primed for another long day on the bike. But my body had other ideas.

Athletes are commonly told, 'When your mind wants to give up, your body still has X% to give!' Sure, I understand this, and have been in the tug-of -war between body and mind plenty of times in my life. During a football match, thinking I was too tired to make another run up the sideline, or in the gym, my body screaming at me to stop and my mind contemplating listening.

But last night my body completely shut down from pure exhaustion. My mind was willing to drag it as far as it needed to go, but my body sternly said 'No!'

Many frightening scenarios came into my head, most ending with me (hopefully) waking up in a foreign hospital. Whether it's a genetic trait, or a result of training my brain, I know I can create an impenetrable mindset ready to face physical pain when it tries to break me down. And when I was weaving erratically on my bike, barely able to keep my eyes open, my mind still didn't want to quit – it only cared about finding a way to cycle to the designated finishing line. My body travelled nearly 80 kilometres with my mind unable to recollect any of the revolutions I made of the pedals. That's seriously insane, and dangerous!

I forced down the rest of my breakfast, took a nap and changed clothes. I was ready to set off – or so I thought …

The crew's job is to get the athlete from A to B, no matter what, but they were extremely uncomfortable with me wanting to get back on the bike, and they made their disapproval clear.

'Luke was in tatters with physical and mental exhaustion, he was in a very bad way – but his will, his spirit, his desire, were all burning as brightly as ever and against all of our wishes he got back on the bike. I hated that decision.'

Warren

I can be stubborn, and put my foot down – I was totally blind to reasoning. I was the athlete who just wanted to 'play'. I swayed and shuffled to the stairs, and used my hands to balance myself as I slid one foot after the other down each step of the four flights of granite stairs.

At that moment, I had two thoughts; firstly, how am I going to cycle over 300 kilometres in this state? And secondly, how the hell did I get up those stairs last night?

The crew waited for me in the parking lot and I could sense their concern. In a slow and deliberate manner (my entire body was hurting), I lifted one leg over the saddle. My left hamstring screamed 'don't do it!' and the rest of my body begged my stubborn mind to reconsider.

Wazza was not happy. He told me he'd be watching me very closely.

I was shaky and my hamstring felt like it would rip off the bone at the next turn of the pedals. I made the left turn down onto the main esplanade of Dénia, and tried to focus on the task at hand – staying upright and cycling in a straight line. It wasn't easy!

My eyes focused on the white line along the edge of the road as I repeated to myself '*stay on the white line*' while I urged my legs to keep the pedals moving in a circular motion.

My head was heavy and bobbing, I struggled to see clearly, and my peripheral vision was limited. I had no idea if there was oncoming traffic. I fixed my attention firmly on my front wheel, and the white line in front of it. I was in a dark and dangerous place.

Time seemed to evaporate, I had no recollection of how far I had cycled that morning, or my surrounding environment.

I heard, 'Luke stop, stop, STOP!' from multiple voices and felt like I was waking violently from a bad dream. I obeyed the commands and slowed to a complete stop.

I had travelled only seven kilometres.

The crew helped me off my bike as I was almost asleep, and managed to guide me away from the traffic. They sat me down on the curb and I immediately fell backwards into the hedge separating the road and a walking path. This woke me up, and shook a little sense into me. Today was done, I needed to rest!

'I had agreed with Luke not to stop him unless there was a serious concern for his life. Some would say that's insane, but this was Luke's dream. I knew where the Ultimate Triathlon stemmed from and in many ways, it was an ending and a new beginning, however painful it would be – I guess he hoped some of the physical pain would heal some of the psychological pain of the past.'

Vanda

The rest of the day was very simple. Sleep, treatment, eat, and sleep. Vanda massaged my legs as I lay motionless on the bed. I felt quite strange. My entire body felt like it was being sucked into the soft duvet and pulled downwards. It was like a magnetic force pulling my bones down into the Earth's core. I felt unable to move a single muscle fibre. This was a whole new state of exhaustion.

By late afternoon without any idea of how long I'd been asleep, I asked Vanda to invite the crew into our room for a meeting.

My subconscious had been processing events as I slept, trying to figure out how I would get to Monaco within the 12 days I'd allocated.

'New plan!' I said with authority. 'Obviously today is a complete rest day,' even though there were only a few hours of daylight remaining. 'We leave early tomorrow, finish the bike leg as planned over the next two days, then attempt to complete the run leg of the Ultimate Triathlon over six days, instead of seven.

This would mean attempting to run the equivalent of 14 marathons in just six consecutive days – around 100 kilometres a day. It sounded logical to me. I love running, it's my strongest discipline in triathlon, and I was excited to see the French Riviera on my own two feet. I got an early night, excited for my 4:45 a.m. alarm. The Ultimate Triathlon was back on!

Completed Cycle: 7 kilometres - forced rest day

DAY FIVE

PLANNED CYCLE: DÉNIA - MIAMI PLATJA 325 KILOMETRES

I lay in the pitch blackness of the hotel room after being woken by the bells of my alarm clock.

'Are you ready?' I asked myself.

It was a rhetorical question, the answer was burning deep inside of me, wanting me to get out on my bike and fly across the tarmac.

I stood up, legs work, nice!

I remembered going to bed, result!

And I knew what I was doing today – great, I'm ready!

Everyone was back into the swing of things. Vanda made my avo mash as I dressed and sorted out the large plastic containers that held my food and my cycling kit. Warren and Erica were packing the van, checking the route, booking accommodation, and making sure everyone was ready on time. Jay got his camera kit ready, replaced the batteries in his cameras, and followed me around as I prepared for Day Five. Game on!

My body has a remarkable ability to recover. A combination of my physiological make up, my nutrient-dense diet, a good night's sleep, and of course the magical hands of Vanda had me feeling pretty much as good as new. It was a similar story 48 hours after the Double Brutal Extreme triathlon I completed in 2014. The day after the race I felt amazing despite just completing 35 hours of non-stop swimming, cycling and running – the talkative and jovial Luke was back! The jury is still out on which version of Luke the crew prefers, the energetic clown, or the one passed out in the back of a van.

Over the first 100 kilometres of the day, I was flying – the road was straight, flat and smooth. The sun was yet to rise, so I followed the friend I made yesterday, 'the white line.' It illuminated nicely as the bright light attached to my handlebars bounced off its glossy finish. I put my head down and found my rhythm. *Work hard for the crew* I thought to myself.

During the first few hours, I reflected on the events of the previous day and a half. I had asked a lot of my crew, and put each of them in a difficult situation. They had been working extremely hard for me, so today, I was going to work hard for them.

We'd started early, so if I worked solidly throughout the day, we might finish at a respectable time, and get an extra hour's sleep. A single hour can make a huge difference to everyone's recovery, so I continued to push.

Physically there were a few things going on. For starters, my bum was hurting, my left hamstring was extremely tight, causing me to alter the force produced through the pedals, and my slightly swollen tongue was still annoying me. The salt burn from the swim made it feel puffy and rough, as if I'd gone crazy on it with coarse sandpaper. It was still very sensitive.

'Need anything?' Warren shouted out from his window as the

crew drove up alongside me.

'Nah, all good!'

He gave me brief directions to get through Valencia, which sounded straightforward, but it's a big city, and we could get separated, so some navigational tips were a good idea. I'm known for having an average sense of direction, hence the nickname 'GPS' from my London cycling mates. If there's a fork in the road, I am guaranteed to go the wrong way.

Exiting the metropolis of Valencia and cycling through the suburbs, I noticed a guy about 50 metres ahead standing close to the edge of the road. I've no idea why he caught my attention, but I'm glad he did.

'Go Luke go, well done!' he shouted in a Spanish accent. It took a minute to register what had just happened; someone who was following my journey online had come out to cheer me on! I couldn't wipe the smile off my face from this chance encounter – it gave me a huge boost of energy.

I was humbled that another person had made the effort to come and stand on the side of the road to cheer me on … wow! Later I found out it was a Spanish fan named Victor who had been following my progress via the live tracker and had been leaving encouraging daily messages for me. Victor, you are an absolute champion my friend.

I met with my crew a few kilometres up the road and told them about my 'super fan' on the side of the road. They were as shocked as I was, but also excited that the Ultimate Triathlon was gathering support. After a quick route check, I was off again.

I was now back in rural Spain, with hills appearing randomly, and tiny villages popping up every so often. I heard some chatter behind me, and turned to see three cyclists coming up behind me, more amigos!

I tagged onto the back of this small group to make a two and two formation, and in doing so, got some nice cover from the wind which swept through this largely deserted area. I smiled at my ride partner and was met with a toothy grin in exchange.

There wasn't much conversation – the cyclists spoke no English, and my Spanish hadn't improved, but we shared a passion for cycling. We all took our fair share on the front of the pack to slice through the headwind that threatened to push us backwards. The landscape was open and exposed with strong gusts of wind shifting our compact formation. It started to rain.

We all fumbled with our wet weather jackets, removing them in an almost synchronised sequence, with one arm wrapped around our backs, and a hand diving into the jersey's pocket to pull them out. We ploughed on through the rain together like we'd been cycling together for years, the four of us moving as one. I enjoyed, briefly, being part of their crew.

Shortly after I waved goodbye to my new team mates, I pulled into a petrol station where my crew was waiting with more delicious salad from the local area, topped off with a few slices of *jamón* – yum!

The timing was perfect, I was getting hungry, my feet were burning from driving the pedals, and my left hamstring felt like it would snap and whip itself into a ball at any moment. I also had a few nasty saddle sores, which didn't enjoy being hard-pressed against my seat for hours at a time.

Vanda treated my hamstring as best she could with a range of techniques – massage, dry needling, manual therapy – to try and release the tightness of the aggravated muscle. My hamstring felt like it was being squeezed in a vice. I struggled to straighten it each time I pedalled but I knew I had to focus and embrace the pain, breathe deeply and keep going. This was my new normal. 'If you don't pedal, no one else will!' I told myself. I constantly thought of my crew sacrificing their time and putting their busy lives on hold, to help me achieve my goal. We are in this together.

As I cycled into the afternoon, the temperature dropped and I felt my energy plummet. It was like towing a caravan – I even looked back a few times in case I was being held back by a weighty load. I needed to find energy from somewhere, so I turned my attention within, and thought of my family, specifically, my two little nephews. I want to be someone they look up to, and are proud to call their Uncle Boof, so I continued to pedal with strength, trying to show these little dudes to never give up!

Slicing through some small hills, and rolling over others, I maintained a solid pace throughout the final few hours of daylight, and into the night.

There is something special about exercising outside at night – not knowing who or what lies around the next corner adds a sense of excitement.

All through the night my crew leap-frogged me, and we exchanged a few words when we could. I'd been going for well over 12 hours and still felt strong. '*Just a few hours to go*,' I told myself.

Once again, I was on a busy dual carriageway, but I'd caught a glimpse of a road sign with my destination listed, so I figured I was close. I knew which exit to take, with just a short ride after the turn off to meet up with the crew. I could almost feel the soft sheets of my bed …

After zoning out and gobbling up miles of road, I realised I was cycling through parklands, with a glow in the distance, and an empty horizon over the Mediterranean.

'Keep your head down and pedal,' I mumbled.

The roads were dark and winding as I kept telling myself, 'Just one more corner,' but it never was. I stopped briefly to check the map on my phone, just to make sure I hadn't had a 'mini' nap and taken a wrong turn – I instinctively knew I should be at the outskirts of the small coastal town of Miami Platja by now.

I had covered more than 330 kilometres at this point, and still no sign of my crew. I went with my gut and continued down the road I was on.

A light shining up ahead at a weird height caught my attention. It started waving at me and had a voice that sounded exactly like Warren's.

'Over here,' it commanded.

I had made it.

Eventually we figured out the hotel was back up the road I had just cycled, but instead of getting back on the bike, I hobbled over to the car for the short trip. My butt was killing me and my hamstring was getting worse. I yelped when the crew helped me into the front seat of the van.

The white marble steps leading up to our hotel could have come from the set of *Scarface*, dropped into a secluded corner of Spain – well we were in Miami 'Beach' after all. The hotel was run by two diminutive Spanish women. Both seemed somewhat overwhelmed to have four guests arrive late at night. We wondered if they'd ever had guests before – it was chaos! All I cared about was food, shower and bed – I was done. I had worked my butt off for the crew today to say a massive thanks.

Vanda started to work her magic on my tired and beaten up body, preparing it for another brutal day ahead. I drifted off to sleep with the thought of just one more day on the bike floating through my mind.

Completed Cycle: Dénia to Miami Platja | 335 kilometres | 14 hours 50 minutes

DAY SIX

PLANNED CYCLE: MIAMI PLATJA TO PERPIGNAN (FRANCE) 300 KILOMETRES

I woke up several times during the night with hot sweats, my hands and feet burning and inflamed from gripping the handlebars and pushing against the pedals. Before I knew it, the alarm buzzed signalling the beginning of my final day on the bike.

Vanda gently massaged my tender extremities as I lay still and focused, mentally preparing myself, visualising how I planned my day to play out, and doing some deep breathing.

My butt and hamstring were in a sorry state, and although the salt burn on my tongue was improving, it still felt like sandpaper. The avocado mash was cool and soothing.

Warren arrived after breakfast bearing unwelcome news. 'I doubled checked today's route to the French border, and we still have 450 kilometres to go, and that's up and over the Pyrenees with 4000 metres of climbing.'

My heart sank. How could I have gotten this so wrong? My emotions started to bubble over, and tears of frustration trickled down my face.

The problem was not climbing over the mountains. I was prepared for what the final section of the bike leg had in store.

The issue was the distance – there were simply not enough hours in the day to complete this type of mileage. I needed to compose myself and create an alternative plan – yet another unexpected twist to the Ultimate Triathlon.

Minutes ticked by as we went through various scenarios, chewing up valuable daylight hours – we needed to decide quickly.

I had triple-checked the distances when researching the Ultimate Triathlon route, but somehow, I had badly miscalculated. I was going to be around 200 kilometres short of what I thought was the 2000 kilometre route I'd designed.

We made Girona our target destination for the day, and worked out I needed to cycle just over 200 kilometres to reach my initial 1300 kilometre cycling goal. I prepared myself to leave, both physically and mentally. It should have been a day of celebration – the last day of the cycle – but I was frustrated and disappointed, and the day was about to get a whole lot worse.

The moment I started cycling, the sharp vibrations from the road caused me to recoil in pain. I was already exhausted, and this morning's revelation had put me in a heightened state of sensitivity. On top of that, my backside was raw with saddle sores, and I could feel the muscle fibres separating in my hamstring. Little wonder my body tried to revolt against each movement.

All I wanted to do was get off the bike and start running, but I still had over 200 kilometres of cycling ahead of me. The route for the day was basically one straight coastal road, but we would have to negotiate our way through the city of Barcelona during afternoon peak hour. The crew needed to source food for the day, so I was on my own for the first few hours. I wasn't too upset about the lack of company – it gave me a chance to get my head sorted. My mind was full of negativity from the route miscalculation. There was nothing I could do other than focus on the job at hand and being alone helped.

'If you don't pedal, no one else will,' I told myself as I worked my way up the coastline.

By Tarragona I was looking for the crew – I thought I should have seen them by now. Next thing I knew I'd come to a dead end. Somewhere along the way, with my head down cycling, I'd missed a turn. By chance, a friend in the UK was checking my progress via the tracker and messaged me with turn by turn directions to get back on the right track. How lucky was that? You just never know who is watching, and willing to lend you a helping hand. Thank you Mr Collins!

If I hadn't already cycled 1000 kilometres in three and a bit days, this smooth stretch of road would have been a dream as it hugged the sparkling coast, and looped around its mini headlands.

There were several climbs as I zig-zagged my way up and around the hills. The panoramic views softened the pain in my legs, before a tightly-wound descent carried me down the other side.

My left hamstring was screaming at me to stop with each revolution during the climbs, and would immediately stiffen when I stopped moving – it had no idea what it wanted.

I reminded myself to enjoy the surroundings, as tomorrow; I'd be done with the bike leg of the Ultimate Triathlon. With the sun high in the sky, I held onto the experience and enjoyed the incredible scenery.

A train line ran parallel to the shore, cutting through the hills via a perfectly constructed tunnel. For a moment, I imagined being on the train that followed this coastline, sipping tea and gazing out at the

Mediterranean, watching boats bobbing as the swell passed through. I even managed a wry smile. It was remarkable to be cycling along the Spanish coast, finally achieving a dream I put in place so many years ago.

The approach into Barcelona was a long, flat, mind-numbing dual carriageway, but with vehicles flying past at close range, I had to stay focused and hold my nerve. One of the main concerns expressed by family and friends was the traffic I'd be sharing the road with on the bike leg. Was I worried about being hit by a passing car or truck? Well, as with any extreme sports, there are risks, and I spent many weeks contemplating them. I had to prepare myself by training on busy 'A' roads throughout the UK to build confidence and bike handling skills. I couldn't control human error, but I also couldn't let it hold me back.

So, I made peace with being a slow moving, unprotected vehicle as gigantic steel bullets whizzed past my ears years before I set off on the challenge. I simply focused on the things I could control, kept my wits about me, and tried, to the best of my ability, to cycle in a straight line.

Before long, I noticed planes above me coming in to land so I knew I was close to Barcelona. My crew was parked in a small layby and I stopped briefly for a chat and bite to eat before we set off to tackle the maze of Barcelona's busy streets.

Cars, trucks, and motorbikes tooted their horns constantly – sometimes at me, sometimes in disapproval at the congested traffic. There were road closures, one way streets, and many sets of traffic lights. Too many traffic lights! At one point, Wazza nearly ran me over as I cycled beside the van when he swerved to miss cars up ahead – I had to be alert the entire time.

We breathed a collective sigh of relief once we passed through Barcelona. I was back on another long flat coastal road that would take me up into the hills surrounding Girona, marking the end of the day, and the cycle leg of the Ultimate Triathlon.

With a small headwind, this stretch of the ride was honest – if I slowed down my pedalling for a second, the bike would stop. As I approached some leg-tingling hills I pictured all the training I had done. The countless climbs I repeated through the hills of Surrey, southwest of London. I'd ride the country lanes multiple times, up, down, up, down, like a yo-yo to strengthen my legs, heart, and my mind – I needed all of that physical and mental strength now as I began to climb.

The sun had set long ago and it was now pitch dark with dense mist. Jay had taped a 'flood light' to my handlebars so I could see through the mountain fog as I crunched the pedals. Each revolution spinning the crank seemed to take forever.

Vanda's concern was growing for my almost-torn hamstring. The hills would put it under more pressure, and she didn't want it to blow.

It started to drizzle as I battled the pedals, and I cursed anything that came to mind – the trees, my bike, the colour red, anything – and now I needed to pee. Normally I would just pull over to the side of the road, pee, and continue on my merry way, but I was crawling up what seemed to be a never-ending incline with only one good leg, in the cold mountain rain. I simply let it flow without skipping a beat.

The moment sparked a memory from years ago with a mate from Bathurst called Barnesy. At the time, he was making a name for himself as a pretty handy Ironman triathlete, qualifying for the World Championships in Kona, Hawaii. I asked him what he did if he needed to pee while on the bike, and he said 'I just pee!' So with that in mind, I relaxed, and enjoyed the warm sensation trickling down my cold and exposed legs.

I was desperate to finish, but today would end when I had covered 210 kilometres. My butt was on fire, my hamstring fibres were separating, and through sheer exhaustion, I wanted to lay down on the side of road in the rain. I continually whispered, 'just one more pedal mate, just one more pedal.'

At the top of the climb, I tucked down over my handlebars to be as aerodynamic as possible on the descent. The rain smashed against the clear lenses of my glasses and the wind was freezing against my flapping cheeks.

Eventually the winding dark chute came to an end and it was time to pedal again, but trying to get my legs to spin, after only a few minutes rest downhill, was excruciating. My hamstring had seized and I whimpered. I'd had enough.

Flashing lights caught my attention and I heard 'take the next right' as I whizzed past. I came off the quiet country road and on to a busy dual carriageway.

'What the fuck am I doing on this?' I yelled at no one.

I had only kilometres remaining and here I was on another dual carriageway late at night. I pushed hard to maintain my speed along the greasy road, dodging small rocks and random junk, mumbling 'this is the last place I wanted to be.' I had no choice but to harness the frustration into pumping my legs, and keeping myself going.

Cars flew by and honked aggressively as if to say, 'what are you doing on here? Get off!' I wasn't overly concerned with their thoughts, but their noisy attention kept my heart rate elevated which produced some much-needed heat in my body, as I was getting quite cold!

I tried reciting the alphabet out loud without letting my teeth come together, which sounds simple, but not when your teeth are chattering! I failed miserably but the exercise distracted me for a few minutes, and got me to where I needed to be – there was the crew waving me onto an exit road.

They overtook me on a dark and desolate road, their taillights disappearing in the distance. I managed a smile, as I knew that I would be off my bike very soon – my watch confirmed I'd cycled the required 210 kilometres. I came up over a rise and saw the flashing amber lights of the day's finish line and heard distant cheers from my ecstatic crew.

I had done it; I completed my goal of cycling 1300 kilometres in just over four days. My crew shook up bottles of sparkling water and sprayed me to celebrate a milestone we'd all worked so hard to achieve.

Completed cycle: Miami Platja to Santa Seclina | 212 kilometres | 12 hours 52 minutes

DAY SEVEN

PLANNED RUN: PERPIGNAN (FRANCE) TO BÉZIERS 100 KILOMETRES (ROUGHLY)

I woke up with way too much energy considering the state I was in the night before. Thanks to more treatment by Vanda and her magical hands, some nutrient dense food, and about five hours' sleep, I was full of beans.

Running is my passion; it's where my endurance sporting career began several years ago, in the southern Saharan desert. In six days' time, when I crossed the finish line in Monaco, the Ultimate Triathlon would be over. I'd have achieved my dream, a dream many had doubted. I reminded myself to stay present and enjoy every moment. The other huge bonus was my butt got a reprieve from the pressure of another long day in the saddle.

The crew was also excited about today. I would be running at less than 10 kilometres an hour, which makes me a lot easier to chase down for food and directions. Perhaps the excitement caused a momentary brain lapse, as they sent me off in the wrong direction, and got me lost after just a few kilometres of running. We all had a good laugh about it – once I was back on track.

I covered my first marathon in just under 4:30 hours – way too fast – but I was enjoying myself and had fun with the crew each time I saw them. The weather was overcast with dark clouds gathering as I ran along the coastline. The wind picked up creating a swell and crashing waves onto the shore. I remember thinking 'glad I'm not swimming in there!'

It was a good day for thinking. I thought back to why I felt the need to challenge myself through this extreme triathlon. I thought back many years to the man I was then – a broken down soccer player, newly retired, battling depression and thoughts of self-harm and suicide. I realised I was still the same guy, just a little further along in his journey of life. I still suffer from depression, but less severely through a lot of hard work on under-standing my triggers, with help from my therapist, my family, and those closest to me. I have an amazing support group. So why do the Ultimate Triathlon?

Here's what came to mind as I ran along the coast of France:

I had a dream, created with clarity, to push my limits, so I could see a glimpse of my potential.

Yep, this pretty much sums it up.

Today's plan was to cover as close to 100 kilometres as possible. Everything was on track until daylight disappeared and with it, my boundless energy. I reached down to my running vest to grab my drink bottle, and discovered it was empty. This was a mini awakening that I was heading for a downward spiral – I had forgotten a vital component of my nutrition. I was now thirsty and my mouth was dry.

Before long, I noticed I had less control over my legs when I needed to detour from a straight line. I tried to negotiate a roundabout on the outskirts of Narbonne, but holding a smooth curve felt near impossible. When I veered to my right it felt like I was leaning heavily to one side, ready to tip over as I shuffled along. I over-corrected and began a pattern of zig-zagging movements that I struggled to control.

I made it to the town of Narbonne, thankfully following the same road. I barely remember passing through – except for one sign that caught my attention: 'PAIN' spelt out in bold neon letters. After nine hours of running with a battered hamstring, my fragile emotions didn't know whether to laugh or cry. I should have remembered (I do still understand some French after living in Belgium) that *pain* is the French word for bread!

On the other side of Narbonne (now known as 'PAIN Town') Vanda came to run alongside me. I didn't ask for the company, but I guess the crew could see how much I was struggling, and thought it was a good idea.

'I jogged next to Luke as the sun went down and the cool night air followed us out of Narbonne. Luke was in his own little world, nattering to himself, talking to his body, convincing it to go on. I didn't say much. There were no lights, pitch black country roads surrounded us. Then Luke started to sway,

he couldn't walk in a straight line ...'

Vanda

'C'mon Luke, keep going mate' I remember thinking; oblivious to anything Vanda might have been saying to me, but happy to have her company.

We were wearing head torches to guide us up what I thought was a drawn-out incline, but it was in fact a long, straight, flat stretch of road. Mentally I was in full motivation mode, but physically, my body was beginning to shut down.

'Great work Luke, you're doing well' I told myself, 'just get to the top of this hill, you can make it, just get to the top of the hill.'

The 'hill' that was as flat as a pancake...

I remember thinking I had made it, I summited the mountain and was now passing over a small bridge traversing a creek. I looked up to see what I thought was another steep section of road. Then I dropped my chin to focus on the tarmac as I stumbled along.

'Luke stopped, stumbled a few steps, and stopped again. It all happened so quickly. He fainted and when he fell, he nearly rolled down an embankment. I had my full body lying down the embankment, holding him up.'

Vanda

The next thing I remember was being bundled into the van by Warren and Vanda with a tearing, stabbing feeling through my left hamstring. My feet felt like burning stumps of flesh, and both hips had hot, sharp sensations pulling the joints shut.

The rest of the night was a blur, and other than the acupuncture needles Vanda stuck in my back, I don't remember much. I'd drained all the energy from my body's tank, plus whatever reserves my mind thought it could squeeze out.

Completed Run: Perpignan (France) to Coursan | 85 kilometres | 11 hours 40 minutes

DAY EIGHT

PLANNED RUN: FROM WHERE I FINISHED THE NIGHT BEFORE UNTIL I REACH 100 KILOMETRES

'Circumstances do not make a man, they reveal him.' – ***Dr Wayne Dyer***

My eyes flickered before opening wide. I rubbed my face with my hands and realised the sheets were, again, soaking wet. While I slept, my body had turned into a furnace, working overtime to maintain something close to a state of homeostasis. I had a new challenge this morning; my legs wouldn't move. I wasn't overly worried, I figured they needed a few more minutes' rest, and who was I to argue with them?

A knock at the front door drew Vanda out of the bathroom where she was drying my kit after washing it overnight. Warren and Erica appeared, surprised to see me sitting up in bed, laughing, and talking about today's run route.

Warren offered me a vase full of water, a little joke after hearing of my night sweats, and we chatted as I ate breakfast in bed – avocado mash of course. I was in good spirits, and ready to run! With my belly full and the beginnings of rehydration kicking in, my legs came to life. They seemed to have a mind of their own.

Warren and Erica struggled to comprehend my overly enthusiastic state after last night's shutdown. They left me to get ready for the day.

On days like today all the mental strength training I'd put in to my preparations paid off. I knew some of the most difficult times of the Ultimate Triathlon would be in the mornings, taking that first step out the front door. I had visualised swimming across the Strait of Gibraltar countless times while training, I'd googled images of Spain's Costa del Sol to get an understanding of my surroundings while cycling, but more importantly, I had dragged myself out of bed to run countless times when it was the last thing I felt like doing. I knew this would be vital preparation for the back to back marathons. But today it was the crew, not me, dragging their feet as we prepared for the day ahead. I was in fine form and ready to go, starting right where I'd finished in a heap last night.

'I think it was about here,' Warren said, pulling over to the side of a country lane. On closer inspection, a flattened patch of grass confirmed he was right. Vanda had held me steady, saving me from rolling into a ditch several metres below. This was where I would start today's adventure. Warren took a photo of me lying on my indentation, giving a double thumbs up, with a grin on my face. But I was quickly onto my feet again as an oversized truck sped down the road towards us.

Even I was surprised at how good I felt, running along small country roads, weaving between homesteads stained with autumnal colours from years of exposure to the weather.

The first 20 kilometres ticked over nicely, and as we were on back roads in the rolling green countryside, I couldn't help but smile and enjoy being completely present in the moment surrounded by nature. There was plenty to be happy about; I was physically able to run and I had my 'family' around me to help me fulfill my dream. After years of trying to understand my true purpose in life, and how I was going to leave my mark on this world, I was finally gaining some clarity.

By living life outside my comfort zone, I hoped to inspire others and help them realise what might be possible to achieve in their own lives, and become the best version of themselves. This clarity fuelled me to keep pushing forward.

But like a swing of the pendulum in an old grandfather clock, my condition changed from good to disastrous. I had a sharp tearing sensation in my left quadricep, which I put down to nearly 1000 kilometres of cycling with a damaged hamstring, and now running over 100 kilometres with an altered running technique. I dragged my body along for a few more kilometres but my left leg was deteriorating. Vanda went to work on it, trying massage, acupuncture, and mobilisation of other parts of my body to try and release something further down my body. Nothing helped. Her main concern was the small lump developing in the muscle, most likely a gathering of muscle fibres that had separated – a tear – not a good sign.

Now my eyelids were heavy and my head started to bob; I was dropping into micro-sleeps as I ran, and I was only a third of the way through today's planned route. The van pulled off onto a small grassy area, and I headed towards them. Even the slight change in terrain stepping from the road to the grass caused intense pain to shoot through my quadricep. I was barely shuffling.

The crew sat me down on the rear bumper of the van for some food and treatment. Within 10 minutes my mind ordered my body to start running.

After the pit stop, I tried to focus on every painful step, the sensation akin to a sharp blade penetrating through the flesh in my upper leg with any slight movement. At this moment, nothing else mattered. I mustered all the strength of my mind to complete the only task I was concerned about – taking the next step.

Next thing I knew I woke up – once again in an unfamiliar hotel room – cocooned in blankets, and Dryrobes, with an aching body, and an intense headache.

My body had shut down again.

I discovered the crew made the difficult call to pull me off the road, bundle me into the van, and get me to the hotel. I had been shuffling in all directions, confused and making little sense when questioned, if I answered at all.

'He mentally wants to run, but he physically can't!' Vanda had said to Warren. I was as limp as a rag doll, a dead weight. It took some wrangling to get all six-foot-two of me in and out of the van, into the hotel room, and horizontal on the bed.

I cannot recall any of it.

When I woke, it was late in the afternoon. I could hear whispering at the end of the bed, and then BANG! As if someone had flicked a switch, my entire body throbbed with excruciating pain. I couldn't move a millimetre. It was an agonising, entire body sensation.

'What happened?' I asked, my voice weak and croaky.

Warren and Erica filled me in and I realised how distressing it must have been for the crew. I was inadvertently asking them to make decisions that could potentially end the Ultimate Triathlon, or risk my long-term health, perhaps my life.

At that moment, I was immensely grateful to my Ultimate Triathlon family. Each one of them endured seeing me in physical pain, had to overcome their own emotional trauma, and make peace with decisions made in the drama of the moment.

I rocked the boat a little that afternoon when we began discussing next steps. For me it was simple. I run as far as I can every single day, until my body switches off and I pass out. Then I rest, and repeat the next day.

I had tunnel vision, oblivious to what was going on around me, or what I was doing to myself on so many levels. All I thought about was how I could adapt to this setback, and overcome the obstacle that was in front of me; I would not be stopped!

The crew wasn't at all comfortable with my suggestion, especially Vanda. She was in a tough spot. As my partner, she had the strongest emotional connection with me, and with her medical background, she felt responsible for my physical wellbeing. What I was asking went against her emotions, her knowledge, and her logic. I was encouraged to call my sister back in England, to let her know that I was alive and OK. She was, naturally, extremely concerned for my health and safety.

Prior to starting the Ultimate Triathlon, I set up a group via an online messaging app for my parents in Australia and my sister in England to have direct access to the crew. The crew had committed to keep them informed, with total honesty.

So, when Vanda messaged the group to say I had passed out again and was not responsive, messages of concern came back. My sister, Amanda (Moo), had tried dozens of times to call and speak to me while I was out cold.

'Are you in hospital, has a doctor seen you?'

I told her I was fine, and that I was just resting.

'Why aren't you going to a hospital?'

To calm her down, I downplayed what I was putting my body through, and said I felt great after a few hours' sleep – I lied.

I understand her being upset. She needed to hear my voice, speak to me, and confirm I was alive! Moo's concern should have affected my approach, but I simply acknowledged her distressed state, absorbed the love, and stuck to my plan of running until I dropped.

Dangerous? Sure.

Should I have known better? Yes.

Would I put everything on the line, and go all in to achieve my dream?

Absolutely, 100%!

I was, however, a little anxious as to what lay ahead. I was confused by the extreme disconnect between my mind and body. Mentally, I was in a good place, and encouraging my physical state with supportive thoughts and words while out on the road.

When my body refused to respond to any of the mental tricks I tried to play on it, I realised the sheer level of my exhaustion, although I was still confused as to why it was shutting down.

When the wheels started to fall off physically, my focus became razor sharp, with a heightened state of self-awareness, attempting to drive my arms and legs forward. But like a puppet with its strings cut, my body collapsed in a heap. My mind – the puppet master – could only look on, distraught and unable to manipulate the motionless figure. I was frustrated with my body, and continued to feel it wasn't fulfilling its true potential.

Completed Run: The outskirts of Coursan to Portiragnes Plage | 34 kilometres | 6 hours 5 minutes

15.

THE ULTIMATE TRIATHLON: SUFFERING AS SALVATION

DAY NINE

PLANNED RUN: FRONTIGNAN FOR 100 KILOMETRES OR UNTIL I DROPPED …

'If I'm alive that means I'm breathing, if I'm breathing that means I can move, and if I can move, I can get to Monaco!'

My morning thoughts.

'Every day he dies, every morning he's reborn.'

Warren's morning thoughts.

It's a curious feeling to lie in bed wondering if my legs would support my body after a few hours' sleep. I was weak and wobbly and for the first time, my entire body, not just my legs, felt completely rubbish. All I wanted to do was lie back down, and not move.

I pondered the battle going on between my mental and physical states. In a way, I was having an out-of body-experience. Physically, I was surrounded by reflections of myself, like a box with mirrored walls. I couldn't see the real world beyond the walls, only an image of myself, on a 'treadmill', constantly moving forward. My brain was on the outside looking in, encouraging my body to keep going when it slowed, urging it to push on when it wanted to stop, and continually reminding it why it was going through such pain.

Inside the mirrored box, surround-sound speakers amplified every comment my brain made – and my body heard every word loud and clear. If my body faltered, my brain screamed louder, demanding correct technique, telling it to soldier on …

But like a light dimming, my body began to fade, my energy levels dropped and normal movement and functions diminished. Extreme fatigue set in, triggering more yelling from the brain, but the volume on the speakers faded out. The body could no longer hear the brain's commands. Frustrated at the body's refusal to co-operate, the brain, still strong and alert, began hammering on the walls from the outside, showing no remorse, but without any reaction from my body.

This new understanding about the detachment between mind and body forced me to question how I felt about my own personal journey through the world of endurance sports. It became clear the strength and stamina of my mind far exceeded the capabilities of my body. Having learnt this, I promised myself to try and help others attain their own version of this state of mind.

I've been an athlete all my life, and I've learnt to recognise the different sensations my body produces, whether I need to address it immediately, or if it's just a niggle that will go away if ignored.

I started the day slowly, shuffling along a residential road outside our hotel. Once again, I had 100 kilometres in my sights. Anything less would not satisfy my ambition. But from the first step I took, I was in trouble. I knew the pain would only intensify. I had to stop momentarily to treat my tearing muscle, but I refused to acknowledge what the injury might mean for the Ultimate Triathlon. I still had more than 400 kilometres to cover, so I focused on one hobble at a time.

Vanda worked on the badly damaged muscle, trying different taping techniques and applying a bandage over a large portion of the affected area. We applied therapeutic liquid, gels and creams searching for a miracle cure.

With my pain levels increasing and my run speed slowing, Vanda wisely planted a seed of an idea in my head before leaving me to see what grew from her thought.

'How would you feel about getting back on the bike?'

She said it with the trepidation of copping a potential backlash, and then quickly ran up the road to meet the crew.

It was time for a decision, as there was too much distance to Monaco to cover at my current pace. The first thought that came into my head when wondered how I would get to Monaco with only one leg functioning was, 'Could I swim?'

This thought didn't last a second, before I called myself an idiot, and began considering the option of getting back on the bike.

Obviously, this wasn't how I'd planned the Ultimate Triathlon would play out, that I forfeit a large chunk of the run – but what other options did I have? As far as I could see, there were no other viable scenarios, and retiring at this point in the challenge didn't even creep into my mind.

The physical pain wasn't going away while I continued to run. I wanted to test myself physically and mentally – this was one of the many reasons I created the Ultimate Triathlon. All my training and preparation was for this very moment. I was in the middle of the biggest physical battle of my life and needed all my mental strength to fight until the very end.

During my childhood, I often heard the saying '*you never know until you give it a go*,' so as I approached my crew to discuss getting back on the bike, I knew I had to exhaust all avenues to achieve my dream. This decision would stay with me for the rest of my life. In the end, what other choice was there? I would cycle the rest to the way to Monaco, on one leg!

The rest of the day's route was flat and winding – an open expanse of farmland exposed to the elements. I pushed and pulled the pedal attached to my right cycling shoe. My left leg was simply a passenger along for the ride.

Each time my left knee bent it felt like a hot knife sliding into my thigh as the muscle stretched. As I pulled the right pedal back up, my left leg straightened, and a sharp pain hit my quadriceps. The result: a crippling vice-like grip grabbing at my left hamstring.

If I stopped pedalling to give my leg a reprieve from the pain it immediately seized up, resulting in a dramatically intensified level of suffering during the next three or four revolutions. Non-stop pedalling was my preferred choice of punishment.

This chain reaction of sensations continued for the rest of the afternoon, punctuated with groans, moans and plenty of colourful expletives.

I had two full drink bottles, and a couple of 33Shake chia energy gels in my jersey pocket for the 60 or so kilometres ahead, so I put my head down, embraced the pain, and got used to my 'new normal'.

It was brain battling the body, mind against the muscles, and the result of this constant conflict put me into a zoned-out state.

All I could do was focus on moving forward.

On occasions, cries from my crew would break my intense concentration as I cycled past. But my eyes didn't waver, I kept a steely gaze on the road ahead.

This was easily the most painful experience I'd had throughout the Ultimate Triathlon, and it took my existing pain threshold to a whole new level. Not something I'm keen to replicate anytime soon.

Cycling into Arles was a huge relief to my mind, body and spirit; my holy trinity was exhausted and needed to rest! First though, I had to get off the bike. My right foot had done all the work and it felt bruised and fiery hot inside my shoe. Get it out!

I rolled up alongside the van, leant over to grab hold of it, and counted down for Vanda to release my poor feet from the pedals.

'Rip it, one, two, go!'

'Argggghhhh, ha ha ha haaaaaa.'

Three people removed the bike out from under me as I could barely move my left leg in any direction. With more moans and groans, Warren and Vanda carried me to the van and as I felt nauseous, placed a large empty Tupperware container next to me, in case the pain led to vomit. Both agreed I was 10 times easier to move conscious than I was in my floppy, unresponsive state.

Using a broom as a crutch, I hobbled to my room. Once inside, Vanda began treating my battered leg, before moving on to treat the rest of my body. A large bucket of ice arrived to try and bring down the extreme inflammation that had swelled my left leg, from my knee to my groin.

It was an emotional evening as the Ultimate Triathlon had altered so much from the original plan I made all those years ago.

The best we can do is to give 100% of ourselves in everything we do in life. I knew I was squeezing everything I possibly could out of my current situation. You'd think then it would be an extremely satisfying experience. It wasn't.

I felt hollow and unfulfilled, like I had failed. My body wasn't living up to my high expectations and this frustrated me no end.

One thing was for sure, I would exhaust every possible avenue, and squeeze whatever energy I had remaining in my weary body to cover the final 350 kilometres to Monaco over the next three days. It was the least I could do to find contentment in my journey.

Completed Run:
Frontignan to Palavas-les-Flots | 17 kilometres | 4 hours 27 minutes

Completed Cycle:
Palavas-les-Flots to Arles | 66.5 kilometres | 3 hours 16 minutes

DAY TEN

PLANNED CYCLE: ARLES TO TOULON | 156 KILOMETRES

'Luke got through this with his strength of mind, strength of body and his refusal to give up – and after that, Vanda. She is an incredible Osteopath. Every night she treated Luke, she put Humpty Dumpty back together again, and every morning he was magically ready to perform at his best again. She has a gift of creating miracles.'

Warren

Day Ten began in the underground car park with my physio, Mo, on speakerphone to Vanda, and the rest of us listening to the pros and cons of me continuing in my current physical state. Mo knows me well, he knows my mentality and he knows my body. He also knows the lengths I will go to achieve my goals.

The purpose of the call was to remove some of Vanda's concerns about releasing me to cycle for nearly 160 kilometres, and to see if there was a specific treatment she could adopt to patch me up if things got worse.

Mo assured Vanda she was doing everything she could – keep the leg taped under compression, and hope my bloody-mindedness could be contained so I didn't use my left leg. If I did, I could potentially rupture the muscle, and that really would mean game over.

I was physically present during the conversation, but I wasn't listening. I had another far louder dialogue going on in my head.

In the four years since the Ultimate Triathlon was first conceived, it naturally evolved based on logistics, but now, with my leg injury, it had changed dramatically, and I struggled to accept the change.

At that moment, the Ultimate Triathlon wasn't living up to my expectations.

Getting back on the bike, rather than running, regardless of my circumstances, diminished the challenge – in my eyes, it made it easier. I felt flat, disgruntled, and frustrated by it all.

Monaco couldn't come fast enough – I just wanted it all to end. I couldn't shake the fact that I was extremely disappointed in my body 'failing' me.

Of course, this was a delusional point of view. The great thing about endurance sports for me, is given some time on my own, that initial knee-jerk reaction fades, and I can look at things from a different perspective.

For the time being though, I couldn't pull back from the negative mindset clouding my thoughts, so I put my head down and continued to grind out revolution after revolution of the pedals, pushing my pain to the same level as yesterday. In a sadistic way, this seemed to lessen the disappointment of altering the challenge.

Subconsciously, this was my way of trying to punish my body for not playing by my rules and staying in one piece. It had been years since I had suffered a significant soft tissue injury that couldn't be fixed with a week of rest and treatment. This resurfaced emotions I'd long buried from the final few years I played football, when my body kept breaking down.

When I was around the crew, I put on a happy face, they had been an amazing support to me and I didn't want my mood to drag them down. I wanted to feel pride and self-satisfaction, but what I truly felt was emotional anguish.

The first of several proper hills was now in front of me, and with my right leg doing 95% of the work, I gritted my teeth and battled with just my right pedal, while I screamed at the growing negativity flooding my mind. On the bright side, it was a warm, sunny day and the French countryside leading into Toulon was spectacular.

Reaching the apex of the long and winding hill seemed to shake out the blues a bit. I thought of the sacrifice my crew and friends and family around the world had made to help me get to exactly where I was right now – achieving my dream!

I knew I was being selfish, I was also doing the one thing I said I wouldn't do before I started this challenge; I was beating myself up. I had promised myself that the 12 days of the Ultimate Triathlon would be a celebration of all my hard work.

My current mindset was anything but!

Before too long, I was able to move on from feeling angry and self-absorbed, to focus on getting myself to Monaco in the best shape possible – physically and mentally.

Randomly, I thought about calling my friend and sports physician, Dr Lorenzo Masci, to book an appointment for my troubled left leg. Not exactly staying in the moment, but I had to let my mind go where it wanted, and it helped.

Riding with a more positive outlook, and an appointment to see Lorenzo the day after I arrived back to London, prepared me for the constant climbing until the final 10 kilometre descent into the city of Toulon, where I would rest for the night.

Forests of giant pine trees covered the narrow winding road during the climbs, with the occasional gap to allow sunlight to shine through, a reminder of just how amazing my life is, on a path to achieving a long-awaited goal, and surrounded by natural beauty.

With some directions from Wazza, I set off to tackle the final climb of the day. I expected to see the crew at least once more as I worked my way through the multiple switchbacks up the hill, but there was no sign of them. The sun was setting, throwing long shadows across the top of the pine trees as I cycled. To my right were incredible panoramic views of dense foliage, eventually meeting the Mediterranean Sea, way in the distance.

The fresh forest air kept my senses alert weaving my way down the other side onto a long flat stretch of road – back into suburbia and heavy traffic.

As I approached the edge of Toulon, I still hadn't seen the crew and was now concerned. I had to decide which roads to take to get to the hotel. My main concern was being able to unclip my pedals and support myself while straddling my bike. I would need the help of the crew – or someone – to dismount. I checked my phone as I slowly cycled, wondering if they'd left a message.

Stuck in traffic, not long behind you, here's the address to hotel.

Not exactly the news I was hoping for!

I copied the address into a mapping app on my phone, gripping it for dear life with my thumb and two fingers of my right hand, while the other two fingers latched onto my handlebars. Luckily, most of the traffic lights en route were green – or green enough – so I wasn't forced to stop.

When I did have to stop, I managed to throw my arms around a post – I have no idea what I'd have done without that support.

The navigator on my phone told me the destination was on my right-hand side. I put my phone away, happy to have made it. Until I realised I had no way of getting off my bike without the crew.

I spotted a pot plant near the front door of the hotel so I cycled up onto the footpath and leant against the wall. Somehow, I managed to unclip my right foot from the pedal, sparking a chain of events that was both comical and painful. Semi squatting with one leg and sliding the bike out from underneath me at an angle, I managed to reach over to my left heel with my left hand, thinking 'this is going to hurt.'

I took a deep breath, then on the exhalation, ripped at my heel in an outward movement to release the cleat from the pedal.

'Arghhhhhhh!' bellowed out from the pit of my stomach, as the torsion of my heel sent a rotating force up through my lower leg, through my knee, and twisted my femur in my hip joint, setting off explosive pain in my hamstring and thigh.

I was now wedged up against the front wall of the hotel, my injured shoulder (from the swim) taking the full brunt of pressure. I took several long deep breaths to settle the pain and regain some composure.

Tentatively, I maneuvered my bike out from underneath me as I slid down the wall, guided by my now aching shoulder, until my tender backside hit the concrete footpath. My ass did not appreciate this one bit.

I was now sitting on the ground, leaning against the wall, right leg slightly bent and my bike lying on its side next to me. I needed to execute one more movement – remove my left leg from the bike. In the process of sliding down the wall, it was now lying on top of the bike. I reached out with both arms to grab my leg below my knee, lifted and twisted, and success! I was now separated from my bike.

I thought about trying to hobble into the hotel, but as it took me 10 minutes to get off my bike, I wasn't sure I'd be able to get up again without help. Luckily my bike is quite light, so I lifted it up without too much hassle, and leant it up against the giant pot plant in front of me, and waited for my crew.

It must have been quite a sight. A sweaty bald man in a Ninja Turtle cycle jersey slumped against the wall at the entrance to the hotel with a bike next to him.

A few people asked if I was OK? One lady walked up, perhaps thinking I was homeless, and pulled a few one Euro coins from her pocket and tried to give them to me. I politely declined and said I was just resting. The entire scene was rather ludicrous – it bought a smile to my face and made me chuckle.

I heard a familiar voice say, 'speedy work!' and looked up to see my crew bundling out of the van. Vanda covered me with a jacket and a Dryrobe, and Jay immediately pointed the camera at me. I was very happy to see them.

I grabbed the pot plant with my right hand, hoping it had enough weight to support me, as Wazza looped his arm under my left arm, and lifted me to my feet. Out of nowhere, I was handed crutches, exactly what I needed, but where did they come from? My chief medical officer (Vanda) had ran off to find a chemist to buy crutches and painkillers reminding me once again how lucky I was to have her in my life, and part of this crew.

I soon realised the extent of my exhaustion, and pain. I had dug deep into my energy reserves, and battled a range of emotions throughout the eight-hour cycle. I was physically and emotionally destroyed.

Completed Cycle: Arles to Toulon | 156 kilometres | 8 hours 10 minutes

DAY ELEVEN

PLANNED CYCLE: TOULON TO FRÉJUS | 95 KILOMETRES

There was excitement in the air today as three of my best mates were coming out from London to support me during the final two days. This should have put a spring in my step, but I was feeling exhausted and battling to keep yesterday's negative conversation out of my head.

I couldn't hide my disappointment as the crew gathered up the kit and packed the van. I hopped down to the lobby on my crutches to meet the guys who'd just arrived.

The always-punctual Tiny was already waiting in the foyer, Seaggs came down next, but Disaster was nowhere to be seen. I was not surprised. He eventually ran through the hotel's front doors, cutting it quite close to our departure time. Normally I would laugh it off, but being in a slightly sour mood, I told him to hurry up, and I was serious. Disaster was cycling with me today on my spare bike, and I wasn't going to set off later than the planned time – not for anyone! I was already extremely frustrated with my injuries, and with a full night's rest under my belt I wanted to do *more*!

One of the amazing contributions Kevin 'Disaster' Bliss brought with him was his infectious positive outlook. I have spent countless hours on the bike with Disaster and shared many good times. Having him around would surely lift my spirits.

It took four people to slide the bike underneath me and clip me in. The moans, groans and screams of agony continued for the first 15 minutes as we navigated out of Toulon and onto smaller country roads.

Cycling with Disaster bought a nostalgic feel to the morning, we reminisced about many of our rides together, and I recalled the first time I met him when I explained I was going to complete the Ultimate Triathlon. It didn't exactly compute in his head back then (I still remember the blank look across his face), but over the coming months as we trained together, he learnt that I wasn't joking. It seemed fitting we were cycling together on the penultimate day.

Beneath the surface though, I felt unfulfilled and deeply frustrated and was still struggling to accept the new normal of cycling rather than running the final leg. Thankfully Disaster lived up to his reputation of lightening the mood. On a narrow winding road, he took the lead to shelter me from the breeze, giving me a close-up view of his cycling shorts.

Normally, if out on a ride with others, I wouldn't pay any attention to the backside in front of me, but today it was hard to avoid – I had as clear a view as you'd ever need of his butt cheeks! Disaster's shorts were so sheer that in certain light, and in certain positions when the fabric was stretched, I could see right through them! I didn't say anything at the time, but the crew couldn't resist pointing out the over share! He certainly showed the south of France more than it needed to see!

The entertainment didn't last long, as the road reared up, and I had a decision to make. Do I slowly push then pull my right pedal with my only functioning leg or, take a breath and go for it, driving both feet down as hard as I can on the pedals?

Without fully thinking it through, I flew past Disaster as the pain in my leg skyrocketed, going after this ascent as if my life depended on it. I used some dark volatile energy from within to push my battered body with a new urgency – it was relentless. As I dug deeper into my physical reserves, my mental strength didn't waver. Maybe I was enjoying this intense extra work.

Sweat rolled down my brow as we cycled under the hot afternoon sun. My body temperature increased with the intensity, it was like a red rag to a bull and I wanted more. I kept my head down, yelling encouragement as the road snaked up and around the Spanish sierra.

The pain was now all-encompassing shutting out everything else but the relationship between my body, my mind and the road. I rolled over the final lip of the climb, where the crew waited, unaware how long my self-imposed torture session lasted. Jay asked about the climb, but I couldn't recall anything specific apart from putting myself deep into a bucket of pain, well past my perceived capabilities, a place I wanted to quickly forget.

Vanda gave me a few painkillers to help the nauseating pain, as I leant up against the van on my bike to gather my composure, and wait for Disaster. Like every day of the Ultimate Triathlon, Vanda did everything possible to relieve, or try to fix whatever state I put myself in. At times, I felt like we were working against one another – I would beat myself up, breaking down my body hour by hour, and all she wanted to do was repair my injuries and try to keep me in one piece. No matter what I threw at her, she always responded with a potential solution.

Every bump in the road, and gear change sent a vibration through my quadricep, hamstring, and bum. I continued my mantra 'If you don't pedal, no one else will!' I was ready for the day to finish, get off my bike, and provide some relief to my destroyed body.

When I finally made it to the hotel car park, I pulled up near a small van, not my crew's, pointed my front wheel at it and applied my brakes gently to slow down. I leant up against its rear doors, still seated with hands gripping my handlebars and brake levers. Warren and Vanda wrenched my shoes from the pedals, and Disaster helped them remove the bike out from under me, letting me collapse in a heap on the warm bitumen where this painful sweat-soaked day ended. The heat penetrating through my body was comforting, like a warm hug – a welcome but brief reprieve.

The impact on my body of today's climb, and the previous 10 days' exertion was obvious – it felt broken in all senses of the word. After a few minutes of me wallowing in self-pity, the crew lifted me to my feet and I hobbled on trusty crutches to my room.

The Ultimate Triathlon would be over in 24 hours and I reflected on what it had taken to get me this far. Years of planning and research, early morning training sessions and late nights working at my laptop, the relentless insomnia and secret eating binges to comfort me in my dark battle with depression. All of this countered by the love and support from a handful of people who truly believed in me.

One big frustration for me was dealing with an overflow of energy after I rested briefly at the end of the day. Cycling within the physical limitations of my injury meant that the amount of energy I could use from my stores was capped. I simply wasn't using everything I had in the tank. Once my throbbing body settled down and the pain subsided, I felt restless with unspent energy. I tried not to dwell on my frustration and made a conscious decision to mark the occasion of completing the Ultimate Triathlon in a positive state of mind.

I recalled a conversation I'd had with one of the world's leading sports and performance psychologists, Dr Michael Gervais, on his *Finding Mastery* podcast, only a few weeks earlier.

'*Your loved ones say you don't celebrate your achievements,*' he said. '*I am wondering if this is going to be a totally different experience at the end for you.*'

'After the 12 days of the pain I'm going to endure, if I can't celebrate there, I can't celebrate anywhere!' I laughed.

With MG's voice in my head, I flipped the switch and decided to use tomorrow's cycle as a celebration of what it had taken to get me here – from the original idea four years ago, to being less than 100 kilometres from the finish line.

I deserve to enjoy this moment! Some of my most favourite people in my life were with me, helping me achieve my crazy dream – what's not to celebrate?

The crew went out to find a bar in Fréjus to relax and watch the rugby World Cup final, so Vanda and I grabbed the chance to catch up. For nearly three weeks we'd been completely focused on getting me through each day of the Ultimate Triathlon and it was nice to have some quiet time together. We decided to watch a movie. Just as the opening credits started to roll, there was a knock at the door.

The crew came barging in, arms full of food and smiles all around. We used the bed as a dining table, and sat around discussing the game, and telling stories from the previous 48 hours on the road. The movie was quickly forgotten, but what a perfect way to prepare for the final stretch into Monaco – friends, food, and plenty of laughs.

One more day to go, let's do it!

Completed Cycle: Toulon to Fréjus | 95 kilometres | 4 hours 57 minutes

DAY TWELVE

PLANNED CYCLE: FRÉJUS TO MONACO | 94 KILOMETRES

I had imagined this day endless times over the past few years, in my dreams, and during the countless hours of training. I felt like a kid again, waking up on his birthday!

Breakfast was the usual avo mash (in bed) while I prepared to take on the grand finale of what had been a life-changing couple of weeks.

The Ultimate Triathlon started as a personal challenge, a massive lofty goal for me to slowly take chunks out of over time. But as the years passed, it became something so much bigger.

So many people played a part in helping make my pipedream a reality and many of them were right here with me. Before setting off from the car park, I took a moment to thank each member of my crew for sacrificing their time to be here with me, support me, and most importantly, believe in me. I hugged each one of these amazing people and whispered just what their involvement meant to me.

Vanda and Tiny slid my bike underneath me for the last time and I had to laugh – I couldn't even mount my bike, and was about to cycle nearly 100 kilometres! Disaster and I rolled out of the car park, and it was smiles all round.

The sun beamed down as we slowly made our way along the looping bays, taking in the sights and sounds of the French Riviera; super yachts docked just off the coastline, and the street side cafes overflowing with locals and tourists. We caught a lift from a large bunch of cyclists for a while, even taking a short turn on the front, before they dispersed as we approached Nice.

We had one final stretch of this 2000 kilometre beast, and a fair bit of it was uphill along the rugged coastline between Nice and Monaco. I knew I had more intense full-body pain coming my way but as we reached the summit of smaller hill and rounded the bend, I spotted the crew's van by the side of the road, and a group of cyclists who must have been out on their usual Sunday ride.

They were lined up along the edge of the road like spectators during Le Tour de France, helmets and cycle shoes on, cheering.

'*Allez, allez, allez!*'

Hearing the French chant of 'Go, go, go!' was incredible, an experience I will never forget. They gave me high fives as I passed by, boosting my spirits sky high. It was exactly what today was all about – celebrating! I couldn't wipe the smile off my face, to the point my face started to hurt. Up, down, and around we went, edging closer to the end of what had been a sun-soaked and fun-filled day.

Earlier, I had told my crew that I would be running into Monaco, not cycling.

'With crutches?'

'No!'

I dreamt of running into Monaco with my multi-coloured cap spinning its orange plastic propeller, and I was bloody determined to make this part of the dream a reality.

'I don't care if it's 100 metres, or one kilometre, just pull over somewhere so I can get off my bike and put on my running shoes.' I instructed.

With several tough climbs remaining, Disaster suddenly decided to become 'Mr Motivator', trying to help me as I winced, huffed, and groaned my way through the uphill sections.

'One pedal at a time, you can do it,' he said, annoying the hell out of me.

I simply don't need verbal motivation. There is no one who can motivate me more than I can motivate myself, and I've been this way since I was a kid.

Coming from Disaster, the words of encouragement were just extra chatter in my ear, and I let him know, politely of course.

'Thanks mate, I really appreciate you trying, but that sort of thing does absolutely nothing for me, I'm not that type of guy.' I said.

On the other hand, having Disaster alongside me (without the chatter) was a huge boost. His friendly company bolstered my strength – he was my ally in this war I was waging. Cycling with a great mate whilst taking in the astonishing views of the Côte d'Azur was one of the highlights of the 12 days, despite the unrelenting and intense pain.

Before long, I looked up and saw the crew and the van parked – the moment had arrived, and with it, a huge lump in my throat.

Erica and Vanda waved me over shouting, 'transition over here!' I slowed right down to fling my arms around a sign post next to the van, and waited for my shoes to be unclipped. Vanda yanked quickly but with enough force to send a jolt of pain up through my left leg and into the pit of my stomach. They pulled my bike out from underneath me as I slowly slid down the pole, rotated around it and collapsed at the base.

Vanda removed my cycling shoes, put on my running shoes, and the crew helped me to my feet. I sat at the back of the van to put on my shorts, and listened to Warren's instructions to get me to a roundabout where the Principality of Monaco started, and the Ultimate Triathlon would finish.

I adjusted my propeller cap, took a deep breath, and started running. My mind was enthusiastic and willing me on, but I was in slow motion and did more hopping than running, putting minimal pressure on my left leg, swinging my right leg through in an awkward jolting motion. I was moving so slowly that people walking casually around me outpaced my efforts.

So many memories flickered through my mind; my parents back in Australia, all the training and adventures over the years, and I was doing my best to hold back tears. I'm not sure if they were tears of joy or tears of pain from trying to run with a badly torn quadricep!

I crossed the road to the island in the middle of the roundabout, not consciously checking for traffic, as Erica and Vanda held aloft a black banner with my sponsors' logos and the words '*The Ultimate Triathlon F I N I S H*' splashed across it.

The centrepiece of the traffic island was a sandy-coloured rock, a couple of metres high and shaped like the head of a spear, with '*Principauté de Monaco*' spelt out in bronzed lettering.

I hobbled over to it, leant over the shrubbery and went in lips first for a kiss.

It was all over, I did it!

'It was a beautiful moment on that little roundabout, after everything that threatened to derail it and every obstacle Luke had to overcome. It was an incredible adventure and I'm so lucky to have been a part of it.'

Warren

All the crew, cheered and clapped, but their excitement was drowned out by the voice in my head, as I pushed back from kissing the rock. I had my eyes closed and my head bowed.

'As soon as you turn around Luke, your life will never be the same.'

I had to be ready for a new normal. Four years in the making, the Ultimate Triathlon turned out to be an incredible period of learning about myself, and realising what I'm truly capable of achieving. I'd had a crazy idea for an endurance event that was a world first, I planned it, and against the odds, I made it happen. I felt like I could accomplish anything!

There were hugs all round and tears of both joy and relief as we stood on that traffic island at the entrance to Monaco. We could have stayed there for hours celebrating, but the local constabulary had other ideas, and we found ourselves surrounded by police who wanted us to stop filming and move on. So, it was back to van, this time with the help of crutches, and with a smile stretching from ear to ear.

Completed Cycle: Frejus – Monaco | 94 kilometres | 4 hours 50 minutes

THE ULTIMATE TRIATHLON FROM MOROCCO TO MONACO: <u>COMPLETE!</u>

16.

EXTREME REALITY

To never give up means you can chase your dreams and turn them into reality. Give up, and they'll forever be just that – dreams.

Steve Waugh, ex-Australian Cricket Captain.

(*Daily Telegraph*, 5.12.02)

Steve Waugh was one of my childhood heroes. I watched his dogged determination with admiration and curiosity. The grit he demonstrated, both as batsman and captain, immortalised him as of one of the most accomplished cricketers of all time.

When I first read the quote above, I was 19 years old and its message grabbed my attention. I cut it out and have carried it with me ever since. The tiny piece of newspaper is almost transparent now, but the message is as strong as ever. Steve Waugh never gave up, and neither would I.

NICE, FRANCE

Within 48 hours of completing the Ultimate Triathlon my crew vanished – back to the lives they'd put on hold for the all-consuming two weeks of the event. I had planned to stay on in the south of France for a few days to rest and recover, but the time-out turned into a battle to remain positive. I wanted to laugh and reminisce, and revisit the incredible 12 days I'd just experienced, but I was alone.

On top of the solitude, I was still on crutches and had to keep my left leg elevated. Conquering the Ultimate Triathlon seemed insignificant and my mood plummeted. I felt no joy and zero satisfaction as I began to feel the all-too-familiar shadows of my depression linger.

I don't know what I was expecting to feel. Journeys of self-discovery and transformation often end with a massive sense of 'now what?' Maybe I hoped the emotional scars and physical exhaustion would magically melt away.

Truth is, I had to stop running from my past. It was time to accept what I'd put myself through and give myself an opportunity to be content with my life.

Very little of what I was feeling was connected to the impact of the two thousand kilometres of swimming, cycling and running I'd just completed. I now had no specific goal to chase, and without one, the realisation finally hit home. It was time for me face up to the truth, accept the past, and find the gratification that would help me to move on with my life.

For as long as I can remember I was always chasing a dream. As a kid trying to strip away the football from my Uncle Phil's foot in the back garden at my grandmother's house, it was the lofty dream of becoming a professional footballer. I pursued this dream relentlessly, sacrificing my teenage years, and my family's time to help make it a reality. Throughout my twenties, I constantly pushed myself to be the best footballer I could be to convince clubs to sign or re-sign me. When I retired from football at the age of 28, I immediately gave myself a new target to become an endurance adventurer with the Ultimate Triathlon as the bull's-eye.

But with that challenge now achieved, anxiety kicked in. Why did I feel so empty and lifeless the moment I had nothing to chase?

Hobbling on crutches through the cobblestone streets of Nice, I passed a wine shop and picked up a bottle of Châteauneuf-du-Pape, a prestigious wine from the Rhone Valley in southern France. Under normal circumstances with a soft tissue injury, I would avoid alcohol as it can thin the blood, which leads to increased bleeding in and around a torn muscle. Tonight though, I didn't care, I desperately wanted to celebrate my achievement – but I had no one to share in the celebration. I sat on the couch with an ice-pack on my elevated leg, raised the glass and said

'Cheers!' to myself. I barely put a dent in the glass of wine, and after about an hour, I gave up and took myself off to bed. The frustration of my injury and my state of mind overwhelmed me, and as I waited for sleep to come, a single tear rolled down my cheek. I knew it was normal to feel flat after such an intense experience, I just didn't expect the sense of emptiness to kick in so quickly.

On the flight home, I made the most of being on crutches and accepted the offer of a wheelchair to avoid standing in long queues at Nice Airport, and again at Heathrow when I arrived back in London.

Normal life resumed – another injury and the all-too-familiar cycle of recovery – this time for a strained hamstring and badly torn quadricep that needed rest, elevation and rehabilitation before I could slowly begin some physical activity to regain fitness. I had years of experience completing this sequence to repair countless muscle tears, I just had to get on with it.

The narrow, winding staircase at my therapist's practice leads up to a small room with a few chairs, a sofa, and a view over London's rooftops. He greeted me with his broad smile, but when he noticed I was on crutches, a look of concern crossed his face.

We talked about the Ultimate Triathlon and how the accomplishment had left me feeling empty and unfulfilled. In previous sessions, we had identified I was putting too much pressure on myself and treating the Ultimate Triathlon as if it was the only thing that mattered in life.

Now with the challenge over, I was at a crossroads. I could choose to head off in any direction, but I had lost my bearings and had no motivation to find a new path. One of the issues that bugged me was that I hadn't completed the Ultimate Triathlon exactly as planned. The tricky conditions in crossing the Strait of Gibraltar had to be respected and I made the right decision to follow expert advice to reverse the swim from Spain to Morocco. Now I just had to fully come to terms with that decision.

I also wondered if I'd missed some clues as to the detrimental impact the whole project would have on my health.

Within a few weeks, I recovered enough physically to get rid of the crutches and before long, my crazy travel schedule kicked in again. First it was back on a plane to Nice for the annual Peace and Sport Forum and charity walk (plus a few business meetings) in Monaco, then back to London for a few hours, before boarding a flight to Los Angeles later that day.

In the lead up to the Ultimate Triathlon, the endurance sports and triathlon communities on the US west coast had shown some interest. I was keen to do follow up media now that I'd completed the challenge. Between interviews and spending time with friends, I took a bit of time at the beach to relax and reflect – but I still had a nagging sense of dissatisfaction.

Back in London, the combination of multiple international flights and jet lag on top of the mental anguish depleted my energy. I gave myself a bit of a talking to. I forced myself to walk taller and put a smile on my face. I tried to get my body to convince my mind that I felt great – once again sticking a Band-Aid on a wound and hoping it would go away.

By mid-January, my physical health began to slide. The first clue was debilitating headaches. I'd wake up with a sharp, piercing pain that lasted for several hours. I figured I was run down so I cleared my schedule for three days and took time to completely rest, but it made no difference.

Every day the following week was the same wake up with a nauseating headache, battle through the morning, feel somewhat human for a couple of hours, then by 3 p.m. my energy levels would flick to 'off' and I'd drag myself around like a zombie until bedtime. I felt like shit.

To combat this, what did I do? I tried to fight the exhaustion by introducing exercise. Subconsciously, I was punishing myself. As I began to cycle and swim (with some pain in my quad) I convinced myself the training was beneficial to my recovery as it was knitting the muscle neatly back together.

Something was amiss, and for the first time in my life I was being amateurish in my approach to recovery. Blood tests from the GP were inconclusive, so by the end of January, I scraped together some cash and took myself off a hyperbaric chamber in London, to try and boost my recovery. The therapy takes place inside a large bean-shaped chamber where I would sit quietly, resisting the temptation to read or listen to music. My only engagement with the technician was to give him a thumbs-up each time the atmospheric pressure increased, to make sure I was still with it.

The sessions gave me time to think about the strain my body was under, as well as the financial impact of the Ultimate Triathlon. I was spending money I couldn't spare to get myself back to a healthier state, and I began to worry about how I would recover. Instead of using the emotional support system I had in place, I stopped going to therapy – another clear indicator that I wasn't thinking straight. I felt it was all up to me to get my act together.

The headaches and exhaustion persisted throughout February, so I asked my GP to refer me to a neurologist. I had an MRI of my brain and the results showed that some of the electric signals in my brain were not 'firing' efficiently due to the extreme stress I placed on my body and brain during the Ultimate Triathlon. It sounded a little dramatic, but I was told it wasn't a major problem. The most important treatment was rest, with a short dose of medication.

I also tried acupuncture administered by Simon Cheung, a traditional Chinese therapist who came highly recommended. I find it fascinating that applying pressure to certain areas of the body can release or enhance other areas. I looked forward to the weekly sessions, and always left with a clearer head, and full of positive energy.

I certainly clocked up a range of treatments to help me feel normal once more, and although the horrendous headaches had dissipated, my extreme tiredness was proving harder to shake. I continued to sleep 12 or more hours a night, and did very little during the day, other than public speaking gigs, a few writing assignments and training a handful of clients. It was nearly five months since I completed the Ultimate Triathlon.

Throughout these challenging months, the one part of my life that continued to shine was my relationship with Vanda. For the first time in many years I had someone in my life who genuinely understood my need to be selfishly focused on my weird and wonderful adventures. She also helped me understand the importance of having a partner by my side for support. The reality of the life I'd chosen was difficult for many people to understand, particularly the all-consuming training in preparation for big events. Most people assumed I must be single, which only emphasised what a beautiful and unique person Vanda is, and her importance in my life.

I was deeply in love with Vanda, and couldn't picture my life without her.

With my overall health still not improving, it was time to get right in under the hood and see what was happening with my body, specifically with my endocrine system.

I contacted Tamsin Lewis, a decorated triathlete and sports doctor who spends much of her time analysing test results of athletes to find the root cause of their physiological ailments.

The first stage was collecting specimens of my urine and saliva and freezing them for future testing. The collection process was mildly amusing and required some precision (try spitting into a tiny vial, it's trickier than you'd think). I'm not sure how much my flat mate enjoyed having my frozen urine and saliva in the freezer.

While I waited for my test results, I cautiously returned to running – nothing too intense, slowly building up from a walk-run, to 30 minutes nonstop, and the occasional hour-long trot chatting with friends. Once or twice a week I would do 20-30 minutes swimming in the pool combining drills and a few laps. It was an enjoyable low-key return to training. My energy levels were OK, but I did feel a slight niggle in my right shoulder when I swam.

A big part of why I do what I do is to motivate others to step outside their comfort zone, which means talking about my adventures. I love that people are curious and want to know more. Several times a week, I'd take an hour or two out of my day to share the story of the Ultimate Triathlon with writers from sports magazines, or podcasters around the world. Whilst I enjoyed re-living the experience and responding to the range of reactions, I was careful to not give too much away as Jay was busy editing the documentary, due out in a few months' time. After each interview was published or the podcast went live, the messages would start to pour in. I love hearing how my way of living inspires others in some way to take on their own adventure or challenge. It makes me happy to know there are so many people striving to be the best version of themselves.

On top of the media commitments, my speaking engagements were coming more regularly. I'd tell my story at triathlon events, schools, conferences, and seminars across a range of industries. I always take time for questions and one of the most common queries was about preparation. I would share the detail of my three years' worth of physical and mental training, alongside the research and organisation needed. I would smile as jaws dropped in astonishment.

Occasionally I would be asked about any long-term health problems from pushing my mind and body to such an extent. I would talk about the soft tissue injuries, the tiredness and the trip to the neurologist and finish up by telling people my health was now fine.

Only it wasn't.

Deep down I knew something was physically off kilter and I had a few kinks to straighten out, but when the test results came in, it was still a bit of a shock. Despite my knowledge of the human body, I'd never heard of a person being so drained of dehydroepiandrosterone (DHEA), or the body not replenishing it. When I first saw the results showing the levels of my DHEA (which is converted by the body into testosterone) and several vitamins and minerals; I realised my body was nowhere near homeostasis.

'You need to completely rest,' Dr Tamsin Lewis told me over a Skype consultation as I lay on the couch with my laptop balanced on my legs. I listened carefully to her explanation and took notes as we worked through the lab's findings. Tamsin then detailed a list of strict instructions that would help shape my recovery. 'No training, get plenty of sleep, and reduce *all* stress from your life. Eat a diet rich in foods to help boost your adrenals and replenish the drained levels of the specific vitamins and minerals in your body,' she told me.

I was instructed to take 10 different supplements each day for the next three months, one of which was custom-made to help encourage my adrenal glands to start secreting DHEA again naturally. It was a lot to take in, and I felt like I'd become a real-life chemistry experiment.

My body had a strange reaction to the news. I felt a severe all-over tiredness settle over me, and even simple, everyday activities exhausted me. I put this down to my mind finally acknowledging the extent of my fatigue, which had a knock-on effect throughout my body. I felt a huge pressure release internally and I allowed my body to be exactly what it was – drained and depleted.

I took the prognosis very seriously and put myself into shutdown mode. I declined most social invitations and missed many special occasions with friends. I made sure I was home by 8 p.m. to unwind and get myself to bed, before my strict bedtime of 9:30 p.m.

All plans for future pursuits were shelved, and unless I was being paid to leave my house, I stayed in bed or on the couch. Most nights I was in bed by 9 p.m., and allowed my body to wake up when it was ready. Blackout curtains blocked any daylight and for the first couple of weeks I slept until after 10 a.m., occasionally later. You know your body is bloody tired when you finish eating breakfast just in time for lunch!

During this period of recovery, the only other activity other than sleep was meditation. I continued my mindfulness practice using techniques that I first learned as a 15-year-old at soccer camp, a practice that's served me well over the years.

My approach was to be present and work towards subconsciously letting thoughts flow organically and allow answers to my many questions come to me while I remained still, and in a relaxed, comfortable position. Mostly I thought about regaining my health so I could continue doing ultra-endurance challenges. In my current state of mind, I struggled to go deeper, I just wanted to fully repair my exhausted body. Sounds obvious, but when it comes to looking after your own body, this can take a little longer to sink in – especially when it means forgoing many of the activities you love. Even as a child I always found it difficult to stop all physical activity, and sit still. The next few months would be tough.

A train station near where I live is a 15 minute walk through the beautiful outer London suburb of Richmond, crossing over the river Thames. It's an easy and enjoyable commute but during my three-month shutdown, I struggled to walk past my front gate. My body quickly went into a state of exhaustion, and I felt like I was carrying a 100 kilogram backpack on tired legs, while trying to stay awake. Occasionally I would fall asleep on the short bus ride home and wake up disoriented, usually surrounded by elderly passengers also nodding off.

Mentally, I had finally let go of trying to finds ways to hold myself up, and drag myself through life. I'd gaze out the bus window, pondering how far I had fallen from the 100 hour training months, barely able to walk the short distance from my house to the train station. It was time to take back control of my life and remove anything that might impact my recovery. I threw everything I had at getting my health back on track.

Physically, this was the best thing I could do, but emotionally, saying 'no' to almost all social and many professional engagements sent me further into decline. The absence of daily tasks left me feeling unbalanced and once again I began sliding into the dark pit of depression.

My mind turned to destructive thoughts, which were so out of synch with the public message I projected, I felt like a fraud. I wanted to give up on life, because I felt I was living a shameful lie. Vanda, my close friends and my family knew something was up and rallied around me, offering support – but I doubt any of them understood the full extent of my misery and I was too ashamed to share my inner torment. I felt unworthy and empty.

Compounding my negative state of mind was the intense financial strain of meeting the cost of medical bills and paying off the credit cards I had maxed-out to fund the Ultimate Triathlon. I had run out of options. Much as I hated doing it, I was forced to ask for help to pay rent and cover the cost of groceries. It was a massive dent to my pride. The Ultimate Triathlon had crippled me physically, emotionally, and now financially.

Was it all worth it?

Did I really need to bury myself in debt to complete my 2000 kilometre dream? Just asking the questions of myself triggered another cycle of anxiety and depressive thoughts. Intellectually, I knew my life was far from dire – heck, I'd met people who struggled to know where their next meal was coming from.

I had a comfortable mattress and warm blankets, and the love of many wonderful people. Yet I had reached a point so low, it felt like my life was in a nose-dive and I was unable to pull up on the controls. I was heading straight into a deep, dark hole, and risked being lost to the world forever.

17.

LIVING LIFE

When I first set my sights on becoming an extreme endurance adventurer I knew I was searching for a life raft after the end of a decades-long dream to be a professional footballer, even if I never actually admitted this to myself. By the time I lined up for the Marathon des Sables I had a clear 'why' for the event – to put myself up against some of the best ultra-runners and see how I compared.

Out in those sand dunes, hobbling on my own in the dead of night, I realised something else about myself. Not only did I *want* to compete at the most extreme level, I *needed* to push myself past my own limits – the suffering made me feel truly alive. It moved beyond punishing myself for not fulfilling my potential as a football player. It proved, if only to myself, that when I was in control of the conditions, I would stop at nothing.

A common question I hear when I speak at events is 'at what point did you want to quit?'

The honest answer is never.

In the Ultimate Triathlon, it simply wasn't an option. If I was breathing I was getting to Monaco. Whatever happened I would adapt and deal with it. Maybe this deep-set belief that I should *never, ever give up* has driven me to achieve feats at levels that seem superhuman. I don't see it that way. I'm pretty stubborn. If I get something in my head, that's it, no-one can stop me doing it. That's not to say my 'why' has always been clear-cut. There were certainly times I was frustrated, angry, upset, sad, and heartbroken and those emotions pushed me to punish myself.

I used these emotions as fuel for the constant abuse I self-administered, and tried to convince the world that I was simply dreaming big in my quest to become an endurance adventurer.

Each adventure had to be more extreme than the previous, it was like I needed to see how deep a hole I could dig, throw myself into the dark, lonely depths and then figure out a way to get myself out.

My parents have talked about this for years. As the people who know me best and who have seen my quirks and personality traits from a young child, I have to admit they're probably right. My Dad, Stan, says I always wanted to 'higher the bar', to achieve something a bit better than someone else, or better than my own previous effort – so I would increase the challenge and push myself even more.

I could have made it so much easier on myself by taking the reins of my life and working hard to give myself closure on my football career, better understand my mental health, and put a lid on my failed relationship once and for all.

But instead, I poured the all-consuming negative energy from these emotional experiences into physical feats so gruelling they were almost sadistic. I challenged my mental strength to create a 'ladder' to climb out of the black hole I created for myself. With each challenge, the hole got deeper so I had to figure out ways to build a longer and stronger ladder. At the time, I considered this to be a positive approach to overcome my setbacks – it became routine to seek adventure, put myself through pain and suffering, and eventually clamber back into daylight. I can now see it was both unhealthy and unsustainable.

I had to find a way to make peace with what I had experienced. Therapy helped, but it wasn't a cure, and as I have identified myself as an athlete for decades, I did the only thing I knew I could trust – physical exertion!

As I slowly came around to this realisation, I felt incredible support from people who had heard my Ultimate Triathlon story. Total strangers would get in touch and share their own triumphant stories. This helped me to realign my own thoughts, and search deeper for the strength to answer the questions I was asking of myself. It helped me find the emotional clarity to pull harder on the controls and get back on an upward trajectory. I had to find a way out, just as I did many times during the Ultimate Triathlon, just as I had during the Marathon des Sables, and just as I had when I was stranded without food, water, and money in Hainan. I needed to get out of my own way for a second and give myself an opportunity to see the bigger picture in life, and grow as a person.

Four years ago, I had a dream of what I wanted to do with my life after football, and the dream was well and truly taking shape. What really excited me was helping others learn how to work through setbacks, use the tools I had developed, and share the knowledge with their own communities. It became a ripple effect of positivity that spread further and further. A beautiful synchronicity was the result. People I had somehow inspired in the past, were in turn inspiring me to overcome my own tough times.

By mid-July I could walk a little further than the front gate and slowly eased myself back into training. I continued with the early bedtime ritual, waking without an alarm when my body was ready. I noticed I was waking up earlier and took this as a step in the right direction. My few running intervals turned into 10 minute jogs around the park across the road from my house. My appetite returned and Vanda commented that I was beginning to look healthier. I know it was said with love, but I wondered just how bad I must have looked.

It was time to start planning screenings for the long-awaited Ultimate Triathlon documentary. I had no experience organising these types of events, so in typical 'Luke fashion', I threw everything at it. I contacted dozens of locations from small cinemas, to cafes, to running and cycling stores, and asked friends if they knew of any suitable venues. The plan was to engage the endurance sports community across London, and further afield. Before I knew it, plans were underway for screenings in the UK, the US, and Australia.

At the start of August, my right shoulder deteriorated. The persistent ache progressed to pain levels that restricted basic movements. The discomfort had started 12 months earlier after my bike crash in France and was exacerbated by my swim training and the 25 kilometre swim across the Strait of Gibraltar. I had to acknowledge there was a serious problem.

I saw Dr Lorenzo Masci, my sports physician, and a day later was sliding into an MRI machine. The following week, I returned to Lorenzo's office with Vanda by my side and after a three-way discussion considering a range of treatments, we agreed surgery was the best option.

Three days later, I was shaking hands with Mr Carlos Cobiella, one of the most respected shoulder surgeons in Europe. It wasn't our first meeting – he had put a plate and screws in my left collarbone after a different bike crash in London several years ago. He got straight into testing my shoulder, asking me to move my arms in different directions, and to resist as he pushed, pulled and twisted. I failed the tests miserably and three days later, I was back wearing a draughty hospital gown listening to him explain the surgical procedure I was about to undergo.

After I woke up from the surgery, Mr Cobiella told me the procedure was a success, and if I could manage to eat and use the bathroom, and felt fine walking around, I could go home. My health insurance covered an overnight stay in hospital, but for some stupid reason, I decided it was a good idea to have Vanda sign me out of hospital and by 10:30 p.m. I was in a cab heading home. I had become so accustomed to having my body put back together under general anaesthetic; I'd forgotten that post-surgery conditions could change without warning. I shouldn't have even considered leaving hospital.

By 1 a.m. I was in excruciating pain – the type of pain that agitates you and causes waves of nausea. I was lying half propped up on the right-hand side of my bed pleading with Vanda through my gaze to help make the pain go away. I knew there was nothing she could do.

The next thing I remember was hearing 'LUKE WAKE UP!' I was hanging over the left-hand side of the bed, face down with Vanda holding me up. I had started to convulse so severely, I shuffled across the bed, regaining consciousness just as I was about to shake myself off the edge. Vanda managed to slide me back on the bed before I flopped onto the floor, and cause more damage to my post-surgery shoulder. The look on Vanda's face told me it had been a close call.

She called an ambulance as I kept blacking out, convulsing and coming to with intense levels of pain. One minute I was breathing deeply to try and control my pain, the next minute I was surrounded by paramedics, facing a barrage of questions as lights flicked across my eyes. The paramedics put me in the ambulance and told me they couldn't give me any morphine for the pain due to my extremely slow pulse and low blood pressure. I definitely remember that conversation! By 2 a.m., I was in Accident and Emergency in a different hospital, stable and coherent – sort of. The paramedics told the A & E staff that I must have reacted to the painkillers from my surgical procedure, and as they handed me over, advised them I needed immediate pain relief. For days afterwards, Vanda praised the swift action of the paramedics. They were amazing.

One of the nurses put me through a few standard tests in the corner of an open treatment room and my pain increased as the minutes ticked by. It felt like mini hot jackhammers going off inside my shoulder joint, and I focused on deep diaphragmatic breathing but it was having no effect. I begged Vanda to get me something for the pain but each time she left to find a doctor or nurse, she returned alone with a furious look on her face. I remember thinking 'I hope I never piss her off so much that she pulls that face at me!'

After two hours, a doctor came over and said, 'We can give you some paracetamol, and that's it.'

With that news, Vanda called the hospital where I'd had my surgery the previous day and we made the decision to go home and wait for advice. I mustered all my pain-coping mechanisms to walk out the hospital doors, protesting silently at the poor level of treatment and lack of concern.

At around 6 a.m., I shuffled back into the original hospital room I stupidly and stubbornly left too soon after surgery.

Mr Cobiella calmly explained that I'd had a reaction to the painkillers, and the immense pain was probably due to not only these analgesics wearing off quicker than expected, but also the nerve block administered during surgery wearing off quicker than expected as well.

The trauma of the previous few hours was soon forgotten as a needle full of morphine was jabbed into my bum and I drifted off to sleep.

* * *

Many months earlier, my mate asked me if I would crew his attempt to swim Loch Lomond two-way, the largest stretch of inland water in the UK. The distance up and back is a gruelling 78 kilometres, and the goal was to complete it non-stop. I had committed to being there, but as it turned out, my shoulder surgery was just a few days before I was due to fly up to Scotland for his event.

My surgeon gave me the 'all clear,' as long as I didn't use my arm at all, so I decided to go. I didn't want to let Adrian down, but in all honesty, I just wanted to stay in bed.

It was a tough day in the water for Adrian, and conditions got the better of him after more than nine hours in the worst swimming conditions I've witnessed. I was proud of his efforts, and proud to be a part of his challenge – but I was over the moon to get home.

Rest was the most important treatment, but for the next six weeks I barely slept. I couldn't get comfortable. Ice and painkillers made little difference to the persistent dull ache I simply couldn't ignore. When it was time to begin a range of exercises, the shoulder joint didn't react well and I was exhausted again from lack of sleep and my inability to settle the pain.

Tickets sales for the Ultimate Triathlon documentary screenings were moving at slower than snail's pace and opening night was fast approaching. It was disheartening but with a lot of hustle we got the word out and ended up with a great list of guests including many respected athletes, and even a few Olympians.

As the lights dimmed at the Olympic Cinema in west London and the documentary started to play, I was beaming with joy. Jay created an amazing film, far beyond my wildest expectations. It was a true team effort. Warren and Erica helped write the voiceover script, my buddy Jason nailed the voiceovers and emceed the event, with Vanda offering plenty of advice on several parts of the film. The documentary was created with the same amount of love that went into their support of the 12 day event. And the feedback was incredible. I felt humbled when two-time Olympic triathlete Michelle Dillon said afterwards that the documentary was 'massively inspiring … it shows you that mental strength can take you a long way.'

Over the next three weeks, Warren, Erica and I bounced around the UK to appear at each of the six screenings, with Jay and Vanda attending whenever they could. With help from two of my buddies in Northern Ireland, Conor and Paul, we made a 24 hour round trip to Belfast to show the film to a packed-out crowd at the MAC Theatre.

Back in London, physiotherapy sessions with Mo became part of my weekly schedule, with exercises increasing in intensity, and slowly but surely, my range of movement and strength returned. The gym sessions reminded me how much I missed the uplifting sensation of endorphins flooding through my body. I was keen to start running and cycling training again, but I knew swimming would have to wait.

One of the mysteries I had yet to solve was why I passed out on three of the 12 days of the Ultimate Triathlon. This bugged me during my challenge, and had stuck in my head since I had finished. It wasn't until I chatted to my buddy James 'Iron Cowboy' Lawrence, a fellow ultra-endurance triathlete who was also confused by my body shutting down, the first time after just three days of exertion. I have enormous respect for James, who completed 50 Ironman distance triathlons in 50 days, one in each state of America. We had chatted via Skype in the past and kept in touch with the occasional text.

After watching the Ultimate Triathlon documentary, he had one question.

'What I don't understand is all the passing out ... what caused this?'

It was the first time someone had asked me that question, so before I responded, I took time to reflect. Most people assumed I pushed myself to my absolute physical limits, and my body shut down through pure exhaustion, and to an extent, they are right. But James's confusion echoed mine when I woke up on Day 4 of the Ultimate Triathlon, without any memory of how I covered the final 80 kilometres on the bike the previous day. I'm now confident that I can answer James's question.

Very few athletes begin an ultra-endurance challenge with a full tank of energy. In most cases, our bodies need longer than we allow them to recover from the amount of training we put them through before race day. I had started the Ultimate Triathlon on nothing but fumes of energy, my reserves as dry as the desert floor I ran across during the 2012 Marathon des Sables. The stress of continually pushing my mind and body without adequate rest throughout 2015 was compounded by battling the demons of my depression and the financial stress to get me to the start line. On top of the training, the relentless tasks of planning, organising and promoting the event pretty much tipped me over the edge – and I still had to work to cover rent and food, and pay for professional treatment to keep my body in one piece. It was a constant hustle to land speaking gigs, pitch story ideas to magazines, write articles, and train clients to achieve their own goals.

If you develop a small blister on your heel, you have two options: stop and take care of the exposed skin, or continue on. If you choose to ignore it, the small 'hotspot' will become a gaping hole of infected flesh that at some point will stop you from running.

I went for the second option throughout my entire preparation. I started the Ultimate Triathlon over-trained, burnt out, adrenally fatigued, and emotionally exhausted. I walked the same tight rope as other endurance athletes, hoping to find the right balance between training, work and life commitments, while getting enough rest. I didn't come close to finding that balance – I failed miserably. Fortunately, Vanda and a few others close to me helped me accept that I needed to stop, and urged me to give myself time to fully recover.

It's not uncommon for ultra-endurance athletes to suffer lingering effects from the gruelling torture we put ourselves through, and like me, many will need surgery for injured or worn out joints and torn muscles – even routine surgery comes with risk.

Australian triathlete Craig Percival put himself on the world map with his incredible #8in8in8 challenge in March 2016; completing an Ironman distance triathlon in all eight states and territories across Australia in just eight days.

I spoke with Craig on the phone before and after his challenge and considered him an inspiration, not only for achieving the #8in8in8, but also for raising over $80,000AUD for the John McLean Foundation (supporting young Australians in wheelchairs).

Nine months after completing his challenge, Craig had knee surgery. There were complications, a blood clot formed and he suffered multiple heart attacks. A week later, Craig lost the fight for his life, and the world lost an inspirational Aussie bloke. When I heard about Craig's shock passing, it hit me hard. After reading post after post on social media paying tribute to the man and his remarkable achievements, I slumped to the floor of my office and sat staring into space. I thought of the number of times I'd had surgery, the latest only months earlier, and realised with a heavy heart from what happened to Craig, it could have happened to anyone, including me. It highlighted how fragile life is, and reminded me how privileged I am to be able to live my adventure-filled life the way I choose.

As 2016 wrapped up, I needed yet another cortisone injection to settle down the inflammation in my shoulder. It had been a massively frustrating 12 months in which I struggled to get going with anything I attempted. The fallout from pushing my mind and body to the limit was laid bare for all to see.

So why do it?

After much reflection and many years of breaking my body in so many different ways, I have come to an understanding of what drives this 'need' to prove that I can overcome any hurdle, no matter how extreme.

Throughout my football career when I trialled for clubs but didn't get offered a contract, or sat on the bench for entire seasons, my hunger to be the best footballer never wavered. I couldn't control these aspects of my career but I had control of my fitness and skills, so I threw everything at developing these attributes – and I mean everything. It didn't matter if I was already working to my physical limits, I would push myself even further – I believed I had the key to the door of limitless potential. This had been a consistent approach since I was very young and along the way it allowed me to develop my own variation of mental skills training techniques.

GOAL SETTING

For as long as I can remember I've had goals to give me direction and keep me on course to continually achieve, learn and live my life. I don't always write them down, but I am clear on what's needed to achieve them.

It takes a bit of work to turn an idea into an actual goal so I start with knowing *why* I want to achieve each particular goal. It needs to be something I'm passionate about, have an emotional connection with, something that will help me and/or others grow and improve.

If it passes this test, then I can begin to understand how to achieve it before setting a deadline. What's more important for me is to set goals with intention, and to be prepared to do the work in order to achieve them!

VISUALISATION

To prepare myself for a physical or mental challenge, I visualise both positive and negative outcomes. Positive visualisation is about helping me feel like I've done what I'm visualising before.

The key to negative visualisation is not to scare myself, but to stay calm while I focus on how to overcome a difficult situation.

In preparing for the Strait of Gibraltar crossing, I visualised a shark swimming beneath me or getting stung by a jellyfish or swallowing diesel from a tanker and created a process of how to deal with each scenario – then I'd flip to the positive visualisation of swimming with dolphins.

I'd go back and forth in my head to make sure my mental framework was strong. This gave me a mental checklist to go through when things take a wrong turn to keep my emotions under control and help get myself back on track.

SELF-TALK, OUT LOUD

It's amazing how different a conversation sounds when you pull it out of your head. When I'm training, or trying to solve a problem, I constantly talk out loud to myself, it helps me quickly deal with negative thoughts and well as tone down overly positive thoughts. I've found it can unlock a deeper level of understanding of what it is I'm trying to achieve, and what steps to take to get there.

MINDFULNESS

Mindfulness has helped me understand my journey through life and the triggers of my depression. I don't have a regular daily routine, but I will always make time at various points through-out each day to simply stop and pay attention to the present moment, without judgement.

I've used a range of techniques since I was a teenager to relax and help calm my mind and body. Sometimes I lie on the floor, completely still, and focus on my breath. Other times I walk through a park with a soft gaze and try to focus on simply being present as I take one step after another. Another way I've found to be totally present is when I'm cooking. My body is on autopilot, and my mind not far behind as I'm engaged in each and every action I take without any internal chatter between my ears.

These simple techniques have, on many occasions, saved me. They have helped me adapt to setbacks, dragged me from the depths when I've put myself through physical and mental abuse, and most importantly, help pull my thoughts away from self-harm and me down from standing on top of bridges at 3 a.m.

After years of reflection, meditation, and simply growing as a person, I now realise being repeatedly exposed to rejection in my early football years created an *external* motivation to prove the coaches or selectors wrong. This soon became an intense *internal* motivation, and the desire to prove to myself that I was good enough.

The external to internal motivation model continued throughout the early years of my endurance sports career, as I struggled with retiring from football. Not only was my self-confidence at an all-time low, but so was my self-worth. When I signed up to the Marathon des Sables and many other extreme adventures, I was repeatedly told '*There's no way you can do that.*' Those words triggered a need to prove to myself that I was fit, strong, and capable of achieving my target. The extreme adventures gave me a sense of control and made me feel alive, which was a gratifying way to increase my self-worth and self-esteem.

Since completing the Ultimate Triathlon, the motivation for achieving goals I have set myself is very different. It's no longer about unrelenting self-punishment, it's become more about curiosity and service. I no longer feel I am running away from my previous life, nor do I feel the need to prove anything to myself – or anyone else. I have a far healthier mindset and a natural curiosity to see what I am capable of – simply to be the best possible Luke Tyburski, in all areas of my life. I want to use what I have learned to inspire, teach, and help others, so they too can become the best versions of themselves.

I believe we are all capable of more than we think, and I'm

beginning to understand that my true purpose in life wasn't just to be an athlete, but to help others find the internal strength we all hold within ourselves, and support them to harness their own abilities to achieve more in their life.

* * *

I have spent many hours, days and weeks trying to understand my mental health. I have come to accept the depression is part of my life, and these days I'm OK with that. I now understand the main trigger for the black cloud is the amount of 'load' I'm faced with in life.

In other words, If I have too much on my plate and am constantly being pulled in many different directions, sure enough, I will begin to spiral into the intense grasp of my disease. On the flip side, if I have too much time on my hands and am not engaged enough with life, or stimulated, this can also send my thoughts down a dark hole.

Sometimes I feel overwhelmed and unable to accomplish anything at all, and other times I feel lonely, like I'm lost and unnoticed in a crowd of people. I respond by slowly and quietly escaping from life as a means of self-preservation.

I have learnt I can minimise the impact of my depressive episodes. Instead of fighting the emotion, I embrace what I'm going through and acknowledge what is happening. I will shut down and give myself an hour, a day, or if I need it, an entire week away from everyday life, to simply be present. At times, I'll try to understand what set me off, and other times I try to remember the people who matter in my life. Most importantly, I am learning to be kind to myself, and I no longer beat myself up.

Punishing myself physically started as an escape and grew into a full-blown addiction. Like any drug, it met my extreme emotional need while I was in the endorphin-filled euphoria of the intense physical exercise – but the crash afterwards was crippling. Apart from the physical exhaustion, I exacerbated my mental anguish. I would then berate myself for being stupid which left me feeling even more distraught and helpless. And each hit of self-administered punishment had to be longer, harder or more extreme for me to reach the emotional high. Eventually something had to give, and in 2015, it did. The Ultimate Triathlon was my overdose.

After nearly two years of reflection, with a lot of self-work, and with the support of others, I now feel like I'm on the road to a life-long recovery.

In the months after the Ultimate Triathlon, exercise was off the table, so my drug of choice no longer existed. I was forced to make a decision – find another addiction (binge-eating momentarily filled the gap) or face up to my demons, and regain control of my inner turmoil. Like any addict, I needed rehab, and regaining control was an important first step. I began to show myself compassion through self-love, and consciously expressed gratitude for all aspects of my life. To some, that may sound a little hippy dippy, but it wasn't until I began to focus on this way of thinking and acting that I was able to see a clearer picture of what I was doing to myself.

The time without exercise allowed me to clearly see I needed proper rest more often – physically and mentally. I realised when I was working at my desk or with my laptop on the lounge I wasn't resting. My mind was constantly wired and putting a continual drain on my batteries. I now understand I need to switch off completely and rest my mind *and* body – every day. This has been extremely difficult for me, but with regular practice it gets easier, and I can see and feel the benefits.

These days I can see when my mental state begins to slide and I feel the dark clouds of depression closing in – well before I'm thrashing around in the black hole. I've made peace with the little man upstairs that life is not perfect, and neither am I. This has helped me to relax and let things go, rather than trying to fix every imperfection or challenging scenario that life constantly throws my way.

Cutting myself some slack, and viewing the world and myself in a more holistic way has helped me see a clearer picture of exactly what is going on in my life. I am learning how to keep my mind from punishing my body and in doing so, maintain a positive outlook on life.

As for the future, I plan to take on more unique endurance challenges, but I've moved on from creating those black holes of self-punishment. The physical challenges I choose will be about reinforcing my message to the world – helping people get out of their comfort zone, live life and be the very best version of themselves.

I feel now I have more wealth in my life than ever before with family and friends around me, and some incredible memories of extreme adventures, but from here on, I don't want to dig down into the darkness, I want to build into the light.

EPILOGUE

July 5th, 2017 was a bright summer's day in London, and a day I will never forget. I stood in a light-filled room facing Vanda who looked incredibly beautiful in an elegant white lace dress. Around us was a small group including my sister Moo, her husband Karl, my two nephews Max and Alfie, as well as Warren and Erica – part of the Ultimate Triathlon family.

When Vanda and I first met, neither of us was particularly keen on marriage, but over the years as our love for each other grew, we realised we wanted to spend the rest of our lives together. So, with little fuss, and telling very few people, we booked the Registry Office at Wandsworth Town Hall, and got married – our way.

The day we became Mr and Mrs Tyburski couldn't have been more perfect, and as I held Vanda's hand for the very first time as my wife, it felt like a new chapter was just beginning – the most exciting chapter yet!

'Today I married the love of my life. To many adventures ahead on the journey of life that I will cherish and share with my best friend Luke Tyburski.'

Vanda White Tyburski (via Facebook)

ACKNOWLEDGMENTS AND LOVE

All the success I've had in life, there have always been many people who have played integral parts in helping me achieve what I've been aiming for. Creating the story within these pages, and then turning it into a readable, entertaining, and hopefully insightful book was definitely a team effort.

Wife, thanks for letting me be me, and for supporting me in ways I didn't even know I needed.

Mum and Dad, you two have always loved me with all your heart, guided me with your wisdom, and clipped me over the ear when necessary, I cannot thank you enough for this.

Moo, Karl, Gremlin, Grizzly, and the extended Tyburski and Cuzner families, you all played a part in creating who I am today.

A massive thanks to Jane O'Connell, this book wouldn't be what it is without the love and attention you paid to my story. You literally took the words that I wrote and shaped them to be *Chasing Extreme* with your writing and editing skills.

Justin Bowyer and Jonathan Hammond, I would not have even started writing this book without you two. Justin thanks for guiding me through the initial stages of this journey.

Mr Brown, I wouldn't have achieved what I have since we met without your constant support, thanks for believing in me.

Wazza and Erica Pole, what can I say, you guys rock and make my life so much more fun!

Graham, we have had so many fun times together mate, and you have always encouraged me while providing your honest thoughts to all my endeavours, thanks for being a top bloke!

To my PRC family, thanks for the laughs, support, and being the best friends one could ever ask for!

Twinkle and Disaster, thanks for all the laughs guys, even when our rock band broke up!

Croc, big love for keeping me warm in the Sahara, and helping however you can, when you can.

Jay and the Cox family, I have so much love and respect for you all, and cannot thank you enough for everything you have done.

Mo O'Connell, you've always been supportive, and never tried to reign in the lofty expectations I have for my body. I appreciate all your hard work.

Lorenzo, your honest feedback of injuries, and direct communication has meant a lot to me over the years.

To my mate Sheila, thanks for providing a light during one of the darkest periods of my life, and for your continued friendship.

Michael Collins, you were the first person to believe I could complete the Ultimate Triathlon, thanks for sticking with me mate.

Tarsh and Happy Tremayne the support, love, and fun times with you both have continued to inspire me, while filling my heart with love.

Much love to my man Jason Bradbury. You have been a constant source of information and ideas during the past few years. I've so much love for you brother, you've given up a lot of your time to help facilitate my projects.

To my Nepalese brothers Aite Tamang and Upendra Sunuwar, thanks for opening up your family homes to me, sharing your local trails, while also showing me what is truly needed to live a happy life.

I would also like to thank Kerri Walsh Jennings, Ann Maynard, Erica Bliss, and Darren Wheeler for contributing to *Chasing Extreme* in the way you all have. Much love team.

I also need to thank the brands who have believed in me over the years, stuck by me when times were tough, and provide me with amazing products and services; you all make what I do so much easier, so thank you for your support.

A massive thank you to those people who refuse to be told that what they want to achieve cannot be done, thanks for not listening to the doubters, but to your heart instead and going for 'it!'

Thanks to everyone who has inspired, helped, or kept me out of harms way on my journey in life so far.

And finally, to the small group of friends I regularly speak with who are spread across the world. You all have celebrated with me, and been there for me when I've been knocked down. Your love and support continues to fill my heart, even if we don't see each other all that often.

Oh yeah, and my wife Vanda once more, I love you.